The Road to Damascus

The
Road to
Damascus

Ralph and Valerie Carnes

St. Martin's Press
New York

Design by Doris Borowsky

Library of Congress Cataloging in Publication Data

Carnes, Ralph L.
　　The road to Damascus.

　　　1. United States—Religion—1960– .
2. Carnes, Ralph L. 3. Carnes, Valerie. 4. United
States—Description and travel—1981– . 5. Great
Britain—Description and travel—1971– . I. Carnes,
Valerie.　II. Title.
BR526.C38　1986　　　200′.973　　　86–17714
ISBN 0–312–68517–3

First Edition

10 9 8 7 6 5 4 3 2 1

To the glory of God,
and with love and gratitude to
The Rev. Dr. Edwin A. Norris, Jr., and
The Rev. Canon George W. Monroe

One catches the spark of love from one who loves.
—St. Augustine, Confessions

Contents

Acknowledgments

It would be impossible to thank all the persons, named and unnamed, who made this book possible. To all our interviewees and those who knew of the project and referred them to us go our sincere thanks for their help.

We wish especially to thank the Rt. Rev. James W. Montgomery and the Rt. Rev. Frank Griswold, Diocesan Bishop and Bishop Coadjutor, respectively, of the Episcopal Diocese of Chicago, for their help and support throughout this project. Special thanks are also due our rector, the Rev. Dr. Edwin A. Norris, Jr., for his many suggestions and information, and the Rev. Canon George Monroe for his information and editorial skills.

The sketch of the crucifix pictured at the front of the book is from the LaSalle Street entrance of the Church of the Ascension, 1133 N. LaSalle, Chicago. Our thanks to the church and its clergy and staff for procuring this drawing for us.

Our thanks to the faculty and students of Seabury-Western Theological Seminary, Evanston, Illinois, and to the Rev. Finley Brown, Chaplain, Good Shepherd Hospital, Barrington, Illinois, as well as to the members of our Clinical Pastoral Education group: Patricia Megregian, Marie Carlson, Keith Zavelli, and Helen McCarthy

Special thanks are also due our curates past and present: the Rev. Richard Nelson (now Rector of St. Alban's, Chicago) and the Rev. Brian Hastings for their support of, and interest in, this project.

And finally, our love and deepest gratitude to the Rev. Robert H. Manning, now retired from the Diocese of Georgia, whose example long ago provided inspiration for this book.

Ralph and Valerie Carnes
Chicago, April 1986

Authors' Note

Interview material in this book is a faithful transcription from tapes of actual interviews with all the subjects. Irrelevant material was deleted and interviews were edited for grammar and in some cases for clarity; otherwise, the style and substance are the interviewee's own. The opinions expressed in the interviews are also the subject's own and do not necessarily reflect the views of the authors or editors.

Most names are pseudonyms, in order to protect the privacy of the individuals. In a few cases, with the subject's permission, the actual first names of the interviewees are used. In the clergy section we have deliberately omitted titles ("Bishop," "Pastor," "Canon," "Archdeacon," etc.) in order to stress the content of the interviewee's presentation instead of his/her position.

Wherever possible, denominational references and names of particular churches have been deleted in order to focus on the stories being told rather than on the church affiliation of the person telling the story. It is the religious pilgrimage that is important, not the particular denomination to which that pilgrimage has led.

Finally, although it is impossible to thank each of them in person, we wish to thank all those who so generously gave of their time to talk with us, to tell their own stories, and in many cases, to lead us to stories of the spiritual journeys of others. We feel privileged to have shared these journeys and their intimate glimpses into so many lives. We feel equally privileged to be allowed to share them with you, our readers.

Ralph and Valerie Carnes
Chicago, April 1986

Introduction

Something vitally important is happening all around us. A great sea change is taking place. People of all ages are turning or *re*turning in increasing numbers to churches and synagogues all across the country. In many countries, it takes the form of "base communities" (in Latin America, *los communidades ecclesiales de base;* in Germany, *die Basengruppen*). As Harvey Cox has pointed out in *Religion and the Secular City,* atheistic parents in Germany are appalled that their children are slipping away on Sundays to go to church.

In America, hundreds of thousands of people are once again turning to the church for answers to questions which, especially among urban business and professional people, have for two generations been unfashionable to ask. People who only five years ago would have laughed at the prospect of going to church are now attending adult church education programs and asking themselves not "Is there a God?" but "What is the work that God has given us to do?"

The long road that has led from the virtual replacement of religion by the behavioral sciences to Tom Altizer's radical Christian atheism and the media-hyped "death of God" has now led us to what may become a new and reversed version of the Renaissance: the reintroduction of religious imperatives into a secular world.

Indeed, the secular humanism that was reintroduced into a morally and intellectually bankrupt theocratic world during the Renaissance may itself have become morally and intellectually bankrupt in our own generation. The natural and behavioral sciences, far from providing us with a modern paradise, have in many ways yielded its opposite: an atomic arsenal that can destroy the earth many times over, atmospheric and oceanic pollution on a planetary scale, morally empty and ineffective programs for social change, worldwide political cynicism, and an amoral business ethic that rewards as virtues what were once listed among the seven deadly sins.

But now, in 1986, out of this malaise has come a return of the religious impulse, a turning away from the secular ideology of modernism to what years ago became an unfashionable, often-ridiculed, and almost-forgotten approach to life. All over the western world, there is a vast turning toward God and His Church as a source not only of comfort and safety in the present, but of guidance through the uncertainties of what some call the "post-modern" world.

And yet, it is difficult for sophisticated people to take all of this seriously. Religion's credibility as a source of enlightenment and practical guidance has been dismissed by many of us for so many years that it takes a genuine act of will for most of us not to be embarrassed by the common terminology of religion.

Even as we write this book, we are still sometimes jarred by the very language that we are using. Three years after our own return to the Church—years in which we have experienced a totally unexpected personal renaissance of intellectual energy and curiosity—we are still sometimes surprised at the sound of such words as "transfiguration," "salvation," "redemption," and (worst of all) "sin." People who have not yet discovered the new religious movement tend to shy away at the first sign of religious language. For them, the concepts that lie behind that language are a kind of archaic mumbo jumbo that has no place in the modern world.

Predictably enough, many of our academic and business colleagues, like the good atheistic German parents mentioned above, are appalled by the turn we've taken: "Ph.D.'s in philosophy and literary criticism; two decades of singular faithfulness to the precepts of secular humanism; seven years as business owners—such promising minds to have gotten mixed up with all this smoke, bells, and organ music, mumbled prayers and sung masses, holy water and sacramental wine." These thoughts are voiced in the same tone commonly used to describe women who still have pretty faces but have let themselves go to fat.

And yet . . .

Even with many of these people, one has but to scratch the surface lightly to discover the same religious impulse we were astonished to find in ourselves three years ago. And once that impulse has been detected, the feeling of obligation to do something about it is hard to escape.

But it is a difficult thing, this turning to the Church, because it calls upon us to do what for many educated, middle-class citizens has for two generations been the Last Forbidden Thing in America: to take religion seriously once again—and to come to grips with the questions about God, freedom, and immortality that many of us left behind with great relief two or three decades ago.

To make this turning requires that we face these questions again, reread from a different perspective the books that drew us away from the Church, and think again what, until only recently, was unthinkable for millions of American business and professional people: that there may actually be something to religion; that there may actually be a God who both loves us and has work for us to do; that there may actually be a better way of looking at the world than the one we ourselves have created; and that modern secular humanism may not, after all, have been the best source of answers to the kinds of questions the problems of the modern world have led us to ask.

The people in the churches, both clergy and laity, who are

aware of the religious renaissance we are describing recognize it for what it is: a genuine and radical shift in the modern consciousness from what might be called "behavioral secularism" to a new Christian humanism. But to the many Americans who have not returned to the Church, what in reality is a broad-based movement often seems only a resurgence of a particularly virulent brand of video-based fundamentalism.

The new religious consciousness is not confined to fundamentalism, however. In fact, this segment is only the tip of the American religious iceberg. Over and above the school prayer issue and the recurrent criticism of evolutionary theory, the chief reason that fundamentalism seems omnipresent is its inspired use not of theology but of the electronic media.

In contrast to the showmanship of the fundamentalists is the quiet progress of Episcopalians, Roman Catholics, Lutherans, Presbyterians, and Methodists toward a genuine ecumenical dialogue not only about ways to draw the churches together but about possibilities for a greater impact on the spiritual, moral, social, psychological, and political lives of all Americans. During the last few years, Roman Catholic and Anglican bishops alike have made public their condemnation of nuclear arms stockpiling. At the same time, they have been addressing ways to become a greater spiritual force in the lives of their parishioners.

This spiritual force is manifesting itself in new religious education programs in churches all over America. At the Church of the Ascension in Chicago, for example, we saw an adult discussion group grow in one year from a handful of spectators to regular and active participation by over 20 percent of the total church membership.

Father Locke E. Bowman, an Episcopal priest and president of the National Teacher Education Program (a Scottsdale, Arizona, organization dedicated to the ministry of teaching), recently became the first full-time professor of Christian education in the history of the Episcopal Church. Father Bowman teaches at Virginia Seminary, but also travels throughout the country giving workshops for church educators. His magazine, *Church Teacher,* invites contributors from all faiths. Religious education is no longer confined to parochial schools or Sunday-school classes for children, but has become an integral part of each church's responsiveness to the needs of its adult congregation as well.

In the midst of all this activity, what is missing, and is greatly desired by people who are themselves starting on this pilgrimage, is a report from the people who are making or have already made their own journey—those who are turning and returning to the Church.

People want to know what others think and feel, what led them back, how difficult the journey was, what they found when they got there. Retreats, workshops, presentations, and publications by and for both the clergy and the laity abound, but publicity and column space is usually given to the activities themselves, not to the thoughts and feelings of the individuals who participate in them.

This book tells the story of the journeys of faith that modern pilgrims have made from secular life back to the Church. It is *not* a book of statistics or sociological analysis. It does not attempt to draw grand conclusions about the experiences that it reports. Instead, it is a intimate sharing of personal stories, told to us by people all across the United States.

We made our own pilgrimage back to the Church on Easter Sunday 1983. One of the first things we learned was that our experience was not unique. People who drifted away from the Church years ago are now returning to recover the sense of community, commitment, and worship that was missing from their lives.

There is an ancient Catholic tradition of "consulting the faithful." The more we realized that there was a vast groundswell of people returning to the Church, the more we wanted to go out and talk to them, ask them personally what had happened in their lives, why they had left the Church, and why they felt compelled now, after all these years, to come back.

In order to do this, we decided to make a different kind of pilgrimage. We packed up our camping gear, a trunk full of clothes, a box of groceries, a tape recorder, and several notebooks. Our rector, Father Edwin Norris, blessed the trip, and our bishop, the Right Reverend James Montgomery, gave us his own personal blessing for what we were setting out to do.

We started out one rainy Tuesday morning, heading west from Chicago. Over the next month, we talked to bishops in Oklahoma as well as to street people in the back alleys of Kansas City, Missouri. We chatted with canons and priests, pastors and preachers, deacons and stewards, teachers and students. We talked to service station attendants, judges, doctors, lawyers, mathematicians, physicists, computer programmers, and airplane pilots.

On the second leg of our journey, we made it all the way to Canterbury, east of London, searching for our own ecclesiastical and cultural roots. We stood at the spot where Beckett was cut down by Henry's earls, and we attended mass in the Jesus Chapel; we tramped around the ancient castle at Rochester, and prayed in the cathedral there; we took communion in St. Paul's Cathedral, and tiptoed through the crypt in the undercroft. Since Valerie had done her dissertation on *Paradise Lost*, we sought out John Milton's grave at St. Giles Cripplegate, and found one of Valerie's ancestors, John Speed, buried beside Milton's statue; we followed Sir Freddie L. Brampton, M.B.E., around Westminster Abbey, made our way to the Royal Air Force Chapel, and wept for the brave men and women who gave their lives for God and country during the blitz.

We came back from our long journey with living proof that

our intuition was right, that thousands of other people are making the same journey that we made back to the Church; that there is a new vitality and a new faith among us; that there is a deep current of a renewed sense of worship, a renewed intuition of the presence of God in our lives. The joy felt by the people who told us their stories reflects the joy that we ourselves have felt since our own return.

As we transcribed the interviews, we were refreshed again as we remembered the people we had met, the conversations we had had, the friends we had made, the insights we had gained: the quiet evening we spent at the home of new-found friends in Louisville; the afternoon that Ralph visited the grave of Thomas Merton at Gethsemane; the lonely street dweller with a broken arm we met in Kansas City; the cathedral Dean in Little Rock who had shared his enthusiasm for his parish with us; the kid pumping gas in a filling station just east of the Arkansas border who really wanted to go to church but felt that he couldn't afford it.

We remembered others: the crusty old woman in the roadside restaurant south of Texarkana who went to church but was wary of two people who would travel around the country talking to people about religion; the jovial motel manager in Des Moines who joked about the church across the street; the intense young urban bicyclists in Oklahoma City, gobbling donuts and arguing about the church building program; the young priest in Zionsville, Indiana, whose vitality and honesty sent sparks into the air; the quiet, intense, and transcendent moment when Father Robert Manning said a private mass for our journey in a 150-year-old church by the Gulf in Ocean Springs, Mississippi.

And in England, there was the pervading sense of history come alive as we looked into the room above the Lambeth Palace chapel where Thomas Cranmer had written the Anglican *Book of Common Prayer*, or chatted with Freddie Brampton about the sixty-two years he has spent guiding people through Westminster Abbey.

We talked to hundreds of people. The stories in this book are theirs. And our own stories are here, too. They shared their experiences with us; now we want to share them with you. What you will read is good news in the ancient Gospel sense. There is an excitement in the air, a feeling of the Divine Presence that some of us have not felt in a long time. As one priest said to us, "Christ is revealing himself to the world again."

One of the oldest metaphors in Christianity is that of Christ knocking at the door. If you visit St. Paul's in London, you will see a larger-than-life-size painting of Christ, standing outside a door with his hand raised to knock. The door has no handle on the outside, which is the point of the painting: He can't come in unless you want Him to. For many of us, the noise of modern life has made the gentle knocking at our door all but inaudible. But we are hearing the knock again—thousands of us—and some of us are opening the door.

This book, then, is the story of people who have rediscovered the gentle tapping at their doors, and, sometimes, in spite of themselves, have made a leap of faith and have opened the door. As you read their stories, you'll hear the tapping, too.

If you are expecting a miracle when the door opens, you won't be disappointed.

Prologue

O Saviour, who hast journeyed with Luke and Cleopas to Emmaeus, journey with thy servants as they now set out upon their way, and defend them from all evil.

—Eastern Orthodox prayer before beginning a journey

O God, our heavenly Father, whose glory fills the whole creation, and whose presence we find wherever we go: Preserve those who travel; surround them with your loving care; protect them from every danger; and bring them in safety to their journey's end; through Jesus Christ our Lord. Amen.

—*The Book of Common Prayer*

Two weeks before we were to set out across the Midwest, the cooling system on the truck went. A week before we were to leave, the transmission went. We feared the worst: we would start the trip full of hopes and then, halfway through the wilds of Kansas, the engine would quit.

Our friend and mechanic, John Mouflouzelis, told us not to worry. He fixed everything in three days, and the truck ran like new. We started our countdown in earnest, and sorted through the stuff we were going to take with us: two trunks of clothes, one trunk of food, cameras, audio tape equipment, tapes, a cooler, a camp stove, sleeping bag, lantern, propane canisters, knives, matches, first-aid kit, books, notebooks, pens, the CB set, extra sunglasses, and tools. Lots of tools.

We didn't use half the stuff we took.

We left on a rainy Tuesday morning, right after Mass. Father Norris and our fellow parishioners waved good-bye to us as we pulled out of the Ascension parking lot. We took Highway 94 east, then 57 west toward Des Moines. Traffic was light, and we had never felt better in our lives.

As we rode farther and farther west, the weather went from hot to sizzling. By the time we pulled off the road for gasoline at Iowa City, the newly fixed air conditioning was barely keeping us cool. We left the freeway and pulled into a service station. When I stopped the car, we got our first surprise of the trip: a gallon of ice water dumped down on Valerie's feet. The condensation catch-basin drain was clogged.

I got out and discovered that the engine compartment was too hot to stick my hand in to find the drain hose. We gassed up and headed west again. Valerie made the rest of the trip to Des Moines with her feet propped up on the dashboard.

We had originally planned to camp out on the way, hence the camp stove, the sleeping bag, and the trunk full of supplies. But by the time we got to Des Moines, it was 104 degrees. The predicted low for the night was 95. We knew that after a sleepless night in the van we would be in no shape for the first day of interviews. We would start the trip tired and stay that way for the entire month.

Since it was still early afternoon, we drove around the Des Moines suburbs looking for the churches we would visit the next morning. When we found the last church, we saw that right across the street from it was the archetypal Low-Rent-Rendezvous motel. It was a one-story, concrete block building, with peeling paint and cracked curbs. Outside, in an ancient, rusting old Chevrolet sedan, a mother and three children waited while the father tried to call collect for money from home. They had car trouble and were stranded.

I went in and asked about a room. Plenty of vacancies. The cashier was a jovial, baldheaded man who looked as if he really enjoyed working in the place. He let the stranded family use the telephone, and offered advice about where they might get help in town if their call didn't yield results.

As I signed the register I told him about our trip, that we were writers from Chicago and were traveling around the country interviewing people who had been away from the Church for a long time and had found their way back.

He grinned, and told us that we ought to visit the church across the street while we were in Des Moines. I told him that it was on our list—indeed, that's why we were in his motel.

He laughed, gave me a conspiratorial wink, and told me that a lot of people went from the motel over to the church, but nobody ever seemed to come from the church over to the motel. Then he allowed as how that was probably the way it should be.

The hallway to our room was long, narrow, and dingy, with heavy scores in the sheetrock made by years of suitcases and trunks.

The room was no more than eight feet wide and ten feet long. There was an air conditioner, but it had been turned off for days. We turned it on full and then walked across the back parking lot to a little bar/restaurant and had a hamburger while watching thunderheads turn dark in the west.

We had just enough time to get a jar of peanut butter and a loaf of bread from the Jiffy market across the street before the deluge came. Thunder and lightning for an hour, then clearing and incredible humidity in addition to the heat. The sudden storm cooled the air all the way down to 92.

After showering, I settled down with the first science-fiction book of the trip. Valerie unpacked and repacked her clothes. On the little black-and-white TV set, a smiling weatherman stood in front of a map, joked with the anchorman and the pretty blonde with the shellacked hair, and predicted highs and lows. Outside, teenaged boys in sixties muscle cars peeled rubber in the parking lot. A mile away, eighteen-wheelers whined down the interstate.

We could have been anywhere in America.

Now as he journeyed, he approached Damascus, and suddenly a light from heaven flashed about him. And he fell to the ground and heard a voice saying to him, "Saul, Saul, why do you persecute me?" And he said, "Who are you, Lord?" And he said, "I am Jesus, whom you are persecuting; but rise and enter the city, and you will be told what you are to do." The men who were traveling with him stood speechless, hearing the voice but seeing no one.

—Acts 9:3–7

And what you thought you came for
Is only a shell, a husk of meaning
From which the purpose breaks only when it is fulfilled
If at all. Either you had no purpose
Or the purpose is beyond the end you figured
And is altered in fulfillment.

—T. S. Eliot, "Little Gidding,"
from *Four Quartets*

The Road to Damascus

I · In the Beginning

A Woman's Road to Damascus

Really, a young Aetheist cannot guard his faith too carefully. Dangers lie in wait for him on every side. You must not do, you must not even try to do, the will of the Father unless you are prepared to "know of the doctrine." All my acts, desires, and thoughts were to be brought into harmony with universal Spirit. For the first time I examined myself with a seriously practical purpose. And there I found what appalled me: a zoo of lusts, a bedlam of ambitions, a nursery of fears, a harem of fondled hatreds. My name was legion.

—C. S. Lewis, *Surprised by Joy*

Midwinter spring is its own season
Sempiternal though sodden towards sundown,
Suspended in time . . .
And glow more intense than blaze of branch, or brazier,
Stirs the dumb spirit: no wind, but pentecostal fire
In the dark time of the year. Between melting and freezing
The soul's sap quivers . . .

—T. S. Eliot, "Little Gidding"

VALERIE'S STORY

There was no single starting point—that much I know. One day I was outside the Church looking in, and the next day inside, a part of all that I had once held in contempt. Yet I can't say precisely when the idea occurred to me.

Except for this: it was late March of 1983. I was aboard a 747,

1

heading for O'Hare Airport on a clear Saturday evening after a three-day book promotional tour of the West Coast. Hours earlier I had been sitting in an outdoor cafe on Rodeo Drive, soaking up the California sun and eating a salad of sprouts, goat cheese, and arugula. And now I was heading home to a city I loved, with a man I loved, to work I loved. And I was unbelievably depressed.

I couldn't have told you why: jet lag, perhaps, or general exhaustion from three days of TV shows and racing from one studio to another. If anything, I should have been exhilarated. Just yesterday, we had been featured guests on the Gary Collins show, demonstrating exercises from our latest book. We had managed to get thirteen whole minutes of air time, a precious commodity by anyone's standards. We had sat with the other guests for an hour in the Green Room, nibbling strawberries and Brie and sipping Perrier, waiting for our turn to come up. And then the culmination of months of overtraining and dieting and running and doing aerobics: I got to put on my skinniest sky-blue Spandex leotard and tights and my matching sweatbands and color-coordinated wristbands and demonstrate a full twenty seconds of wrist rolls and overhead presses. A heady experience: it should sell books, and book sales mean royalties and money in an author's pocket.

And yet, flying home that bright afternoon, I was unaccountably fatigued and depressed—no, not depressed; something stronger. I was saddened, and about what, specifically, I didn't know—but mostly about the long chain of circumstances that led me to starve and fatigue and beat myself into someone's (whose?) ideal body type for those few minutes of on-camera glory. Saddened, too, for a world in which the apex of someone's dream might be lunch in a Green Room with out-of-work starlets and TV actors down on their luck, and a stroll down Rodeo Drive.

I didn't know; I was too tired to articulate it that night. But

I fell asleep against the airliner's cool window with a question running through my head: *Surely there must be more than this?*

Scene: It is late October 1982, and I am riding down Michigan Avenue on a southbound bus, on my way to my evening writing class that I teach at the university. Suddenly, for no apparent reason at all, I remember that it is All Souls' Day. It is all quite perfect: the yellowing leaves, the fading light, the cold wind, the darkening sky. I feel what C. S. Lewis used to call "the Northernness" coming upon me. From nowhere in particular a phrase comes into my mind: "May their souls and the souls of all the faithful departed, through the mercy of God, rest in peace."

I don't know why I am thinking of this line, nor why it brings a sudden mist to my eyes. Not for any personal grief or loss: not for my grandparents, long dead, nor my uncles, or even for my dear friend and mentor, more recently gone. No, what moves me almost to weeping at the words is my own sudden yearning for perpetuity, for a kind of immortality beyond mere celebrity, for something—anything—lasting. The words run counter to everything that my own life has become in the past half-decade: transient relationships, quick deals, precipitous moves, crash projects, hasty good-byes, throwaway disposables, here-today-gone-tomorrow. And in the midst of this impermanence, an almost palpable craving for some order, something to stay the flux; some fragments to shore against our collective ruin, Eliot might have said. May their souls, and the souls of all the faithful departed, through the mercy of God, rest in peace, amen. . . .

Scene: It is mid-November, approaching Thanksgiving. I am sitting with my husband, having coffee in the little shop we call the Rusty Bucket, at the fringes of Chicago's regentrified Uptown. It is a gray, desolate November morning, damp, full of bedraggled, raincoated commuters waiting for the Number 36 bus. Sodden leaves in gutters; long fingers of rain on the windows. I am scanning the newspaper for something to read while my coffee cools. I settle on Bill Granger's column. Some light reading.

Ah, here's a fun story: Granger repeating a section of an earlier column bewailing the state of church music in the 1980s (as if anybody cared!). Distressed because in Sunday school his kid Alex has learned to sing a tune entitled, somewhat irreverently, "Hi, Jesus!" Granger goes on to tout the joys of traditional sung masses and lists a couple of Roman Catholic churches known for their music. And at the very bottom of the column, a rejoinder from a man who writes, "Without attempting to convert you, let me point out the sung mass each Sunday at the Anglican Church of the Ascension, 1133 N. LaSalle."

I take a sip of scalding coffee and scan the article again. The music sounds interesting. (Good liberal cop-out word, that.) At least it's free. What with the price of tickets in these early post-recession days—maybe a little Solemn High Mass on Christmas Eve? Might be amusing to see what's going on. I realize that I am skating on dangerously thin ice and decide to read the entertainment pages instead.

Scene: It is a Lenten Friday. February; the snow is a thin winter blanket over the city. I'm walking from a client's office on Division Street to catch the 156 bus on LaSalle Street. My arms are loaded with textbooks from my classes, papers, shopping bags, a briefcase full of brochures. I am standing on the corner, waiting for the lights to change, when I suddenly find myself staring up at a small French Gothic church.

An average Chicago Gold Coast church: white limestone, a sparsely elegant planting of shrubbery in front, a tasteful plaque on the cornerstone—except for one thing: a life-sized crucifix, a figure of a man in a loincloth slumped from a cross, his compassionate eyes downcast, his head sagging in pain. Overhead the pigeons roost and defecate on his crown of thorns, on this icon of suffering hanging in his eternal wooden agony at the northernmost end of LaSalle Street, over the thousands of accountants and ad execs who rush past every morning and night.

It is the church I had read about in the November Granger column, the Church of the Ascension. And the early-afternoon crowds might not read the legend under the figure, but now I do: IS IT NOTHING TO YOU, ALL YE THAT PASS BY? the figure asks. And I have no answer for him.

But I am stopped short by the question. I recognize it as one that troubled me long ago, one that I put out of my mind more than a decade ago, in order "to free myself," I said, for other, more important things. But now I am nailed to this spot on the sidewalk as the figure is nailed to his wooden cross, riveted by the inscription. No, I cannot say it is nothing to me: quite to the contrary, it is Something very real indeed. It is almost palpable, it is so real. I feel it thickening the winter air like snow, freezing the tears on my cheeks in the biting Lenten air. It is *not* nothing to me, even though I have been for so long one of the passers-by who never look up.

I stand there until I feel embarrassed to stand any longer, looking past the man with his thin mantle of new-fallen snow, to the red doors of the church beyond. I would like to go inside, sometime—but to do what? Pray? Sit? Kneel? Announce to all and sundry, "I'm home"?

I don't know. I feel that if I ventured inside, some grand gesture would be required of me, and I don't feel up to it. As a matter of fact, I don't believe I could speak to anyone. Besides, there would be *clergy,* priests, for heaven's sake, and official people of all sorts, all *believers.* The kind of people I haven't spoken to in ten years or more. I don't know what I should say to them. And it is growing late; Ralph will be worried, afraid that I have been robbed or mugged or murdered in these fashionable streets where no one dares walk after dark.

But before I leave the spot, I stoop down on the sidewalk in the snow and make the sign of the cross for the first time in over a decade. The statue's face is awash in melting snowflakes that run in tearlike streams over the finely carved features. But I have the feeling that it—no, He—and the pigeons, and the sky, understand why I am here.

I grew up in an average American home of the Fifties: a little smaller than the norm: one child (me), two parents, grandparents who lived into my teens. For a generation that later was to be labeled Baby Boomers, my peers and I were a pretty secular lot. We went to Sunday School whenever our parents forced us to, wriggled through church services, yawned and fidgeted through opening exercises at school—this was in the days before the Supreme Court ruling, when it was customary to start each day with "a word of prayer," which I loathed almost as much as I hated school itself.

My father was a deacon in the Baptist Church and was described by everyone I knew as "a pillar of the church." My mother, a Methodist, never "converted." So for the first ten years of my life, I more or less commuted between the two traditions. I went to the Baptist Sunday school because that's where everyone who *was* anyone in my particular elementary school went. There I wore stiffly starched cotton dresses with crinoline petticoats in summer, velvet dresses with eyelet petticoats in winter, white knee socks or lace-trimmed anklets, black patent-leather shoes.

I sat for hours on scratchy, faded, hunter-green plush cushions and listened to adults drone on about God and heaven and hell and something called The Trinity that seemed quite as incomprehensible to me as it had to Dorothy Sayers. I read the fine print on the backs of innumerable cardboard fans in summer ("This fan presented to the Red Bank Baptist Church by Lane's Funeral Home"), sang Christmas carols with other red-cheeked, scarfed and mittened carolers in winter. The rest of the week, I went about my business: the real stuff of going to school and digging holes to China in the playground at recess and clothing my twenty dolls in outlandish costumes of my own making.

Still, on balance, I rather liked Sunday school. The music was fun. It was good company. I liked it when it was my turn to read the lesson, for I read well and liked to show off my skill in public. I was secretly appalled at the reproductions of the Bible pictures in my Sunday-school books; somehow the syrupy-sweet portrayals of Mary and the Christ Child didn't fit my conception of what I read in the Bible.

For I was fascinated with the Bible, which I learned to read at an early age. One of my earliest memories is of having learned to read the story of Jesus casting out demons and being asked to read it for my great aunt, who was amazed when I glibly rattled on about "whited sepulchers."

Then, as now, I hated bad "religious art." But certain things I learned to love, even as a child. My father, then supervisor of instruction for the county schools, used to bring me reproductions of paintings that had appeared in his education journals. So the walls of my nursery were crammed with reproductions of Raphael and Botticelli Madonnas, Jean Baptiste LePage's *Vision of St. Joan,* Holman Hunt's *The Light of the World,* that amazing painting of Christ standing before the door which opens only from the inside. I adored that painting as a child; when I recently saw the artist's own copy of the Cambridge original hanging in St. Paul's Cathedral, I felt the old pull I had felt as a child to enter into the painting and open the canvas door from the inside to the waiting Man.

Then there were the lovely Irish and Welsh hymns my
grandmother sang for me: "The king of love my shepherd is,"
"Lord of all hopefulness," "Let all things now living," "I bind
unto myself today/The strong name of the Trinity." And the
big leather-bound family Bible, crammed with Gustave Doré
drawings of Moses and the Promised Land, Elijah being translated into heaven in chariots of flame, the Resurrection and
the road to Emmaeus—all that I loved.

My problem was that, even then, I simply could not make
this connect to the raspy-voiced Sunday-school teachers who
made us sit painfully still on miniature pews with scratchy seats
while they told us "God doesn't like little boys and girls who
don't put money in the collection plate or who go to movies
on Sunday afternoon or pull their doggie's tail." My private
opinion was that the Almighty, if He existed at all, probably
had matters of more cosmic concern than whether or not I put
my quarter in the collection plate and teased my collie.

By the time I was in the third grade, I was getting somewhat
more sophisticated theologically. I remember being called on
the carpet more than once for asking the wrong questions in
Sunday school. "If God made everything, then who made
God?" I once asked a nice gray-haired lady who was busy
putting little paper cutouts representing Moses, Aaron, and the
children of Israel on a flannel board. She told me I shouldn't
ask questions like that; just shut up and listen to the Bible
stories. I got sent to sit in a corner when I refused to memorize
the Ten Commandments unless someone would tell me the
meaning of "Thou shalt not commit adultery." Over and over
it was the same message: don't ask questions, keep quiet, don't
make waves. God doesn't love little girls who ask the wrong
questions in Sunday school.

I finally severed my relations with the Baptist Church in the
fall of my last year of junior high. I had a series of bouts with
the flu, a severe middle-ear infection, and was out of circulation

for several weeks. Unfortunately, this coincided with an "every member canvas" perfect-attendance drive. My friend Betty was the captain of the girls' Sunday-school team. Betty was a tough player even at age eleven and she knew that my three Sundays' absence would spoil her team's perfect record —no gold stars, no coveted trip to the lakeside resort that went to the winner for the year.

Betty and a delegation of girls came to visit me under the guise of "visiting the sick." Actually, the real purpose of the visitation was to cajole, plead, shame, and, yes, bribe me into coming to Sunday school. I promised I'd be there next Sunday, largely to get rid of them and return to *Anne of Green Gables*.

But next Sunday rolled around and I was sick again, this time with strep throat. I literally couldn't get out of bed. When I returned to school the next week, no one was speaking to me. The entire girls' team from the church, furious at having lost the contest because of me, had decided to ostracize me. Four years later, when we graduated from high school, they still weren't speaking to me.

For a long time, I didn't go anywhere. Then, in the fall, when I entered high school, I decided to try the neighborhood Methodist Church. By that time, a friend of my mother's and father's was pastor of the church. I got involved in the youth group, played the piano for my Sunday-school class, sang in the youth choir, even taught a Sunday-school class of my own, composed of fidgety first-graders who ate the flannelboard cutouts and threw the lesson books at one another. I tried to integrate with the church community, and to an extent, I did. Once I joined the adult choir, I was much happier: I got to sit through the long Sunday services from the choir loft—a much better view and better company than the gigglers and paper-airplane-flyers who peopled the youth choir.

By the fall of my senior year, I was involved in all sorts of church activities. The most involving one was the new youth

director of the church, whom I was dating. We were seeing
one another regularly, on choir nights and during the week at
Wednesday night services. Only one thing bothered him: his
father, a Methodist minister at a church across town, was
deeply concerned that his son was dating a girl who was not
officially a member of any church.

Until he raised the question, church membership had never
occurred to me. Most people in the Baptist church had "joined
the church" at the age of about ten or eleven. But you were
supposed to "feel the call," answer the altar call one night, and
I had never felt anything—certainly not what I thought you
were supposed to feel. When people asked me if I were
"saved," I was tempted to ask "From what?" Now I was past
the usual age to "join the church," but still not particularly on
fire to join anything.

But I listened to John's arguments and acquiesced. I agreed
I should be baptized: I did indeed believe in God the Father,
Son, and Holy Spirit. I certainly repented of my sins, of which
I was painfully aware, and wished to be "saved," whatever that
might entail. And so, on a Sunday in March, after talking with
the minister, I added one more name to the membership rolls
of the church. That night, instead of taking me home, John
took home Ruth, a junior-high choir girl with a high-pitched,
breathy soprano voice and an amply filled-out pink angora
pullover.

I cried myself to sleep and tried not to think about the
unrepentant, unconverted core inside me where a "religious
feeling" should have been. Somewhere I knew there was a
strong belief in me—at least, a desire to believe—but this
church had not touched it, and neither had the brief, perfunctory baptismal service. I felt more than ever like a masquerader,
a pretender in the midst of all these good folk who sincerely
felt all the conviction that I lacked.

Spring came on, and with it, graduation. I was elected class valedictorian and had to prepare a valedictory address and class poem. I won a scholarship to college. And my beloved grandmother died, just a week before her ninety-second birthday. I picked the music for the service. John sang a hymn and the pastor preached a totally uninspired sermon— the very kind of eulogy my grandmother would have loathed. I could almost see her thin lips curled back in scorn: "Oh, come now, how do you know I have entered into the Kingdom? You hardly spoke a dozen words to me in my entire life." I grieved for her with a wild, childish, un-redeemed kind of mourning that took no comfort in the platitudes that the Church had to offer. I rejected them without even recognizing the rejection.

The final piece in the puzzle fell into place during a fund-raising drive that the church held the summer after my grand-mother died. I was engrossed in preparations for college and I was growing impatient with the constant pitches for money. The pastor was a good man but had the art of preaching sermons that could have lulled a saint to sleep. Three Sundays he spent preaching on money. The third night, after the evening service, I told my mother, "If he preaches one more sermon about money, I'm walking out and never coming back."

The following Sunday the good reverend ascended the steps to the pulpit, looked out over the congregation, and sniffed. A thin, nervous little man, he constantly sniffed and cleaned his wire-rimmed spectacles while he talked. Now, looking out at a congregation of potential donors, he said, innocently enough, "Now friends, I knew we've talked a lot about money lately. But we haven't said quite enough, so today we're gonna talk just a little bit more . . ."

I didn't walk until the end of the sermon. And I doubt that anyone noticed my grand gesture of adolescent defiance. But I was true to my word on one score: I never went back.

Besides, it was already fall and a new life was beginning. I was now a college student.

My first year in college at the University of Tennessee was spent in typical pre-Revolution Sixties college style: sorority rush week, freshman "rat week," fraternity parties, pledging, keeping up with six classes, trying desperately to maintain an A average and party at the same time. I joined the staff of the literary magazine and the school newspaper. And I studiously avoided all the campus religious organizations. Sunday mornings I studied or slept. I had long since resigned from the choir and my Sunday-school teaching. I didn't have time: I was much too busy becoming an intellectual.

Because, by now, a new factor had entered the equation. I was in a college environment for the first time, learning things I had always wanted to know. For the first time, I fully understood that there was an entire universe of things that I knew nothing about; that in order to be an *intellectual,* to be the kind of person I wanted to be, I needed to know these things. And that, more than the sororities or the parties or the new-found freedom of living alone, became the *raison d'être* of my life.

I vividly remember small but telling details: sitting in a college political science class, early in January of my freshman year. The weather was cold, the hour early. I wore a raincoat to class over wool pants and a sweater and still froze. It was barely eight A.M. and just beginning to grow light outside when Professor Prescott walked into class. He finished his introductory remarks, telling us what we needed to do to complete the course. Just as an afterthought he threw in a comment that changed the course of my life for the next half-decade: "By the way, I assume you will all watch 'Face the Nation' this coming Sunday. I'll assign you to watch these programs several times during the term. And I'll also assume it's no problem for any of you—none of you go to *church* on

Sunday?" (This last said with a fine sneer on his face.) "Good
—I'd hoped not. That's often the last relic of anti-intellectual-
ism to go. Just remember, no self-respecting intellectual worth
his salt would ever be caught dead inside a church. It's just
intellectually dishonest self-delusion, all lies and fairy tales,
that's what."

That hit home, and hit hard, with me. I had been thinking
about looking up a church near the campus, more out of the
vague conviction that it would be nice to do something different on Sunday mornings than out of any profound religious
conviction. Besides, it would make my mother so happy. But
Dr. Prescott's comment turned my head around in the other
direction. An intellectual: that was what I aspired to be. And
if no self-respecting intellectual ever went to church, then
neither would I!

So passed my first years in college. I pressed several other
professors for answers about the relationship between religion
and the quest for knowledge, and got much the same answers.
The church was the enemy of learning, the force that has kept
men ignorant and unenlightened down through the ages. The
church, Catholic or Protestant, keeps adults children; fosters
sloppy thinking, bad art, sentimental writing, and superstitious
attitudes. It is the instrument of conformity and acquiescence
while the social sciences and the liberal arts promote change,
growth, discovery, freedom of person and spirit. The church
is conservative, the arts and sciences liberal. Religion stifles
man's spirit; education broadens and enlarges it. And so on.
Those were the beliefs of American college students in the
mid-Sixties and I adopted them, whole cloth, as my own.

And then an amazing thing happened. In my junior year, I
became friends with a tall, ascetic-looking boy named Joel who
was a painter and an organist, choirmaster and harpsichordist
of some distinction. He and his artist girlfriend, Pat, became
fast friends with my old high-school chum John, now a candi-

date for honors in romance languages, and his good friend Stewart. Together, the five of us sat up late night after night, closing down campus coffeehouses and listening to hours of Bach and Vivaldi and Purcell on one another's dorm-sized stereos.

Joel, it turned out, was organist at a small Episcopalian church in a nearby suburb. I knew next to nothing about the church, but Joel waxed eloquent about its beauties. It was an entirely different kind of religion than the Baptist and Methodist faiths I had grown up with. He kept inviting me to come with him. When I protested—"Me, go to church? Why, I gave that up long ago"—he countered: "But you've never seen anything like this. It isn't your normal Baptist church. Come with us just once."

So I finally accepted the invitation, for a Christmas Eve midnight Mass at St. Paul's Church.

Joel had explained some of the practices to us already—when to stand, when to kneel, when to genuflect, when to make the sign of the cross, when to reverence the cross in procession and recession. So I was prepared for much of the unfamiliar activity that I saw going on around me. What I was *not* prepared for was the way I responded to all this. I remember the completely contradictory sense of something totally alien and yet somehow entirely familiar, as I watched the procession with crucifix, torches, thurifer, vested choir and clergy.

I was most affected by the church's difference in emphasis. I was used to Protestant services in which the whole focus was on the sermon. Here the sermon was a very brief homily, preached informally from the crossing in front of the chancel steps. The service culminated in a celebration of the Eucharist. The whole concept was strange to me—in the Methodist church we had "the Lord's supper," as we called it, only once or twice a year. Here, Joel told me, it was a weekly, even daily, observance.

It was all so different: the unfamiliar, quintessentially English hymns, the way of reading the Gospel in procession, of celebrating the Eucharist. The church, Joel told us, had been stripped of flowers all during Advent; now the altar was decked in poinsettias and garlands of greens and berries. At midnight, the bells in the great steeple pealed out over the cold city streets and the choir burst into the Hallelujah chorus from Handel's *Messiah*.

While the rest of the congregation knelt, lost in their post-communion prayers and meditations, I crept out to sit on the back steps of the church, where I gazed up at the starry Christmas Eve sky and cried my eyes out. I simply couldn't believe what I had experienced that night.

It was perhaps the first time in my life when I had felt, with any force of conviction, that I had had a "religious experience." Other people had talked about such experiences. (Protestants, I had noticed, talked about "witnessing" or "testifying.") Even girlfriends of my own acquaintance had talked about the emotional experience of being baptized or of "joining the church." But until that night, I had never felt a shred of it myself. Now religion, once a remote and theoretical thing, had become something real to me.

I stayed out late that night. Once the Mass had ended with a jubilant peal of bells, my friends came and picked me up off the steps of the church. To their credit, they didn't ask too many questions; they understood what had happened. John and Stewart, ordinarily the skeptics of the crowd, were strangely subdued. We bundled ourselves into coats and gloves —it was cold with a drizzly southeastern penetrating cold, and a light rain was beginning to fall. We went to an S and W cafeteria, the only place open at two A.M., and ate lemon meringue pie and drank coffee until nearly breakfasttime. But even my parents couldn't protest too much when I told them where I had been. I hadn't darkened the doors of a church since

I had left the neighborhood Methodist church. Now it was all I could talk about.

The next few months were a strange time in my life. I was now in my junior year of college, holding an unprecedented (for me) 4.0 average. Next year I would be a candidate for Honors in English and classics. I felt keenly that my newfound interest in the church was a betrayal of all the intellectual tenets I had come to hold. I simply couldn't reconcile the two.

And yet, I found myself returning, Sunday after Sunday, to various churches around the area. I started first with St. Paul's, where my Christmas Eve epiphany had happened, then moved, at Joel's recommendation, to Christ Church, an austerely beautiful Anglo-Catholic church whose rector was the Reverend Christopher Morley Jr. For the first time, I felt I had found a religious tradition I could embrace.

But I was not yet confirmed, so I could not take Communion. I remember vividly going in to sit, invisibly, I hoped, in the back at Morning and Evening Prayer, trying desperately to learn when to sit, when to kneel, when to stand, when to genuflect—it all seemed hopelessly complicated to me. I still felt very much the outsider; I found myself longing for the time when I, too, could go to the altar with the rest.

Yet I don't think that I felt anything profoundly religious, at least not in a specific way. I would be less than honest now if I claimed that I had mature theological or spiritual insight. I was, quite simply, a bright college student who had discovered a way of talking about and looking at religion, a language and style and ritual, different from anything I had encountered before. I was mesmerized by the liturgy and, more than that, by the sense of being in a sacramental church for the first time in my life. I had always hated the emphasis on sermons and personal interpretation of scriptures that most Protestant churches stressed; now I found the emphasis shifted to the central Sacrament of the Eucharist. And suddenly it made sense to me: I understood why people went to church.

At Joel's suggestion, I approached Father Morley about attending his confirmation classes. I didn't end up in a room of ten-year-olds as I had feared. There was actually a class for college students. About this time, coincidentally, I met several faculty members at the university who were also members of Christ Church. Reading about T. S. Eliot's and C. S. Lewis's conversions to Anglicanism also helped—perhaps I was not, after all, betraying my intellectual integrity in examining the church?

But I found myself torn: there was so much there I questioned, could not accept. My friends and the clergy were marvelous in dealing with those doubts. The rest of the parishioners, however, seemed not in the least interested in all the knotty questions involved in free will, the problem of evil, the nature of the Trinity, and the interpretation of Scripture. They mostly wanted to come to church, "say" the Mass, get through the liturgy, and go back to drink coffee and chat about dogs and children and work and other everyday concerns. To me, ever the disenchanted idealist, this was appalling. I thought that a church should maintain a sort of intellectual and religious fervor, a passionate white heat that would boil and seethe continuously twenty-four hours a day. I couldn't conceive that anyone would want less than that kind of peak experience.

It was coming time to decide whether or not I would be confirmed, and I was still wavering. My heart told me yes; my head told me no. I was only half-convinced by the thought that T. S. Eliot had become an Anglican; like all college juniors, I secretly thought I was exempt from judgment by the same standards that one might use to judge even the great *literati* of the age.

Fortunately or unfortunately, circumstances allowed me to postpone the decision. I came down with a terrible case of swollen lymph nodes, tentatively diagnosed as mononucleosis, later diagnosed as simply a bad ear infection. I had to drop out of confirmation classes two months from the end of the instruction, thus postponing indefinitely the question of confirmation. What little energy I had left went into completing my Honors thesis. I simply swept the whole issue of confirmation under the rug; I'd deal with that later, I decided. My new boyfriend, nominally an Episcopalian, thought the whole thing rather silly and childish. I was secretly relieved that I had never taken the final step toward confirmation.

My first quarters in graduate school passed in a whirl of activity. I was much too busy trying to maintain the average required for my fellowship and adjust to a higher level of anxiety.

But that second year in the graduate program brought important changes. My fiancé and I began drifting apart, partly over the issue of religion; I had announced I wanted a church wedding and he was violently opposed to it. I met Elizabeth, a girl who had just converted. And she, in turn, introduced me to the Episcopal chaplain on the Emory campus, Father Robert Manning.

At first I attended Mass mostly in a perfunctory way. Since I couldn't take the Eucharist, I came as an observer to keep Elizabeth company. But I began going to the daily office five or six days a week. When Father Manning organized monthly Sunday trips downtown to the Episcopal Cathedral (the Cathedral of St. Philip, Atlanta) or to the Church of Our Savior, I often went with him. At his invitation I picked up Inquirers' classes again and, almost without realizing it, found myself preparing seriously for confirmation. In May of the next year, I was confirmed at St. Philip's Cathedral in Atlanta, along with two good friends, Michael and Ron. A third friend, Bill, was confirmed six months later at Holy Trinity in Decatur.

For nearly a year, I was a faithful communicant. I attended

the daily office on the Emory campus, went to daily Masses whenever I was free, went to Sunday-morning services with Father at Our Savior and then to Evensong at the alumni building's small chapel where we held our daily services. Father gave of his time unstintingly; the beautiful little log cabin on Lullwater Road that he rented was always open to his students. I spent many a night there, sitting by his fireside, listening to Puccini operas or to his newest baroque record, looking at the arresting crucifix above his little shrine, talking about the very problems that had always engaged me: the nature of God, immortality, freedom, justice, the relations between the races.

And then, abruptly, it all ended. Father was transferred by the bishop in the late spring to a large Gulf Coast parish and our little flock was left without a shepherd. I cried all afternoon the day he left in the black Fiat we had christened Christine. The log cabin was boarded up until new renters could be found.

Since we had no chaplain on the campus anymore, we had no parish. The little campus mission of St. Athanasius was, consequently, inactive. I tried to find a substitute. I started attending a small Anglo-Catholic parish across town. But the liturgy was unfamiliar, transportation was bad, and the parishioners didn't know what to do with a single woman, barely in her twenties, who wanted to talk about imagery in the Metaphysical poets and the problem of time in Milton. I was simply too young and immature to know how to integrate with a parish full of adults, and they had no model for accepting college students in their midst. Over a period of two or three months, my friends and I all drifted away.

At Christmas, when I went home, I went back to Christ Church, but it was like attending a wake. My undergraduate advisers, Professors Connors and Stuart, were gone, and Father Morley was on sabbatical in England. John had gone to

Spain and Pat had decided to go back to the Roman Church.
I sat watching the lights blink out on the family Christmas tree
and felt more lost than ever.

The rest is history: I once again left the Church. But this
time, it wasn't so much a premeditated, deliberate act as a slow,
painless drift. Years later, I would read Father Holloway on
modern apostasy and recognize myself in that slow, almost
imperceptible drifting away from things sacred that he describes. For I defected, not only from the church, but from
religious concerns altogether. By now, I had finished the
course work for my degree and I felt the responsibility lie
heavy on me: I had to be not just an intellectual, but a *scholar*,
an example of secular learning to the young. I had my reputation to uphold. It was time that I put childish things behind me.
An adult at last, I had outgrown religion. And that was that.
Or so I then thought.

More than once in the years after we were married, Ralph
tried to discuss religion with me. What he got, mostly, were
flip answers ("Heaven for climate but Hell for society") or the
request to drop the topic altogether. I simply didn't want to be
bothered with discussions of God, freedom, and immortality,
as I put it. I wanted the sense that this matter was settled once
and for all, that it was all behind me. Several times, we went
for one reason or another to visit churches in the area—for
musical events, speeches, dramatic productions. I remember
once attending a Sunday morning service at St. Luke's in
Evanston and marveling at how alien and remote the once-
beloved liturgy now seemed to me. I was proud of what I had
achieved: I was a secular woman, liberated not only from
housework and "feminine" preoccupations, but also from silly
religious superstition.

And yet, there was that part of me that still was incredibly
moved by the words of a Donne sermon, a fragment of a
Herbert poem from *The Temple*. Once, visiting the Notre

Dame campus at South Bend for a conference on Renaissance studies, I walked into the chapel early, just at the close of a solemn Evensong. I was so moved by the fragment of plainsong chant I heard and by the blessing and dismissal that I couldn't wait to get out of there and back to the safe objectivity of the conference.

And so matters stood that spring of 1983 when, for no reason at all, I found myself standing speechless in the snow before a worn crucifix on a LaSalle Street church in Chicago. And that is where our story begins in earnest.

April 1983

Though these things, as I ride, be from mine eye,
They'are present yet unto my memory,
For that looks towards them; and thou look'st towards mee,
O Saviour, as thou hang'st upon the tree;
I turn my backe to thee, but to receive
Corrections, till thy mercies bid thee leave.
O think me worth thine anger, punish mee,
Burn off my rusts, and my deformity,
Restore thine Image, so much, by thy grace,
That thou may'st know mee, and I'll turne my face.

—John Donne, "Goodfriday, 1613. Riding Westward"

Winter in Chicago hangs on intolerably. Like a low-grade fever, or a late-spring cold, it refuses to go away. In the morning you awake, your head clear of winter fever, to a room drenched in sun; by afternoon, the familiar gray is back and you are once more exhausted, in the fever's grip. Next morning, it is iron-cold again, but with a hint of spring warmth in the air reminiscent of Lawrence Durrell's line "In the midst of winter, we feel the inventions of spring."

Such was the onset of my own late-winter madness, so deviously did my Adversary set his snares. I seldom walked past that imposing crucifix the rest of the Lenten season—because it was out of my way, I said. Actually it was because I, a fully grown-up woman in full possession of her senses (or so I thought) was frightened to death of it. I often thought back to that day in the snow when I had been almost struck dumb before the statue and tried to assess my feelings. But I found they simply would not be assessed.

The Presence, as I came to call it, hit me at odd times, with no apparent provocation. I would be riding the bus on the way to my university classes, of a late March afternoon, when suddenly the shape of a bare branch against a wisp of cloud, the form of a budding leaf, the slant of the afternoon sun, would recall the corpus on its cross, and my eyes would mist over again. I was almost angry that the Presence now held me so powerfully in its grip. Once, passing a handsome church on Michigan Avenue, I had the most uncharacteristic impulse to leave my seat on the bus, rush inside and—do what? I couldn't say: I only wished to be inside, where I might sit and think and perhaps look at Something. Or Someone. I didn't know what else one might call this vague but persistent Presence.

By the last day in March, winter was losing its grip and I felt that something in me was coming back to life. Slowly, the lump of ice in my heart was melting. A year later, in a Lenten meditation, I was startled to hear Father Norris use the same analogy for the slow progress of Lent toward the Easter season. But I am already getting ahead of my story.

Along with the new melting and thawing sensations, though, came a new conviction. I knew that I had to go into the church with the crucifix sometime in the near future. I kept setting dates and letting them slip inexorably by ("We will go the first Sunday in Lent," "Perhaps Palm Sunday," and so on). Mercilessly, the statue drove home its question: "Is it nothing to you, all ye that pass by?" Ye watchers and unholy ones on

LaSalle Street, perhaps you can say it is nothing. I cannot. But if I fail to act on this new fragment of self-knowledge, am I no more than they?

I didn't know any of the answers: I tried to dismiss these new and unsettling thoughts. But they wouldn't go away. Increasingly I felt that some sort of action was called for. And I became obsessed with the need at least to enter those red doors, to go past that limestone facade, and encounter my Presence on its (I still would not say His) own terms.

And so I set myself a kind of research project. I looked through the Yellow Pages and systematically sorted out (under "Churches—Episcopal") the places that lay within a ten-mile radius of our lakefront apartment. And finally, on a bleak Holy Thursday morning, I got down to the task of calling up all the parish offices to locate an Easter service. As fate would have it, the only one where I got an intelligible answer was the church that housed the crucifix I had stood before in the snow.

When I called to inquire—this time, a little less diffidently, I imagined—about the time of the Easter Sunday Masses, I got a live human being. Instead of the obligatory bored teenager ("Huh? Easter Day? Well, I dunno, just you know, the usual schedule, I guess . . .") or the equally baffling recording: ("Hello! You have reached Saint Hrosvitha's in Suburbia, Illinois. No one is in to answer your call at present . . ."), at this church I got a live human being who had a lovely, most unclerical-sounding voice and read me the full schedule of Easter Masses and hoped, or said he hoped, to see me at one of the services.

Friday and Saturday passed in a frenzy of indecision. On the one hand, my rational self (Valerie the liberated writer-businesswoman-urban-dweller-rationalist) was thoroughly appalled at what this other, emotional, and totally irrational self was about to do. (For example, I now realized, with a sharp jolt of recognition, what the black hat I had bought so "impulsively" a month ago was really for.) On the other hand, this other self, impulsive and irrational, stumbled through pages of research, sorted wash, bought jellybeans for Ralph's Easter basket, and typed like a madwoman to make time for the next day's excursion into the higher mysteries.

By the time my journalism class was over on Holy Saturday (how quickly I had slipped into that strangely familiar rhetoric), I would no more have given up my secret expedition on Easter Sunday than I could have flown. That damp, sodden Saturday, slopping through the Loop in rubber boots, my hair plastered with freezing rain, my arms burdened down with books and packages, Easter candies and cards and new gloves (yes, gloves: one does it right or not at all), I was at once the most terrified and happiest of women.

But Sunday morning threw a very different light on my excursion. I woke up to a cold, dismal rain that chilled even our warm apartment. I had a splitting headache and the beginnings of a cold. As I made coffee, I threw myself into a sofa chair, overwhelmed at the silliness, the sheer foolish anachronicity, of what I was about to do. Why had I ever dreamed up this latest idea? It would all end in disaster, I was sure. We would be drenched. The church would be cold. I would look as miserable as I felt. Ralph would be put off by the liturgy. The incense would make us sneeze. We would be late for brunch. The *Times* would be sold out by the time we left Mass. No, it was a disaster all the way around, and even at this eleventh-hour I hit on a plan to rescue us. First, I decided, we would go to Vie de France and have a croissant at the counter, read the *Times,* then go on to a full-scale brunch when the restaurant itself opened.

Fortunately, the Presence was more astute than I. I called Vie de France and got a charming little recording telling me to call again at eleven o'clock, when they opened for Easter croissant and baguette, not to mention beignet, and wished me a happy Easter in three languages.

So that was it. It was by now nearly eight A.M. The die was cast; I was already committed. The alarm had gone off, the coffee was made, and Ralph, strangely alert (apprehensive?) for this early hour, was already shaving. Feeling myself increasingly trapped in snares of my own device, I surrendered and got dressed in my red jacket and black skirt. The hat, my only real concession to the occasion, I could put on at the last minute.

The details of the next half-hour are still vague. I assume we drove down Lake Shore Drive, turned down LaSalle Street, and parked about a half block from the church. By then, the early deluge had subsided into a thin drizzle. We walked through that fine green mist of buds and bloom in our raincoats and stopped before the crucifix for a moment, transfixed by another sight. On the ground under the stained-glass windows to the north lay a heap of broken, colored glass. Someone had broken out the bottom pane of the third window during the night.

The sight of those slivers of broken glass moved me, strangely, in a way that even the spire and cross did not. For someone, at least, all this really was nothing. To some passerby, one at least, this place of Mysteries so vivid that I was shaking as I stood outside was merely physical: stones and wood and colored glass. But I felt the Presences closing in and I was outraged at the broken glass, afraid and ashamed that I was outraged.

Later, we would learn that the intruder had come on Holy Saturday before the Great Vigil, had broken out not one but two windows, had stolen coats and wallets from the rack in Wheeler Hall, and had laid waste to the rector's office. But that all belongs to a different story. For now we must follow the man and woman walking up the narrow stone steps and through the red doors that face onto LaSalle Street.

The church is damp and cold as I walk in and I am seized by nostalgia as I walk into the narthex and smell some familiar mingled scent of mustiness and incense and candle wax. I walk in and take a seat in a front pew. I cannot bring myself, out of some self-conscious remnants of pride, to genuflect, nor do I pull out the kneeler. Instead, I sit stiffly, self-consciously in the pew, staring straight ahead at the altar, trying to take in all this strangeness. It is a beautiful, small French Gothic church with an arresting rood screen, a marble high altar with two exquisitely carved alabaster angels on either side, a shrine to the Blessed Virgin to the left of the chancel, and another to St. Michael to the right.

I sit, pretending to read the program and the bulletin insert, but in reality I am fighting for my very existence against the Presence. And when the music starts, I know that I am irrevocably lost. This is bad, very bad indeed. It is Kierkegaard's sickness unto death. I am in the throes of a life-struggle with my Adversary and I know I won't escape unscathed.

I cannot describe many details of that service. I remember that the processional hymn was "Come, Ye Festival Day." I managed to get out a croak or two and then ceased singing, or attempting to sing, altogether. The occasion was all but festive for me. I was being battered by tidal waves of emotion. I was drowning in the Presences (there were now considerably more than one of them), and felt powerless to come to safety. Things were going from bad to worse. What had begun as a light exercise in nostalgia and aesthetics had turned into a major battle.

I fought unsuccessfully and lost. The *Kyrie* devastated me, the *Gloria in Excelsis* destroyed any shreds of cynicism left in me. By the time the lector rose to read the Old Testament lesson, I was hiding behind my sunglasses and veil, looking for all the world like a Sloane Ranger funeralgoer in my efforts to look somewhat normal.

One paradoxical thing about my perceptions of that day: my journal tells me that it was cold and drizzly, yet my observations are only those of light. By the time the Gospel was read, I was sufficiently recovered so that I could timidly respond along with the rest, "Praise to you, Lord Christ." But then the rector came out, a tall man in a plain white alb like a monk's robe and a white stole for Eastertide. He stood facing us, simply, on the lowest step of the chancel, lifted his hands in greeting, and began: "Why are you sitting here? Why are we all here? Either the Resurrection is true, or we're all just fools, every one of us." Three sentences, and I was off again.

"Batter my heart, three-person'd God," the poet John Donne had pleaded. But I, less masochistic than the divine poet and preacher, could only beg for mercy. I too was broken, burned, bruised, and could not save myself. Mercilessly the rector's lovely voice ran on and on, like something in a dream, weaving more nets to catch the unwary. When I glanced over at Ralph, I saw at once that the Presence had caught hold of him too.

I regained enough composure at the Offertory to get through the second hymn. The bustle of collecting plates, the rustling of money and envelopes, coughing, presenting the Elements, moving of kneeling pads, gave me just enough cover so that, faking a discrete sneeze, I could blow my nose and dry my eyes. But the onslaught escalated now with renewed force.

The Sanctus and the Agnus Dei left me unable to speak, much less sing. When the celebrant spoke the closing words of the Consecration ("He stretched out His arms upon the cross and offered himself . . . a perfect sacrifice for the whole world"), I could stand no more. I put my head in my arms in what I hoped would be taken by my neighbors as an attitude of extreme piety and gave myself over to wrenching tears. *"Lord, I am not worthy that you should come under my roof; but speak the word only."*

". . . speak the word only, and my soul shall be healed." My soul, healed? I was so devastated, so overwhelmed by the sense of

something irrevocably lost, the emotion that I had felt once
before, that Lenten Saturday before the crucifix, that it now
seemed inconceivable to me that my soul should ever be healed.
I had to struggle now with that paradoxical sense of loss and
the first faint, distant beginnings of something else: a kind of
wild joy that in the midst of all this sadness, there was something else so palpable I could almost reach out to touch it. Yet
it also was fragile, and I recognized its delicacy.

I kept a respectful distance and refused even to make polite
overtures to it. This other Something counterbalanced the
lostness, the isolation, the devastation, the broken-heartedness,
and beckoned me toward it. I felt myself, as I watched the Holy
Eucharist prepared for us, drawn as if through a vast tunnel.
At the end was one small light, so tiny that one would lose it
forever simply by averting one's eyes for an instant.

But if one fought the waves of fear and darkness rushing in,
if one simply continued breathing, keeping one's gaze on that
dot of light, walking not by direction but by (that was it!) a
kind of primitive blind trust, one came eventually to the place
where the light was, to a place flooded by Light. I had no name
for this place yet, but I recognized some of its inhabitants. The
man in the white alb with the incredible voice, he was part of
it, and so was the chime of the sanctus bell, and so were the
curate's hands, holding high the consecrated chalice.

None too soon, the Mass is over. Five more minutes of this
and I would have drowned myself and the whole congregation. I resisted the temptation to take Communion (the altar
might have blown up in my face). I dab at my nose, apply fresh
lipstick, adjust my hat and sunglasses to cover the damage, and
file out. The rector is standing in the doorway with the rain
blowing in on him. He seems oblivious to the mini-monsoon
outside; he is busy hugging children, old ladies, couples, everyone. Even in the darkened narthex he seems to give off some
fine, almost invisible light. We shake hands and introduce

ourselves and he invites us back for coffee. We refuse: the idea seems unthinkable, preposterous. All I want is to get out of there, away from all that, away from the Presences that have ganged up on me, are assaulting me now, even as I am almost safely to the door. "Not this Sunday, thanks, Father, maybe next week," I mumble and make my way to the other side of the red doors. Safe at last! A narrow escape, but an escape nevertheless!

I have depended throughout on Ralph for some comfortingly cynical words, but he has none. Indeed, he is strangely silent. We drive north in the city, in a sort of a daze, both of us, going nowhere in particular. An hour later, we end up at brunch in a small, cold bistro in Lincoln Park, picking over the omelette *du jour* and talking, or trying to talk, about what we have just experienced. Ralph, the family skeptic, for the first time has let me down: he is as devastated as I. As I dissect my dessert crepe, he drops his bombshell.

He looks me straight in the eye over a cup of espresso. "I know what we gained by leaving the Church so long ago," he is saying. "We gained the freedom to do any damned thing we wanted to do. But I never understood until now what we lost."

April 10, 1983

It is a clear, sunny, chilly Sunday, very unlike the wet Easter of a week ago. All week long we have fenced around the issue. Are we going back or not? Ralph said (jokingly? seriously?) yesterday morning, "Want to go to church tomorrow?" I decline: too much work, I said, but we both know that isn't the reason. I don't want to deal with that storm of emotions again so soon. Maybe next Sunday, I say, and although it is a statement, it always ends up as a question.

I deliberately drag my feet on the project we're doing for *Consumer Guide*. I *want* to have too much to do this Sunday:

I want to go back to the safety of my usual Sunday routine, the bagel-coffee-and-*Times* ritual that I have held sacred for so long. I'm terribly protective, suddenly, of my freedom. I don't want any demands placed on me, don't want to have to answer to anyone or anything, don't want to have to change the way I live. Above all, I don't want to feel myself under any obligation to be anywhere—least of all, at the Church of the Ascension—on a Sunday morning.

So this particular chilly, bright day, I put on my jeans and sweatshirt with a special sense of relief. No more hats with spotty veils and silk dresses for me on Sunday! I am free. I have escaped from the clutches of this—this Presence, whatever it is. I am Valerie-the-free-spirit again.

With a sigh of relief I grab up my *Times* at the newsstand and slip into a window booth at the Parkway coffee shop, right in the heart of Lincoln Park's Yuppieville. A perfect seat, this: a view of the graystone-lined sidewalks of Fullerton Avenue, joggers running against the cold spring wind, pavements still damp from the melting snow, kites high against the brilliant sky.

I am sitting with my toasted bagel in front of me, sipping coffee and leafing through "Fashions of the *Times*" when it hits me: *I don't want to be here. I want to be somewhere else.* And I am afraid to admit, even to myself, where it is.

I keep up the pretense well, ordering second and third cups of coffee, feigning interest in next season's fashions, joking with Ralph about our "narrow escape" last week. But all I can think of is the Man, hanging there on his wooden cross above the haunting legend, now with the first dogwood blossoms of April budding beneath him. And the people for whom that corner of LaSalle and Elm is just a street, that white limestone building just another church.

I wish that we had gone back today. I wish that I were there now. Most of all, I wish I didn't have to think about what I am going to do now.

April 24, 1983

Another clear, cold, bright Sunday. This time we have done it: we are back on our way to the Church of the Ascension.

I can't reconstruct in my mind exactly how we decided to go back. But last Sunday we went to another church, quite near our favorite coffee shop. It was a bit larger, a bit "lower church," as we used to say, rather friendlier and less formal, I thought. But nothing special; just another church. No strange Presences there at all. I sat through the service, largely unaffected by it all. And that in itself was a good sign.

I felt rather better for it. It was, after all, just a passing phase: maybe the result of my Easter cold, or the rain, or loss of sleep, or the sight of those piles of broken colored glass on the sidewalk.

At any rate, all that is over. And so we have decided (or rather, *I* decided) that it is safe to go back to Ascension today. So back we go, through the now-familiar red doors, and back to the third pew where we had sat three weeks earlier. I am confident this time, rational, self-assured, in control. This time there will be no tears, no violent emotional upheavals. All that was a passing phase, mere nostalgia for an reclaimable past. But now I am back in the real, the rational world, and I am here today to prove it.

This time I remember, and practice, my church etiquette. I genuflect when I enter the pew, kneel briefly, feigning prayer, before the Prelude starts. My morning devotions go something like this: "Dear God, don't let me make a fool of myself again, let me see there's really nothing to this except some nice music, Amen."

The Prelude is over and the Sanctus bell rings, summoning the faithful to worship. We all stand and the procession enters through the side doors: acolyte, master of ceremonies, the rector (the tall man whom I recognize from Easter Sunday), and last, a large white-haired man in simple brown monk's robes.

The service is by now halfway familiar: opening hymn, Kyrie, Gloria, opening Collect, lessons. At the opening Collect, I listen to the rector's lovely voice intone, "Almighty God, to you all hearts are open, all desires known, and from you no secrets are hidden, cleanse the thoughts of our hearts by the inspiration of your Holy Spirit."

The voice is simple, direct, completely without pretense, and yet somehow so absolutely genuine in its pure unabashed acceptance of the truth of those words: "To You all hearts are open, all desires known, and from You no secrets are hid." An amazing line: am I, a woman of the 1980s, to believe that to Someone, anyone, my heart is open, all my desires known, my secrets laid bare? I was never prepared to accept such an idea, and yet this man with the incredible voice full of such utter conviction is telling me so, with no pomposity, no bombast, no cheap theatrical tricks. He is simply stating these revelations that so shatter me in the same tone of voice he might use to talk about buying detergent or watching the ten o'clock news.

The man in the brown monk's robes is no less remarkable. He speaks with a charming, cultivated British accent. Father Norris (for that is the rector's name) introduces him as Brother John Charles, the former Anglican Bishop of Polynesia, now a Benedictine monk who is here conducting a retreat for clergy and is guest preacher today.

The service proceeds: Old Testament lesson, Epistle, Gospel. Then Brother John Charles mounts the lectern and pronounces "In the name of the Father, and of the Son, and of the Holy Ghost, Amen."

The sermon has to do with his experiences as Bishop of Polynesia, and there is about it some peculiarly, distinctively Anglican mixture of homely humor, wit, erudition, Scriptural acuity, and simple holiness that stirs up the Presences—yes, and something more: a genuine nostalgia for, and pride in, the church I abandoned a decade ago. I find myself delighted, in a proprietary way, at the charm and force of personality of this extraordinary man: he is *one of us,* a quintessential Anglican. I lean over to Ralph: "He is the perfect monk, this is the perfect Anglican homily," I begin, then lean forward not to miss the next part of the sermon.

Brother John Charles tells of his experiences among the natives, of his own only half-successful attempts to cultivate charity toward a certain priest in his diocese: "I asked Our Lord to give me charity toward Father ———, and I tried very hard to find something about him to love. He was one of those sorts who knew everything, *and in the most unpleasant way.* But finally I meditated and meditated and at last hit upon his one great and singular virtue: *he took regular baths.* And that was a decided virtue in this rather steamy tropical climate . . . and all too rare in the diocese as a whole, alas."

Then he goes on to draw, from this homely morality fable, a stunning discourse on the dangers of knowing everything, especially "in the most unpleasant way," on the wisdom of knowing that we do not know. I am quite sure he is talking about me; he surely is describing half the academic colleagues I have known. By the end of the short homily, I am utterly captivated. And I am even more astonished to realize that I have just sat through an entire sermon and relished every word of it.

And now it is all getting out of control again. The Prayers of the People are preceded by an invitation from the curate to attend the Henry Chadwick lectures at Seabury-Western Theological Seminary next week; Chadwick, a noted scholar on the early church, will give two lectures on his specialty which are free to members of the parish. Then we pray for Ronald our President and James our governor and Harold our mayor and James and Quentin, our bishops, and for the faithful departed (Grandmother! Papa! Suzanne!), "for our families, friends and neighbors, and for those who are alone." I am touched by the simple dignity of the prayers, the sense of the larger world that lies behind the red doors. For an instant, LaSalle Street and church, Mammon and God, business and spirituality are knit together in this strange blend of sacred and profane that I find so extraordinary. And the Eucharistic prayer for the day includes one stunning line: "we pray for this fragile earth, our island home."

Then comes the Confession of Sins ("things done and left undone . . . we have not loved You with our whole hearts, we have not loved our neighbors as ourselves . . ."). I am overwhelmed by a sense of my own faults: a decade and more of petty jealousies, greeds, small-mindedness, intolerances, resentments, deceptions, dissatisfactions rise up before me. Secular society tells me, *It's whatever you can get away with, get yours, go for it, never mind the consequences to others.* But this is something different, and I don't know how to respond. Even as I say the words, I realize that I half-believe them: more than half, were I honest with myself.

Then after the confession, the absolution: Father Norris, with his usual beautiful simplicity, signs the Cross and pronounces what the old prayer book was pleased to call the "comfortable words" of absolution from sin. And then an innovation: the rector greets the congregation: "The Peace of the Lord be always with you." We respond: "And also with you," and then I am surprised to find a dozen hands extended to me, voices that whisper "Peace! The Peace of the Lord to you!" People are going up and down the aisles exchanging the peace with their neighbors. I can't help contrasting this simple gesture of trust with the world in which we live and do business, the dog-eat-dog and rat-eat-rat universe of businesses, big and small, where we are daily betrayed for the proverbial thirty pieces of silver, where contracts are made to be broken, and where a man's word is good only until he gets out of the door. And once more, I am immensely touched by the gesture.

My skepticism and cynicism are wavering again. After the exchange of the Peace, Ralph and I, seeing other couples hug, pull one another close for a moment. The offertory hymn begins. It is an Irish air, one that I love and which was a favorite of my grandmother: "The King of love my shepherd is." I remember that it was sung at her funeral, at my request. I could not bear to sing it then, at sixteen. I can hardly sing it today.

Now the Eucharistic liturgy is beginning and I am shaking again, half from the spring cold but mostly from the Presences that are assailing me again. I am kneeling next to Ralph, in an attitude that I hope simulates devotion. But this time I am, quite simply, torn apart. I have not taken Communion in over a decade. Ralph had said to me earlier in the week that if we returned, he thought we should take Communion ("Look, we can't go just halfway. If we really believe in what's happening to us, we've got to make a commitment"). But I am afraid to go near the altar.

Alone, those few minutes on my knees, I wrestle with every emotion known both to the faithful and to the infidel: pride, bitterness, fear, nostalgia, longing, isolation, dread. I want to go to that altar more than I have wanted anything in years. But I am also desperately afraid of what might happen if I do. Broken phrases from the 1928 *Book of Common Prayer* come back to haunt me: "Ye who do truly and earnestly repent you of your sins and intend to walk in love and charity with your neighbors." Do I intend to do that?

Do I repent? Do I want to—can I—walk in love and charity with my neighbors? Do I repent? And if so, of what? And in that moment I know that if I go to that altar today, somehow my life will be irrevocably different. I don't know if I want that, don't know if I am prepared for the changes that that act will effect in me, the demands it will place upon me.

I don't know if I will do it; if I *can* do it. My mind is teeming with jumbles of words and phrases and half-forgotten scenes:

Father Morley long ago telling a confirmation class of bewildered students that to approach the Sacrament in anything less than a spirit of religious awe is to desecrate the Sacrament. I think that for me in my present state of sin to get within ten feet of the Blessed Sacrament would be a desecration. I am sure of it. In fact, I think the altar will blow up if I go near it. Surely a loud thunderclap will sound and the heavens open up if I even approach the altar rail.

But as I am kneeling there, torn apart with indecision, Father Norris elevates the Host and I suddenly hear that fragment from St. Augustine's Prayer Book: "Lord, I am not worthy that you should come under my roof, but speak the word only, and my soul shall be healed."

And all at once, I know what I am going to do. I can do nothing else: in that split second of mingled sunlight and tears and smell of incense and bone-chilling cold comes a flash of recognition that almost knocks me from the kneeler. If I were about to desecrate the Sacrament, I would not be kneeling here paralyzed by fear of desecrating the Sacrament. The fact that I put it in such language means that I am, have been, much closer to it all than I ever realized.

And so, when the Sanctus bell rings for the last time, calling the faithful to the altar rail, I have no need to look over at Ralph, no need to hear his whispered, hoarse, "Let's go." I find myself meekly folding back the kneeler, moving toward the center aisle, up the steps and onto the long blue-green kneeling pads.

There is no time left to consider; already I can feel a slight breeze from Father Norris's vestments as he moves toward my place. Hurriedly, I make the Sign of the Cross, cup my hands and, head bowed, watch him place the tiny Host in my hands, hear him pronounce, "The Body of Christ, the bread of heaven." So this is it: there is to be no turning back. I am committed. Humbly, I bow my head to my hands and take the

Host, choking it down quickly so that I can dab at my eyes before the Chalice comes around. For here follows Brother John Charles with an intricately carved silver cup: "The blood of Christ, the cup of salvation." I drink. There is nothing else to do. And the altar wine burns my aching throat as I swallow it.

Back at my seat, kneeling again, I glance timidly at Ralph. He is fumbling for a Kleenex too. I pass him one; we hold hands like children. We croak through the communion hymn, read the post-Eucharistic prayer in whispers ("And now, Father, send us out into the world to do the work You have given us to do, to love and serve You as faithful witnesses of Christ our Lord"), and kneel for a moment of silence before the organ peals out a jubilant postlude.

At the door, strangely, we are no longer strangers. Brother John Charles greets us warmly, the curate remembers us from Easter and reminds us of the Chadwick lectures again. Father Norris starts to shake hands, then spontaneously reaches out with both arms and hugs us both at once. He has a way of leaning back slightly, looking at us with his head tilted; he holds us at arms' length for a moment and moves us toward the door of Wheeler Hall. "So you came back after all! Do come and have coffee with us and visit with Brother John Charles, won't you?"

"No, Father, thanks, not this time, we're so sorry, we have all this work to do." *Escape, escape;* just get me out of here, away from the Presences, somewhere so that I can think. I have to assess all that has happened to me, to come to terms with it somehow. But this time, when I say good-bye to him, I know that, one way or another, we shall be back.

Outside in the car, I am shivering, half from the spring chill, half from . . . whatever it is that we have just experienced. I try to get out some wise, witty, and cynical sentence that begins "Well, that was quite something . . ." But I get no further: I break down into sobs. "I don't know what is happening to me," I cry into Ralph's shoulder. "To me, either," he says, burying his wet face in my hair. "To both of us."

May 1983

It's now mid-May and I'm sitting in the lobby of the Mayfair-Regent in Chicago. It is a chilly Tuesday afternoon, with a thin wash of rain streaking across the window. Inside, a fire, the last of the season, I hope, burns brightly. I sink into velvet and chintz and sip tea. It's my custom these days to meet my friends on the first Tuesday of each month in this haven of faded elegance. Six or seven women, all professionals, working women, all childless; two married, two single, the rest divorced, divorcing, separated, or in transition. Here we come to chat, sip tea, view impossibly luxe fashions from the Michigan Avenue carriage trade, and compare notes on our recent, albeit chaotic and complicated, lives.

Today the news varies: one woman is ending an intense platonic affair with her mentor, breaking up with her husband (who in turn is ending an affair with his lover, male), and is moving to a new section of the city. Another confesses to us that her affair with a local *artiste* is ending and she's reconciling with her husband, who is just ending five years' worth of therapy to help kick an expensive cocaine habit. Another, recently divorced, talks candidly of her new liaisons, the pain of her divorce, her bisexual lover who's planning a sex-change operation for next year. A fourth talks of co-workers who are planning fantastic boondoggles with company cash, sleeping their way to the top, faking expense reports, and dipping into the company pot for extra perks.

We are the quintessential urban liberals: smiling politely, we sip tea, murmur the predictable Baby Boomer formulas. "Poor Alvie, he had such a rotten childhood, no wonder he's so hostile. . . . " "Oh, Ian is such a genius, such a free spirit, you have to excuse him his little fling in Greece. . . . " "Charles's father *beat* him, no wonder he abuses his kids. . . . " "Well, after all, Lester *would* make a beautiful woman, it's not as if he were hung up on being a man."

All is forgiven, all forgotten, all understood, in terms of repressions, obsessions, fixations, deviations, neuroses. Nothing is too risqué, too liberated, too outré, to be commented on, understood, and forgiven.

The talk wanes briefly. I cannot just sip tea like a stump any longer. I'm expected to say something. The organizer of this monthly ritual, I am strangely silent today. But I am reassured by their broad-mindedness. They are such accepting, loving, open women, so tolerant and generous to flaws in others, so funny and warm. Surely they will understand what is happening to me (they like *feeling* and *sensitivity*, they will at least relate to the Church's social message, I hope). Encouraged by this insight, I take a sip of tea and drop my bombshell. Elsa opens the way by asking me what I've been shopping for.

I hesitate. Our curate has just graduated from seminary and has been ordained deacon, and my tiny Tiffany's shopping bag holds his ordination gift. I am tempted to lie. I am suddenly overwhelmed by the silliness, on the one hand, and the enormity, on the other, of what I must explain to them. Briefly, I am simply too tired to tell them anything. But I rush ahead out of some fantastic devotion to the god of Letting It All Hang Out. These are my friends, I don't have to lie to them.

"Shopping? Oh, yes, this—well, it's for a friend's ordination."

Karen breaks in with a low-pitched sniff (snort?). "An ordination? You mean, to the priesthood or something? For God's sake, how *quaint!* But then you always did have interesting friends. Whatever in the world is this *new* thing you're into?"

I hesitate, then plunge in. "Well, Richard, our . . . curate, he's just been ordained deacon and he's to be ordained priest next month." (Blank stares, open mouths, the sound of teacups

clattering to rest on saucers.) "Well, maybe I should explain
. . . I've—we've—been attending the Church of the Ascension
—since last month, since Easter, really—this really incredible
place, on LaSalle Street—gorgeous French architecture,
stained glass, wonderful music, very high church—and these
really fascinating lectures on the primitive Church."

More blank stares and polite jingling of teacups and demi-
tasse spoons. I pause, stunned, ashamed at how utterly incapa-
ble I am of describing the Presences to these women, my
friends, some of them dating back a decade or more. I have
experienced something that, quite simply, has transformed my
life, yet I am tongue-tied with cliches and dodge all around the
real issue when I speak of it. I am angry at myself for hedging
with polite lies about the architecture, the music, the lecture
series. All of which have attracted me to be sure, but what I
want to say is that I now feel a sort of wild wonder and
astonished joy in the created universe that I had once thought
gone forever. I feel as if someone had just dropped me into the
midst of the prelapsarian Eden. But none of this can I articulate
for my friends.

"It's a *what?*" Lynne shrieks. "Oh, an—Anglo-Catholic
Church! That's not the same as Episcopalian, is it? Well, will
wonders never cease! I thought you hadn't been near one of
those places in years; didn't even know you were one of them
before. Sorry, didn't mean it that way. I just can't see you as
a *Catholic,* that's all. But then you always did have this taste for
the bizarre!"

My teeth are set on edge by my conversion being described
by the word "bizarre." (Surely no more unusual than a sex-
change operation? An affair with the boss? Beating one's children?) But I persevere. "Bizarre? Not really. At least, you'll
have to admit I'm in good company. You know, T. S. Eliot
converted. And in case you've forgotten, John Donne, George
Herbert, Andrew Marvell, Richard Hooker . . ."

Karen and Ronna break into laughter again. "Oh, *God!* All those Metaphysical poets. No wonder you got hooked on this mumbo jumbo. Whatever do they *do* in this place, the Black Mass?"

I am now positively cringing and furious at the same time. Is no one capable of taking me seriously? Even Caterina has turned to me with her best Baltimore-catechism look: "Do they do all that stuff in your church—you know, going to confession and saying the office every day and the feast days and fasting, and all those goddamn saints?"

But something in me has turned, grown brave at their ridicule. I hear myself saying, as if I were quite another person: "Yes, it's the whole nine yards, the Masses and feast days and incense and vestments. But that isn't all, it isn't all vesture and gesture and posture, as Bishop Michael Marshall [the Bishop of Woolwich, England] would say. It really is something quite special. I feel something there I have never felt before. I just can't explain to you how devastating and marvelous and beautiful it all is."

Lynne shakes her head in genuine disbelief. "Well, I never would have guessed it. You, of all people. Well, you'll get over it; you'll never sit through the summer in such a hot, musty place. Did I tell you, by the way, that I'm going to Portugal with Mike and the cat in August?"

So much for the Higher Mysteries. The talk dwindles on, glides over Andrea Pfister shoes, new luggage, new houses, careers, lives, loves. People begin getting up and saying their good-byes as it approaches five-thirty. Karen and Elsa have aerobics class, Ronna has a client, Lynne has to get home to feed Chardonnay, her cat. Others have their therapy sessions. We pull on gloves and bright, short coats against the chilly spring dusk. But I am strangely saddened again, this time for a different reason than before.

They are again warm, loving, funny; we hug and cat-pack-kiss good-bye. They will forgive me, tomorrow, my little eccentricity ("God, poor Val, she thinks she's getting old, getting religion like this—never mind, it'll never last"). And it is precisely this that saddens and enrages me. For them, my friends, this is simply the latest and last in a string of fads and fancies, the newest In Thing, like a sudden passion for Perry Ellis towels or buffalo bags, for white cookware or cone-shaped heels with white hose. They have suffered through these little affectations of mine, so they will suffer through this *amusing*, if irritating, penchant for incense and tapers and other things liturgical, assured that sooner or later Val will come to her senses again.

Perhaps if I told them that I had seen the light on the road to Damascus and had been struck blind. . . . Metaphorically, at least, that is what has happened to me, and I stand, isolated and saddened in my knowledge of a revelation that, for the time being at least, I cannot share. Marriage, pregnancy, sudden riches, a new job, a trip to Paris, a best-seller: these they could comprehend and rejoice in with me. But if I told them that for the first time in a decade, my starved soul is being fed again: no, they simply cannot cope with that.

A half hour later; the night is foggy and cool. The Magnificent Mile is a blaze of light in the early spring dusk. Caterina stands with me at the bus stop. Our breath makes small white clouds in the chill, damp air when we talk.

"Well, you really broke up that party, didn't you? They didn't know what to say, you know—and neither did I. Why didn't you tell me, a month ago, when I got back from Boston? I'd no idea all this was going on."

"Couldn't talk about it, Cate. I will, later, honest. Right now, I can't tell you anymore than I have already. Except that I haven't been so happy in years, and neither has Ralph."

Caterina looks at me, her beautiful broad Italian face breaking into a smile. "That's all that matters, isn't it?"

Later, on the bus, we are sitting watching the lighted shop

windows, talking about trivial things, when and where to go on my husband's birthday, Ronna's birthday. Suddenly I say, "You know, Cate, doesn't it strike you as strange what went on this afternoon? Think of what we talked about: a sex-change operation, an office romance, VD, drugs, child abuse, artificial insemination, every psychosis and neurosis imaginable—and I break up the party with my news that I've gone back to church. That's it, Cate, it's the last forbidden thing in America. Religion is no longer the opiate of the people; instead, it's the last real conversation-stopper, the last thing that can truly amaze and shock your liberal friends."

Cate shakes her head with a sigh. "I'll never understand all of this. . . . but if it makes you happy, I suppose it's all right."

Later, after she gets off the bus, I stare out of the bus windows at the street lamps wreathed in haloes of fog. "The last forbidden thing in America," I muse, to no one in particular.

May 22, 1983

It is nearly seven o'clock. The house is quiet, so quiet that I can hear the living room clock ticking as I stand in the kitchen. A rare moment of peace: our work in neat stacks on the desk and drawing board, dinner bubbling on the stove, a vase of red tulips on the table, Pachelbel playing on the small tape recorder nearby. And I am sitting at the dining table in the late April sunlight, staring into the heart of the biggest of the tulips, when it hits me: *I wish I were there again.* I wish I were back in that miraculous place, hearing the man in his monk's robes and listening to those chants that strike so deep into my heart and soul, that it seems that I was born, or reborn, listening to them.

And, gazing deep into that endless red and pollen-dusted heart of the tulip, I realize that, just this minute, just today, I have come home.

May 27, 1983

We have finished a marathon two days at Seabury-Western Theological Seminary. Of all the unexpected places we have been in the last month, this is by far the most unlikely!

But we got there by a perfectly straightforward route: our new curate, who is just graduating from Seabury this month, invited us to come to three lectures by Henry Chadwick, the noted British theologian and writer on early Church history.

The whole experience was marked by a sense of *déjà vu*, beginning with the moment we first parked and walked through the campus in the twilight: very reminiscent of Emory and Oglethorpe College in Atlanta it was, with the gray Gothic buildings, the first trees budding, and a pervading sense of peace and order that has been missing from our lives for a very long time.

Nostalgia? Disillusionment with the world of business? I don't think so: we were genuinely enchanted by Chadwick's wit, humor, erudition, and humanity, enlightened by his insights into early Church life and thought. And pleased to be part of a conference in which no one, for once, talked about "the bottom line."

Walking back through the wet grass of the campus, under the stars, with the library lights still burning dimly behind us, I wondered again: *What is happening to us?*

And I don't know the answer. I can only reply, as I answered myself last Sunday evening, when I looked so long into the heart of the red tulip and listened to the Pachelbel Canon: I feel that I—we—have come back home after a long absence.

May 30, 1983

I saw Father Norris in his office this afternoon to talk about joining Ascension. Ralph and I were both surprised to find ourselves sitting in that room, talking about redemption and baptism and corporate worship in completely matter-of-fact tones to this incredible man.

A cold spring afternoon; I am wearing a sweater and am still grateful when Father turns on the space heater in his office. Very characteristically a priest's office, I think: crammed with books and photographs and memorabilia, icons and statues and cards from parishioners and friends, and dominated by a big carved desk piled high with papers.

We tell our story and he listens intently without interrupting. This man, I note, knows how to listen. There are no deprecating or condescending remarks. He doesn't try to make a joke of the prodigals' return. He doesn't scold us; he doesn't try to play God. He doesn't exert "authority," although in his quiet way he exudes it. He is, simply, a very good man talking to two fellow beings who, like him, are engaged in the universal quest for God: pilgrims together, all three of us.

I like him instantly. There is absolutely no pretense about the man. He tells us a little about himself: He was formerly an Anglican Benedictine monk at St. Gregory's Abbey in Three Rivers, Michigan. He plays viola in the Evanston Symphony. He adores Wagner—most opera, in fact. He has been at Ascension for fourteen years.

We leave with stacks of books and a reading list a mile long. Despite his lack of intellectual pretensions, this gentle rector of ours is awesomely well-read. Ralph will have to study for confirmation this summer. And I have asked for reaffirmation at the same service. We don't know a date yet, but meanwhile there are books to be read, a million questions to be asked, dozens of late-night conversations over dinner and past, into the wee hours.

We stay for Evening Prayer and the Low Mass that follows. This place is beginning to feel like home.

June 28, 1983

Another milestone: Ralph's confirmation and my reaffirmation.

Sunday, Father ran up to us at coffee hour between the Masses and asked, "What are you doing Tuesday morning at seven A.M.?" It happens that the bishop was to celebrate a Mass there, with several other confirmations. We said: of course, we'll be there.

At 6:45 this morning, the church is dark. The weather is unseasonably cold; when we get there, the canon is sitting in Wheeler Hall alternately smoking a cigarette and warming his hands over the lighted end. The church is full of the Sisters of St. Anne, kneeling in a row in the front pew like so many devout doves in their gray habits. Father hugs us both and gives us a flurry of whispered instructions in the sacristy two minutes before the Mass begins.

The Mass is a simple daily Low Mass, with the Sacrament of Confirmation just before the Peace. I try not to catch my heel in the uneven tiles of the floor when I go up the altar steps. Together we promise to continue in the apostles' teaching and fellowship, in the breaking of bread and in the prayers; to persevere in resisting evil; to seek and serve Christ in all persons, loving our neighbors as ourselves; to strive for justice and peace among all people and respect the dignity of all human beings. The bishop lays hands on Ralph and signs him on the forehead with the Sign of the Cross. To me he says, "Valerie, may the Holy Spirit who has begun a good work in you, direct and uphold you in the service of Christ and of his kingdom, Amen."

Afterwards, we all hug—Ralph, the sisters, the curate, Father Norris, even the bishop. And then, all the parishioners—people I don't know who seem to know me—Jim, Roger, Steve, Jane, Cynthia. Mother Mary Margaret takes both my hands and whispers, "Welcome!"

Later that evening, we are going to dinner at the curate's cottage with some other guests, including the bishop, so we rush away for our daily meetings and work on several clients' projects. We make time for a quick breakfast at the Oak Tree: more kisses, a few tears, an astonished laugh at our own astonishment. And a surprise—we have both gone out to buy each another small gifts: cards, a medal depicting the Four Gospelists, a new Prayer Book, some paperbacks from the tract table.

The day passes like a dream. I can't seem to connect this with the need to rush around, see clients, meet deadlines, Xerox manuscripts, get together samples. Tonight my evening term class for the summer starts. By class time, I am *still* rushing, trying to get to the curate's house on time.

A student asks me a question and I am about to ask her to call tomorrow, there isn't time tonight, when all of a sudden, an image flashes into my head: Father Norris at the Eucharist last Sunday, handing the chalice down to a blind woman, bending exactly to her height with infinite care, infinite attention, before moving on to a child who is fidgeting at the rail, waiting for his blessing.

So I tell the student, of course I have time tonight. And I try to listen to her problems with a little of the care that Father lavishes on us all, Sunday after Sunday.

And I get to the curate's house on time, after all. At dinner the bishop proposes a toast to us, the newest of Ascension's parishioners. We tell him a little of our experiences since Easter and he says, "You know, it's always amazing to me how many adults, otherwise sophisticated people, try year after year to live with a five-year-old's conception of God. That's not what the Church asks of people. We don't require that you check your brains at the door."

This is my kind of church, I have decided. I had forgotten —if indeed I ever knew—how much one can *think* here.

II · Consulting the Faithful

Personal Stories of Spiritual Journeys

A monk was once asked: What do you do there in the monastery? He replied: We fall and get up, fall and get up, fall and get up again.

—Tito Colliander, quoted in Father Kallistos Ware,
The Orthodox Way

Under the pressure of a very great love, or in the darkness of a conflict that exacts a heroic renunciation of our whole self, or in the ecstasy of a sudden joy that does not belong to this earth, the soul will be raised out of itself. It will come face to face with the Christ of the Psalms.

It is the flash of a flame that is touched off by an immediate contact of the substance of the soul with God himself. In one terrific second that belongs not to time but to eternity, the whole soul is transfixed and illumined by the tremendous darkness which is the light of God.

Thomas Merton, *Bread in the Wilderness*

GEOFFREY

For Geoffrey, a university administrator with a master's degree in education, the road to Damascus was literally that. He is one of those who speak of apocalyptic experiences—and not without some

48

cautions and reservations. He was willing to share his story with us only on the condition that his identity would not be revealed. "It could be professionally disastrous to me. Some of my colleagues . . . they'd laugh me off the campus if they ever recognized me in your book." Geoffrey was born of upper-middle-class, educated parents in a large and affluent western suburb of Chicago. He was a cradle Episcopalian who grew up in a tradition he describes as "very Morning Prayer/low church" in approach.

I was never taught to see the Sacrament as central; it was very typical perfunctory low church. I saw a new side of the Church when we got a new rector, an Anglo-Catholic with a degree from Nashotah House [an Episcopal seminary near Milwaukee, Wisconsin: *Eds.*]. And I got interested in liturgy and was an acolyte and altar boy and all that. I was taken on a "field trip" to St. Gregory's Abbey as a high-school student, but I recall no specific details of the trip.

I majored in philosophy at Oberlin College and decided that there was simply no intellectual substance to the faith at all. So, in the early Fifties, I stopped going to church at all. And starting in the late Sixties, there was a ten-year period when I literally didn't go into churches at all, not even for weddings and funerals. I just stayed away, out of a conviction that there was nothing in the Church for any self-respecting intellectual.

Between 1971 and 1975, my comfortable life began to change. There were political problems at work—campus unrest, violent confrontations with students, internal tensions in my department and college. The "tennis-shoe liberal" approach was being called into question. And my personal life was a shambles. I had grown up in a very well-bred family, typical WASPs. When I saw the film *Ordinary People,* I was devasted for days; that's exactly what my family was like, exactly how I was brought up. We never learned, never were allowed, to express our feelings at all.

In 1975 I made a trip to England—just an ordinary trip, chiefly to visit museums and listen to concerts. I did go to visit some cathedrals, just as any ordinary tourist would, I told myself. Now I realize that I was still interested in them, in what they represented. I'd been before, on previous trips, and those were my only real or meaningful exposures to liturgy.

So in 1975, I made my annual pilgrimage to England in a more than usual state of emotional turmoil, but without any hint of what was in store for me. One afternoon, I had heard of an excellent concert in Canterbury Cathedral, so I went there for the afternoon. I went in and sat down. I had nothing more in mind than just listening to music casually and looking forward to a beer in a pub with some friends afterward.

That afternoon, sitting there in Canterbury Cathedral, I had the most incredible, ineffable experience of my life. I can only call it, without exaggeration, a conversion experience. I realized that previously I had gone to church, been confirmed as a teenager, gone through all the motions, without a profound conversion taking place. Now, I suddenly realized, in the most profound insight of my life, that I had found my roots. I found myself shaken to the very foundation of my being.

Geoffrey didn't know why, but he suddenly felt the compulsion to act, to bring his life into line with the new insight he had gained. Then within two days, Geoffrey was stricken with the first of two cerebral strokes. With the first, he lost the peripheral vision in his right eye. The second stroke, occurring a few weeks later, wiped out the hearing in his left ear. He was hospitalized for a month, with impaired vision and little hearing, and was away from work for six months.

In this long quiet period I began to make connections that I had never made before. I saw the meaning of my experience at Canterbury in relation to my strokes, the present crises in

my life, in a way I had never done before. And I recognized
a need in myself—a need to experiment with religion.

I started walking regularly as part of my rehabilitation program. I just walked, I told myself I didn't know or care where.
But I know now that I was walking to church. I went a bit
farther each day until finally, the Tuesday before Thanksgiving of 1975, I walked to the seven A.M. Mass at a church nearly
five miles from my apartment.

The following Sunday I went back, but had to leave—the
volume of the organ and choir was so intense, it hurt my ears.
I still couldn't hear in my left ear. But I started going regularly.
And I also started reading everything about religion I could get
my hands on. I made friends with a Roman Catholic priest. He
gave me two books that made a profound impact on me: *The
Jesus Myth* and *The Sinai Myth*.

At first, I made no real effort to integrate with the church
community. I'd skip coffee hour altogether, or just stand
around without making an effort to know anyone. I found
myself shy with the people here. But several people made a real
effort to get to know me, and the rector took every opportunity
to make me feel welcome. Soon I felt he was a friend as well
as a spiritual adviser and priest. In 1976 I transferred my membership, some thirty years old, from my suburban parish to a
church in the Near North of Chicago.

*Today Geoffrey is just finishing his term as senior warden of the
church. He has served two terms on its vestry and has just completed
writing a history of the parish. He continues to be active in the
parish, although he carefully restricts his activities to those which
do not interfere with a self-imposed rule of life that includes prayer,
regular confession, and participation in daily and Sunday masses.*

My training is in psychology, so I'm well aware that there
are all kinds of psychological explanations for what happened

to me. But that doesn't bother me. I simply don't consider them applicable to my experience at Canterbury and the subsequent months. To me the experience was a genuine conversion experience. It was completely credible, and it continues to seem valid to me, even as I try to analyze it. The fact that it could be "explained away" in psychological terms doesn't mitigate its force.

ALEXANDRA

Alexandra is an attorney in her late thirties who lives in a high-rise in Chicago with her husband, James. She has recently returned to the church after more than ten years of absence and credits her newly rediscovered faith for helping her deal with the bitterness she still feels toward the priest she identifies as "Joe" in this story:

I wasn't reared in any church. My father was nominally Presbyterian and was an elder in the church. I went with him off and on while I was in elementary school until he and my mother were separated while I was in junior high. So then I started going with my mother to her church—she was a southern Baptist. I went with her a good deal while I was in high school. I mostly went because I was sleeping with the assistant pastor. He was such a hypocrite—but I guess so was I. I felt no real commitment to that church or any other, or to my faith, for that matter. I just went to church out of a sense of duty—and to see Tom, of course.

After we broke up, I didn't go anywhere at all. I made a few stabs at going to a campus church the first year I was in college. But the Baptist Youth Fellowship seemed full of all these *churchy* types who didn't drink or smoke and thought going to dances was the work of the devil. I just didn't seem to connect with any of it.

The way I connected with a church again was strange. A

group of my friends and I took off to New York, without my mother or any of the parents knowing about it. My aunt and uncle covered for me; Mother thought I was staying with them in Washington. We drove all night to get to New York. While we were there, we went to St. John the Divine. It was the 1960s and we were all smoking pot and drinking wine and getting high, and one of the boys with us said, "Why don't we go to church tonight?" It was some saint's day, I forget what. That was the greatest experience of my life. I loved all the ritual and ceremony of carrying in the cross and banners and tapers. So once I got home, I started to take instruction and was confirmed a year later.

But then even that soured. I got into this very political parish where they were fighting these incredible battles over the prayer book and the liturgy and everything. The rector—I loved him, he was my mentor, the father I never had. I know that. But he was gay and I guess someone in the bishop's office found out: at any rate, he was removed as rector and sent to some small rural parish in another diocese. It broke my heart to lose him. I felt the Church had let him down—had let *me* down. I was moving out of town anyway, but I was just as glad I wouldn't have to go back. I didn't like the new priest at all.

I moved to a university town the next fall to go to law school and started dating James B., a man on the faculty whom I'd known in college. We fell in love and decided to get married. He was divorced, with three children by his previous marriage. While he was waiting for his divorce to become final, we lived together, like everyone else in the Sixties.

I wasn't formally a member of any church in the new town. But I wanted, *really* wanted, to be married in a church. I had always had this vision of the sort of wedding I wanted: the medieval-looking wedding dress and the baroque music and the sort of service I would have. There was no church of my denomination in the town, but the head of the university's humanities department was a priest who had just graduated from seminary. Joe was his name; he wore his collar to class sometimes. So we asked, kind of indirectly through a friend of ours, if he would marry us. I planned to use the university chapel and have him celebrate a Eucharist.

He didn't even do us the courtesy of talking directly to us. He sent a message back through our friend that he couldn't marry us because James had been divorced. He wouldn't even consider it, he said.

So I went to his office. I thought there was nothing to lose at that point. I asked for an appointment and asked him point-blank *why:* why couldn't he marry us?

I'll never forget what he said; I was crushed by it. I still wake up at night angry about it, almost ten years later. He told me that I was formally renouncing the Church. By my decision to marry James, I was cutting myself off from the church and all it stood for. He said that our marriage was not a sanctified union and that I would always be barred from the sacraments. I would never be able to take Communion again if I married this man. And no, he would not marry us.

I asked what he would do if we appealed his decision, but he said that was no good: we would have to take our case to the bishop of a nearby diocese and he would never support it as a priest. The case he laid out was this: you marry him and you become a pariah in your own faith. As far as he was concerned, the case was closed.

The odd thing was, he wasn't much older than I. He was a young man, in his late twenties or early thirties, perhaps, with a sort of silly smirk on his face. But his manner was so pious, so holier-than-thou. He didn't speak to me as a human being at all; he talked to me as if I were a bad child instead of a woman with a professional degree. He talked only in the official jargon of the Church; I felt that I was talking to an institution instead of a human being.

I'll never forget his eyes: he never once looked me in the face while he talked. Instead, he played with a letter opener in the shape of a cross while he told me that he would not marry us nor appeal the case for us. I felt that I had just become the Scarlet Woman.

So that was that. I didn't have the knowledge—or the heart —to pursue it any further. Our friend, who served as James's best man, introduced us to the university chaplain, a sort of bland man in his early fifties who muttered and grumphed his way through a "pre-marital counseling" session with me. He told me that he thought I was making a big mistake in marrying James. He agreed to marry us. But he clearly didn't approve of the match at all.

So we got married in a very quiet ceremony in a friend's living room. I cried, and not entirely for joy. All the time, I felt cheated out of the wedding I had wanted: the long medieval gown and the baroque music and the nuptial Mass. This seemed like just another day. I had found the love of my life, and yet I couldn't get married the way I'd dreamed of since I was a tiny girl. I felt the Church had failed me for the second time in my life. I knew the union was holy—in its own way; I felt that our marriage was a sacrament, just as I had always been taught. But the church said otherwise.

Ten years later, a friend invited me to go to church with her and I did. I'd suddenly been thinking, for no reason at all, about how different my life might have been if Joe had given us a different answer that day. What if we had been married in a church? What if we had kept up that connection, that side of our lives? I realized that that had been one of the big reasons we had never had children of our own—I had no real tradition to offer children, nothing. . . . I couldn't even ask for my baby to be baptized, if I had had one. I was beginning to question myself, the kind of person I had become. I didn't like what years of being a lawyer had done to me.

So I went back to church with my friend and at first I didn't dare to take the Sacrament, of course. I still remembered what Joe had told me that day a decade earlier in his office. It was only after weeks of indecision and talking with my friend—and talking with the rector, who is a wonderful, gentle, and compassionate man, nothing at all like Joe, and learning how differently the Church now views divorce—that I finally went to Communion again.

James started going to church with me and he was confirmed last year. We've since learned that all Joe would have had to do was to file a petition with the Bishop in that diocese for a clarification of James's marriage. We could have waited six months and been married in the church after all.

Of course I've forgiven Joe; what else could I do? But I still feel cheated—out of the wedding I wanted, out of all those years in the Church, out of the Sacrament I felt I was barred from—even from having the children I realize that I wanted. It colored so many of the decisions I made in my life, and some of those things can't be undone.

The irony of it all is that just two years ago, we learned that Joe wasn't a priest after all. He had been ordained deacon but never priest. I wonder how many other lives he ruined with that false piety?

JOAN

Joan, a recent graduate of an Ivy League university who is now in the word-processing division of a large and prestigious Midwestern legal firm, is typical of the new breed of churchgoer. She comes from a family of prominent Lutheran theologians; in fact, her father, now living in St. Louis, is working with other theologians on a project called Crossings II, a project to integrate theology with daily life and work. Joan moved to Chicago three years ago. At first she attended a "progressive" church on the city's South Side, but found herself increasingly dissatisfied with the form of worship.

* * *

I didn't hear Gospel preached, there was little or no emphasis on the Sacraments—in short, it just didn't speak to me at all. I found myself going less frequently, skipping whole weeks altogether, and finally becoming, once again, a church dropout.

Then, I ran across Pastor Brian of the Lutheran School of Divinity at the University of Chicago. Pastor Brian had close ties to Bishop Brent House at the University. Although it represented a different denomination, Brent House proved to be a turning point in my spiritual journey. It was all there again: Scriptures, ritual, the correct use of liturgical worship. I felt I was returning to my roots in a certain way, although it was a totally different denomination. That didn't matter: I felt at home there in a way I never felt in the "progressive" church. And for the first time in my life, I realized that at heart I was very traditional about religion.

Later, through my association with Father Sam Portaro of Brent House, I came to visit an Episcopal church. I felt my personal demand for liturgical worship completely satisfied. At first it was enough to sit and immerse myself in the liturgy; later, I came to sing in the volunteer choir and to serve as lector and acolyte. When you walk in there, you sense the Holy Spirit working in that place. Sometimes, still, I can hardly talk about it without crying.

Somehow, still, joining the Episcopal Church seems to be turning my back on a whole family tradition of Lutheranism. I still feel deep roots in myself to the whole thing; when we sing "A Mighty Fortress Is Our God," I can hardly hold back the tears. I can't just turn my back on all that. Yet I feel comfortable, okay, about taking the Sacrament with Anglicans. I have come to be much more ecumenical in the way I feel about worship.

I guess you could say I am just looking for the perfect place that's both Lutheran and liturgical, but I'm willing to look, for

months or even years, if that's what it takes. Formal membership isn't very important to me. I'll worship wherever I find
something that answers my personal needs.

*Within the last year Joan has returned to the Lutheran Church,
although she maintains close ties with clergy and friends at the
Episcopal parish.*

MIKE

*Mike, a tour guide with a major transit company in suburban
Chicago, didn't have a single conversion experience. Rather, a series
of coincidences led him back to the Church—or more accurately, led
him to search out a church where his own needs could be met.*

I was a cradle Episcopalian who went through the usual
things—confirmation classes, confirmation, a drifting away. In
the Sixties, when things were so turbulent and unsettled, I
switched over to evangelical churches because they seemed
more charismatic and "renewed." Somehow I ended up attending the Philadelphia College of Bible and giving serious
thought to being ordained.

The courses at Philadelphia were in some ways liberating:
I learned some things about Scripture that I had never known.
But I left school at a point of crisis that was both personal and
intellectual. I had been a conscientious objector, totally against
the Vietnam war. Now I enlisted as a matter of conscience.

Later, I got to the point where my life seemed empty and
without meaning. I got out of the Marine Corps and started
driving a school bus and that brought me into contact with
school-age children for the first time. That made me have to
come to terms with the child in myself, to realize that I've got
to be a human being first and a Christian second.

I also started reading like mad, especially C. S. Lewis—in

fact, I was reconverted, or maybe really converted for the first time, by reading *The Pilgrim's Regress*. And then, by coincidence, I went to visit a friend's house and there was a man there at dinner who said, "I just read the most marvelous book that I'm dying to talk about to somebody." It turned out to be *The Pilgrim's Regress*, and I stayed up half the night talking with the man about Lewis.

Finally, and this was the most amazing thing of all, I met a professor at Trinity College in Deerfield who had just weathered an emotional crisis very similar to the one I had just gone through. He invited me to go to church with him and his wife the following Christmas Eve.

As I left work that Christmas Eve, I remember telling my boss, "I am about to do the most amazingly stupid thing of my life: I'm going to church." Well, it turned out to be the most memorable one of my life. At that one Solemn High Mass, I felt as if I had stepped right in the eye of a storm. All those primitive chords in me were stirred, all those bits of half-buried liturgy and music, and I couldn't fight it all anymore. I finally surrendered and the rest is history.

Now, four years later, Mike is a regular communicant of this church and chairman of its library committee. But he is not "religious" in a conventional sense. Like many of the yuppie churchgoers his age, he is less committed to the Church in the abstract than to a particular church.

I don't think I'd be in another church, I can't see myself going regularly anywhere else. If this particular church weren't here in this city, I think I just wouldn't be going anywhere right now. It was all just providential: the place, the church, the occasion, the rightness of the experience, all the coincidences that led up to it. But it couldn't be just any church; it had to be this particular one. If this place suddenly vanished off the face of the earth overnight, I'm not sure what I would do. I don't think I'd go somewhere else in the same way that I come here now.

DAN AND GINGER

Dan and Ginger are almost textbook-case urban professionals. They're early- to mid-thirtyish, successful career people who juggle work and family obligations to their two children, Ginger's daughter, five, by a previous marriage, and Dan's son, fourteen, also by a previous marriage. Ginger is away doing Saturday-morning errands when we first begin to talk. Dan, an attorney in a large Oklahoma City firm, keeps an eye on Ginger's daughter as he talks with us.

We were inactive, just totally out of the Church for years. So when we first came back, we were sort of susceptible to all sorts of sales pitches. We both had been baptized as Disciples of Christ and we kind of wanted to get away from the fundamentalist thing. We heard of this Church of the Master [a large nondenominational Protestant church in the suburbs: *Eds.*], and we went there.

At first we found the people very involving and—well, the people captured us. I was always bothered by the lack of doctrine, or a real theology, and I think so was Ginger. But we became very active in the Church and felt somehow it was all to the good to get so involved in a church, any church.

But something was missing. I felt very uncomfortable there, although I couldn't put my finger on why. I just knew something was wrong. I didn't feel the whole church was religious in a true or concrete sense. I've always related to the humanistic approach to religion, and I've always dealt with it that way myself. But I also knew that I didn't feel a direct contact with God.

The whole experience was very cathartic at first. I found myself crying for the first time in years and that was a very healing experience. I was going through—am still going through—very difficult circumstances in my own life, my divorce, family problems, all that, and I don't see how people can face adversity without some sort of faith. And at that time I was on trial, literally, on legal and political matters, and I went from being a public official to an attorney in private practice and that was a big change in lifestyle.

I guess we were attracted by the people there. The Church of Master had a lot of younger people there, and they were attractive, good-looking people, it was all sort of upscale and lively and a far cry from the old blue-haired ladies' ice-cream social type of thing. The church was very liberal politically, and we liked that. But something was missing. One thing was —and I became progressively more aware of this as the second year wore on—that the church was entirely built on a kind of cult of personality. Pastor Jones [not his real name] was a big charismatic figure and as time went on, he got bigger and bigger. There was a whole cult developing around him. People literally worshipped him and hung on his every word. It got to be so it was a bad day when he preached badly and everyone was high as a kite when he preached well. Everything hung on him.

And he was no TV evangelist. He was a bright, intelligent man with a string of degrees, eminently respectable. But it was Jones, Jones, Jones, until the whole church was lost, submerged, in his personality. People came just to hear him. And I was turned off by that.

As luck would have it, one of Ginger's friends was a single parent and her daughter was being christened at All Souls' a little ways out from the city. This was around late October or early November of 1982, and was just about the time that Ginger's mother died from a brain tumor, really a horrible thing. When the surgery and chemotherapy were over, little was left of her dad's life. And somehow, he had started going to All Souls' and then this woman, Ginger's friend, her daughter was to be christened there. So these two things happened quite close together: Ginger's dad was confirmed and the baby was christened.

And both times we went, and we were literally just knocked out by the liturgy. Both the services—the language was unlike anything we both were used to. I've always had a great love for the English language and its words, and this was the most beautiful use of that language I had ever heard. It was involving, real and concrete and intimate in a way that services at the Church of the Master never were. Here there was little or no emphasis on preaching. I can't recall if we even had a sermon, but we spent a lot of time *praying*. And we both were knocked out by that.

So we started going, first to All Souls' and later to St. Paul's Cathedral. And eventually we left our former church and entered confirmation class, just like kids, you know, and were confirmed at the Cathedral. Another thing, unlike that church, the people at the Cathedral knew all our problems and they cared. It wasn't just pretty people being pretty together, these people really cared. They were very supportive to anyone with serious or trivial problems. I think now in retrospect, that without the church I might have made it through with a private faith. But that congregation—that parish—certainly made it easier.

Ginger, a pretty blond social worker in her early thirties, breezes into the room, laden with the staples of an affluent household: fresh daisies, loaves of Italian bread from a gourmet bakery, designer jars of exotic mustards and chutneys, a bottle of Pinot Noir Blanc for dinner. She tells her story in much the same way as Dan: simply, directly, but with an obvious love for her adopted faith.

* * *

Several things influenced me to get back into the church, I guess. I had been working for the state and I wanted to get into private practice as a social worker. I'm now with a mental health center as counselor and find I prefer it to government work. And my daughter Erin was born, and about the same time, my mother died. And I started to shop around for a church, to feel the need for some religious tradition I could believe in.

I flirted with Roman Catholicism, and I liked many aspects of it. But I couldn't buy the doctrine of papal infallibility. And while I liked the hierarchical organization, I found it much too rigid and absolute for my tastes.

DAN: Sure, we were both interested in Roman Catholicism. Historically, it's been a great force for good—but also for evil. Just look at the Inquisition, all the other great persecutions. There were just so many things we were both uncomfortable with.

GINGER: Well, unlike Dan, I had kept a membership with my folks' church. And I had this experimental Catholic period where I went to this sort of outer fringe Roman Catholic Church. It had a wonderful priest and a congregation that was a mix of Catholic and non-Catholic that I liked. And I felt completely comfortable there. But I got further and further away and never was confirmed, and after about a year and a half I left.

So like Dan I was searching for something and so I went to the Church of the Master and began to get involved. I was very active—except that I think now that Dan really tried harder than I did to make it work, to be a part of the church. A part of me never really felt secure there.

You see, at that time my mother was ill, very ill, with terminal cancer. And the people at the Church of the Master didn't do a very good job of ministering to us. It was just this young, young, very yuppie suburban population. Their whole focus was on belonging and not belonging, who fit and who didn't.

And there was something else. I liked Pastor Jones—*excuu-use* me! *Dr.* Jones! He went off and got a degree and suddenly he had to be *Dr.* Jones. And about that time there was a subtle shift in the congregation. It got to be a cult, where they all worshipped the minister and his personality. But the members of the Church who were in trouble were all but forgotten.

When Mother was dying, Dad and I weren't able to be there every Sunday. And we felt very isolated. No one was there for us. No one came to visit us. It was very much a young suburba-nites' church. There was no mix of ages, there were no older people, no people ending their lives. It was just all these beauti-ful people being beautiful and successful together, not having problems, thinking positively and scaling the corporate ladder. My mother was dying, and no one seemed to care.

I remember once a woman in the congregation shot her husband, who had been an FBI agent, and everyone tried to pretend it hadn't happened. They just had no way to cope with grief or loss.

Dad felt the same thing. He needed ways to deal with his grief after Mother died, and a friend of his took him one night to this seminar on coping with grief at St. Paul's. There he found a real permission to cry and grieve and be who he was, in the midst of people who really cared. And eventually he took confirmation classes and this man in his mid-sixties was confirmed. And that was how we got to where we are now.

Like Dan, I was deeply moved both by Dad's confirmation and by Debra's daughter's baptism. I was moved especially by the liturgy. But I wouldn't say that our move to St. Paul's away from the other Church was a "high," a peak sort of experience. We just kind of got up one morning and went to St. Paul's, and have been going there ever since.

DAN: We both like the active worship—the sense that you don't just sit, you actively worship. We have been out of town several times and gone to other churches and felt a little uncomfortable. If a part of the liturgy is left out—the General Confession or the Peace or the Absolution—it's as if you feel cheated, as if something were left out of your life that day. I like the lack of emphasis on personality. Here the sermon is less important than the total liturgy, the total worship experience. When the focus is on the Sacraments, any individual person becomes unimportant—and at the same time the most important thing in the world. And I guess that paradox expresses what it's all about for me.

SUSAN

Susan is a pretty brunette who is in public relations with a major Atlanta firm. She talks easily about her experience in converting from a southern Baptist background to Roman Catholicism.

I graduated from high school about 1972. I had grown up Southern Baptist. I stayed Baptist while I was in college, at least nominally. Actually, I was nothing. It was just whatever I could get by with. I went to church as little as possible, mostly on holidays with my parents, or when someone got married. I got married, and my husband's family was Roman Catholic. But he was a sort of nominal Catholic, he didn't insist that we get married in the Church. We did, but I didn't convert right away. We sort of went, and when our daughter was born, I just wanted her to grow up a different way than I had grown up. I didn't want her to be brutalized by all the Southern Baptist guilt trip.

Eventually I got divorced and I felt that was the end of my association with the Roman Catholic Church. I had heard that divorce was forbidden, that they frowned on it. But I could never go back to being a Southern Baptist. My heart was in the Roman Catholic Church and I couldn't leave it.

I made friends with David, a young TV producer who is acolyte at a small Roman Catholic parish in his neighborhood, and we starting seeing each other. And so I came with him to his church for a Christmas Eve Mass. And one thing led to another, and I went to talk to the priest. And I discovered this whole new thing. There's a newly formed group to get people back into the church who are divorced or separated.

I was so surprised I could hardly speak. I had expected the priest to tell me I was banned from the church, something like that, you know, "Never darken this door again." Instead, he invited me to come to this group and think about starting confirmation class.

I thought a little about going back to the Southern Baptist church; I will admit it seemed like a lot of hassle at my age (I'm almost thirty) to start going to confirmation class like a kid again. But I couldn't go back. I'm just not comfortable with hellfire and brimstone and sin and guilt and singing all six verses of "Just as I Am" while they lead people up front, just like a herd of sheep.

So I started confirmation class, and I got through it and was confirmed last fall. Now I just about live here on weekends and in the evening and so does my daughter. It feels very much like a family, a place that feels like home. For us it's especially important since there are only the two of us. I no longer date the man I came here with, but we're still friends. It's as if Gabrielle, my daughter, had one big extended family with dozens of aunts and cousins and grandparents—the kind of thing you used to see in the old South but we've gotten away from—it's here in this parish. I think I must have been born to be a Roman Catholic, it just took me all these years to find it out.

MELINDA

For Susan's friend Melinda, the transition was equally hard but rewarding. Melinda, also a young divorcée, without children, was never baptized as a child.

I pretty much grew up without benefit of religion of any kind. No Sunday school, not much of anything. My parents, like Susan's, were Southern Baptist, and the custom in our community was that children were not baptized until the age of twelve or so. So when I reached what they call "the age of accountability," I just slipped through the cracks—just vanished. I never went to church enough to let anyone get to me. And my parents didn't keep up with that kind of thing. They were too busy playing golf at the country club and getting over Saturday night's hangover.

Well, I got married, and my husband had no religious background either. We got married in a civil ceremony and went out and got bombed with our friends, no religious overtones to any of it at all. The marriage lasted only two years and then we split. And for the first time I had to make a living. I lucked up and got a job in Atlanta, making good money. But I felt something was missing from my life. I went out to singles bars every night, not really looking for a man so much as looking for someone to talk to.

In my department there was this woman whose husband had been an Episcopal priest. He had died the year before, and this woman was a professor, part-time, at Georgia State. I took one of her courses finally, and got to know her better, and we started talking, of all things, about God. It was all very new to me, I hadn't talked about God to anyone since I quit Sunday school years ago. She wasn't holier-than-thou, or falsely pious. She was just—just different, so different from anyone I knew. One Sunday she invited me to her church and I went there and

—I don't even know how to describe it. My whole life turned around from that moment on.

I didn't start confirmation classes right away. I didn't feel I was even on that level. I just began to read Scripture and to meditate and talk with Fiona at length about things like, "What is the nature of God? And what does it all mean?" I was baptized last May, and Fiona was my godmother. It was a very special time to me.

I now intend to start confirmation classes this fall. I think I'm ready to go that far. I still have lots of doubts and problems but I think I am at a level where I can resolve them, or perhaps learn that they aren't that important. And I've met Susan and David, Susan's friend, and other single and divorced people here. And older people like Fiona are very much a part of our group. It really is a family—what I was looking for in the singles bars, I think, and didn't find.

This fall, I'm buying a house in the neighborhood and moving in and fixing it up. Maybe I'll remarry, maybe not. For the first time, my own life is in order and—I've found where the Spirit is, that's all.

DICK

Dick is an affable and engaging person who spent most of his life as a career military man. We first met him at a diocesan-wide educational conference, and within ten minutes of our meeting we were sharing our respective stories. At the time we met he was a student in a local theological seminary.

I'm thinking about how to introduce my own journey back to the Church, and as I reflect, it's more than that: it's a spiritual pilgrimage. And if you want to understand that pilgrimage better, you need to understand a little about my personality type. According to the Briggs-Meyer Personality Inventory, I am a personality type known as E/N/F/J. I am extroverted, intuitive, feeling, and judgmental—that is, I often make judgments instead of simply perceiving things. So because of who I am and how I operate, I spend little quiet time with myself reflecting. I am a mover, a hard worker, a person who becomes enthusiastic easily, and who generally lives without much reflection or self-searching.

I grew up in an evangelical, rather conservative denomination. God was never an issue for me. I was a rather middle-of-the-road perfunctory trinitarian. But somehow, I knew from childhood, deep down, that I was called to be a minister of the Gospel. I don't know how or why I knew this. Certainly I didn't feel that I had any special gifts that fitted me for this role. All I knew was that someday, somehow, I would be ordained.

But my life and educational path took me pretty far afield. I went to a university whose whole history and tradition and values were about as far away from conventional religion as you can get—you know, the standard "small liberal arts college for small liberals." The subjects I took both fought with and neutralized the belief patterns of my denominational background. I was in an interesting life situation at the end of college. I was about as far away from any sort of profession of faith as you can be, yet I still firmly believed that I would be ordained someday.

Still, after graduation, I had no contact with any church. I met and fell in love with a Roman Catholic girl, and eventually married her. Yet I also remember telling her that I could not convert and we could not be married in her church because someday I was convinced that I must be ordained in another church. And she accepted this, somehow. Yet we still, even after this, found ourselves without a church, without any formal religious affiliation of any sort. All of our close friends accepted the validity of the call that I felt even then, yet they were baffled by it. How can a person who is—practically speaking—an agnostic feel such things, they wondered.

I entered the Air Force and became a pilot. It was a career that was to last over twenty years. I loved it. I was good at it and I enjoyed nearly every minute of it . . . yet I never really felt that it was my career. As a hobby, I began reading theology and biblical criticism and everything I read weakened my faith rather than strengthening it. It all ran so counter to my former denominational training.

My wife and I made some perfunctory attempts to find a church. We attended a small church in the suburbs late in the 1960s for about six months. The priest was very socially active and made us feel welcome and we became involved to an extent, but we eventually drifted away. Then we joined the Lutheran Church in America and that was really the start of my spiritual journey in earnest. And yet, since I am by nature not a reflective person, I didn't reflect much on the meaning of this—I just involved myself in a church again because it seemed the right thing to do at the time.

A big change happened in my eleventh year of military service. I was selected to go the Air Force Command and Staff College and was also assigned to fly a combat tour over Vietnam. I was stationed in Thailand, actually, but was also flying regular missions over Vietnam. There in Thailand, through a series of coincidences, I became a sort of minor expert in drug abuse and rehabilitation. I found myself being asked to run a drug-abuse office at the Air Force base where I was stationed.

This was a real turning point in my encounter with the church. Because at that time it was considered appropriate to have affective educational expertise, especially intensive group experience, to prepare one for such counseling. At this school, then, I got the first introduction to the affective side of myself. "The system" for the first time demanded that I use my affective side, my feelings. For someone who had spent little time in feeling, reflecting, or speculating, this was a real turning point. I began to look at myself as a father, a husband, a friend, a career military man, a human being, and to question whether I liked what I saw. And I judged myself too harshly on many points. I judged myself to be more egocentric and selfish than I would have guessed. And I recognized that this is not who I want to be. I was becoming more and more aware that I was not who I thought I was.

Eventually I was sent to an Air Force school for training drug counselors for world-wide duty, located in San Antonio. I attended a series of very intensive training seminars to become a group facilitator myself and then to train other facilitators. In one of the first experiences I had with these sessions —I'm sure the military would have died had they known. One of the sections in any military person's orders is marked "Clothing." But this school refused to put clothing into my orders because the recommended attire was T-shirt, jeans, and sandals. A delicious irony! But that's all I had to bring with me to my training seminar.

It was the end of the great era of groups, about 1973. I learned a lot about myself, about groups and group dynamics. I worked hard and was highly motivated. But what it led to for me was an incredible encounter with God, when I least expected it. God was always waiting for me, I now realize, but since one might surmise God was having a hard time getting through to me, I had to be prepared for the encounter first. If God speaks, the very least we can do is to listen!

One day we did the classic guided fantasy. We were told: you are alone in a field, on a beautiful spring day, in the grass. You notice the smell of the cool spring air, the feel of the grass, the freshness of the day . . . then become aware, slowly, almost accidentally, of a person sitting on a log. And then you grow curious and approach, slowly, quietly, to see who this other person might be.

I should say here that this entire seminar was about as non-religious and nonsectarian, as totally devoid of religion in any form, as anything you can imagine. They were all secular people, secular humanist types. There was not a trace of any invitation to spirituality in the seminar.

So religion was the last thing on my mind as I started, a little skeptically, on this fantasy. But I did the fantasy as I was told. I stood in the field and sniffed the grass and felt the cool spring breeze. And then I became aware of a shape sitting on a log across the field and I felt an incredible fear. I first saw the shape of a person, then a robe, then a beard. And I began to shake. Something was happening that was out of my control. And the group leader said, "Go ahead, walk over slowly to the person, work through the fear." And I did. I walked across the field, over to a person that by now I knew to be Our Lord.

I felt so out of control, I looked first at the expression on this person's face. For some reason that was a real issue with me. I saw a non-negative expression. Now I would describe it as somewhat neutral, leaning toward me a little with a warm, slightly curious look. Perhaps the head was tilted a little, I don't know. And He asked just a simple question, but it devastated me so much that it took months before I could even talk about it with my wife: "Where have you been?" Just that, nothing else: "Where have you been?" And obviously I had no answer for that. It was not that I felt punished or intimidated, just devastated by the question. I still had no answer except, "Yes, where *have* I been?"

So I encountered, in a very warm and loving yet ultimately spectacular way, a person who I believe to be Our Lord. And that was the start of a reorientation in the pilgrimage I had been on. Now the Lord became very real for me, in a much more integrated way. It was all so real to me that I chose to cherish that encounter and use it as a starting point to look again at my life.

But I didn't immediately retire from the Air Force. I kept on doing what I was doing—this particular experience happened at a training seminar in Indianapolis. I stayed in the Air Force—in fact, I resisted the temptation to retire after twenty-one and again after twenty-two years. I just believed in some strange way that I was being *formed*. Yet it was two more years before I was confirmed in the church, and that only because it seemed to me I had found a church where I could survive and grow. This would not be true of everyone, but the great gift of the church for me personally was that it allowed me to grow and stretch in the ways I needed.

So I actually stayed in the Air Force for another eight years. My whole orientation was different, though, after this experience. Not "Will I make the next rank?" or "Will I get that assignment?" but "Who am I and why am I here?" and "Am I really being called, Lord, to do your work?" A lot of rebuilding took place in those years. My real priority was not to make the next rank or even to be ordained, but to become a true child of God, in a more intense, directed, and serious way than I'd ever done before.

That's about all there is to the story. In 1981 I retired from the Air Force and all the doors opened so that I could start seminary in the fall. But that is almost incidental to the story. The real story I want to tell is the spiritual journey I made and the way I learned finally to listen to Our Lord.

(Author's note: Dick was ordained priest in 1984 and now serves as curate in a small-town Midwestern church.)

GARY

Gary, a judge in Oklahoma City, talked to us about his personal experiences in the Church and away from it. He is a modest, unassuming man, whose pilgrimage is typical of thoughtful laypersons. He begins his story with a bit of personal history.

* * *

Well, I'm not sure what I can add. I can tell you about me, and if that's illuminating, it's great. Okay? I was not raised as a child in a particularly religious family. My mother was a Methodist by church affiliation, and my father—I don't think had any particular affiliation at all. He may have, at some point in time, been a member of some church or other, but it didn't come out at any time in my life.

But both of them were concerned with education because neither of them had any to speak of. So they wanted me to go to parochial schools. So I started off. The only parochial schools that existed around here at the time were Roman Catholic. So I went to Catholic schools from the time I was in kindergarten. I was not a Catholic, and neither of my parents was Catholic. But I went to a Catholic school anyway. And of course part of the process is the religion class and the Baltimore catechism, and all of that—with the nuns and the priest coming in once a day to teach religion.

So I grew up essentially a Catholic, although unbaptized. And then when I left grade school and got out of the eighth grade, of course all of my friends were going on to the Catholic high school. And so naturally that was where I wanted to go. That was fine with my parents; they had long since divorced. They divorced when I was about eleven or twelve. They both wanted me to go to Catholic high school, and that's where I wanted to go, so I went.

And about my sophomore year, I decided I would become a Catholic and sort of formalize the relationship, and be baptized. So I was. I was a fairly faithful Catholic at that point. I don't think I was ever a real gung-ho-get-involved-in-the-Church type, but I did the things you're supposed to do.

As a senior in high school, I met a girl who was not Catholic and we ultimately married when I got out of college. I went to college at Ohio University. I didn't see any point to any more Catholic education. And while I was in college, I just pretty much stopped going to church. I had other things to do on Sunday morning—mainly, try to get over Saturday night. And so that's kind of where my religious connections came to a screeching halt right about then.

We had children and for much the same reasons I had gone to Catholic schools, they went to Catholic schools. They were baptized as infants, and they went to Catholic schools. They started out in public schools, but I put them into Catholic schools. And then my wife began to take instruction and converted and became a Catholic and was baptized herself.

We started going to a church. But frankly, I just didn't like many of the people who went to that church, and that's just the way it was. But it was the parish church and where our kids went to school, and that's how it was. So I sort of, after reestablishing a brief contact with the church through the children, I sort of drifted completely away.

Then in 1981 when I was divorced, of course I had nothing to do with the Church, but my kids continued go to Catholic schools. In fact, my oldest is enrolled to start at the end of this month at McGinniss High, where I had gone. And they still remained faithful to the Catholic Church, as does their mother.

My ex-wife's older sister, who died in 1979 of cancer, converted to Catholicism on her deathbed. So her family started out with very little connection with religion and got all involved in it, while I seemed to go in the opposite direction. So as luck would have it, after I was separated and was in the process of getting the divorce out of the way, I began dating a woman who was active in my present church.

I resisted any involvement with the Church. On Saturday nights, she would say, "Why don't you come to church with me?" And I'd say, "No, I'll see you after church. Call me when you get back from church and we'll go to the zoo or something." But I didn't really want any part of that. So that continued for about maybe six months. Then she finally talked me into it. She said, "Won't you at least come to the service and sit down in the pew and just watch?" And I said, "Well, all right, I'll at least do that." And I did just that. And everybody made me feel very welcome. It seemed to please her that I did that. So I came back to church.

And I continued to come back pretty regularly but never went to communion because I felt very much the lifelong Catholic. And I couldn't imagine anything that would be more destructive to that image than to receive communion in any other church. So I sort of hung on to that image of being the fallen-away Catholic.

Finally, I said, "Well, okay, I'm coming here every Sunday morning. I might as well get in the act or get out of it." So I went to the confirmation class that they had here. Although I had been confirmed as a Roman Catholic, I felt like I ought to at least learn a little something. And I did, and I was received here in 1983. I've stayed here ever since.

I'm now a regular communicant, I'm on the vestry of the church, involved in quite a few of the other activities, and no longer date the woman who brought me here, although she's still very active too. So that's the history of my return.

The reason that I stayed away so long? Well, it wasn't a matter of loss of curiosity, it was just that I didn't see that there was anything that religion could do for me. There didn't seem to be anything there that would cause me to want to go, to become a regular part of it. And at the same time there were some very negative things that caused me *not* to want to go.

The people condemned me for the divorce. And, at least as I perceived it, every time I went to church the sermon had to do with how much money the church needed. At that time the Roman church I belonged to was trying to build a sanctuary, trying to build some new buildings, and it was this constant drive for money every time. I felt that really all we were getting in church was a series of commercials.

I found that it had changed enormously from the time I left it in high school until the time I went back six, seven years later. Because it happened to be in that period of time that the Roman Catholic Church underwent the great change from Latin to English, the great change to the participatory Mass, and all the other functional, procedural changes: Vatican II, and all that. So when I went back, I didn't recognize that church as the one I had left. It just wasn't church anymore.

In coming to this church here—I don't know how many people you have talked to about St. Paul's, but if you have talked to three people already, you have heard it three times and I'm going to say it the fourth time. It's an extremely warm, personal small church. People here are a family. And that's important. You can't go to a church that's got five or six thousand members and have any sense of belonging there. It's more like shopping than it is going to church. It's not a community. Here, the *people* are the Church. I think I've learned a lot here by osmosis. I am not one to learn much from a sermon, but I can see people doing things that reflect what they've learned from the sermons and from being part of this family.

Of course, Bill, the canon of the cathedral, is wonderful. And George: I don't know if you've met the Dean, but he's delightful. Everyone who is connected to this church is just— well, there's nothing of the foreboding, disciplinary atmosphere you find in some churches. This is not a place that one comes either to be told what he's done wrong or to be forgiven for it. This is a place where one comes to be a part of a community.

The irony is that we're in the midst of the business district. It's amazing. If you could survey the people who come here on Sunday morning, you'd find that many of them drive past at least one other church to get here. And that brings me to another point: if this church disappeared from the face of the earth, or for some reason I decided to leave, I cannot in all honesty say I'd go to another one.

I can't say that I wouldn't, either. Maybe this is not what you want to hear for the book, and maybe this is not what your book is about. But I don't see myself as a part of the great return to religion in the Eighties. I don't see myself as a member of the great mass that has turned away from whatever they were turned onto in the Seventies back into the spirituality of the Eighties the way that magazines talk about in their religion articles.

No, I just simply got to a place I liked. I didn't turn away from anything. I'm not saying that everybody who made that turn was doing the same as I was. But I wasn't an alcoholic, I didn't have a drinking problem, I wasn't on drugs, I wasn't doing the singles-bar scene. I was living pretty much the same life I am living right now except that I didn't have any of it focused on a church, on a community outside of the people that I worked with.

I'm not qualified to comment on the state of American society in terms of the collective spirituality of the people. I just know that I meet, on a day-to-day basis, more and more people who talk about church as opposed to talking about the club, or something like that.

You have to remember that you're talking to someone who was born and raised and lived the great majority of his life right here on the buckle of the Bible Belt. People have been going to church in Oklahoma for a long, long time.

As for people who go to church just to get away from it all, well, I think that no responsible person would ever teach that the purpose of church is to help people hide from the world. And that's another one of the things that I like about St. Paul's: the people here are very involved in the world. I mean that the people who come here are involved in many other things that have nothing to do with the Church. They have very rich and satisfying lives away from here, but they also seem to carry something away from here to their lives and they bring something from their outside lives back here with them.

This is a very old church in terms of years. There are many people who have been going to church here since childhood. And there's a gap here. There aren't that many people my age here [early forties: *Eds.*]. We're getting more younger people, in their late twenties and early thirties, and we have a declining number of people over sixty. And then in the middle we have a very small group of people, thirty-five to fifty-five.

I guess the upshot of all this is that I took a very circuitous route back to the Church. Maybe my motives for coming back weren't all that spiritual. But you know, in the final analysis, I don't think there is a *bad* reason for going back to church.

PRESTON

Preston is a thin, almost emaciated young man in his late twenties who was diagnosed in early 1985 as an AIDS victim. Although he is not formally affiliated with any church, he has, since his diagnosis, experienced a renewal of his own faith and has developed an active ministry of speaking to hospital and church groups on his illness and on death and dying. We first met him when he appeared in a city church in Chicago speaking on "Spirituality and Death and Dying." His faith was obvious and so was his dedication to the ministry he has developed in the last year and a half.

The time was February 22 of last year [1985] when I was diagnosed as having AIDS and pneumocystic pneumonia, a pneumonia which is very common among AIDS patients and is also a killer. So I have to live with that all the time—it's very scary. It's changed my life; it's changed the way I think. It's changed my everyday living. It had made me a much stronger person. I think I'm much closer to the Lord now.

I don't get any support from my family and that's tough to have to deal with. That's also pretty common among AIDS victims. For the parents, finding out first that a child is gay, and second that he has AIDS, is too much for them to deal with, which I think is really sad.

I can't work, so I'm living on unemployment and Social Security, which sort of puts a crimp in my style. I take a lot of comfort from my faith—if I didn't have that, I'd feel as if I had nothing. I feel good now. I feel good that I've accomplished what I have in the past year. Maybe by listening to me, people can realize that maybe their own sons and daughters could start and end up at the same place.

The way I came to be here is that one day your curate got a call saying that I would be willing to come here to talk on spirituality and death and dying. He got my number through an AIDS task force. And so for the last few months, he and I, to varying degrees, talked about some of these things—where I was before and during the diagnosis, and then since.

I grew up in a Christian church in my hometown. My grandparents were Baptists, but my parents were members of another Church. I was active in the Church—I was choir director, and for a short time I was youth director for youth groups. This was all in Florida, before I moved to Chicago.

The church where I grew up was sort of Fundamentalist in outlook. They didn't call themselves Fundamentalists but they acted like it. I came to Chicago in 1977. And I had a really bad experience at a church as soon as I got here.

The minister and his family had been doing everything at the church—being youth director, choir director—so they decided, which I thought was good, that other people ought to get more involved. I got a little involved and then it all fell apart. I handled the choir much better than the minister's wife had—it was just because I knew what kind of songs the people wanted to sing: gospel!

But the minister's wife was a real la-de-da lady who liked anthems and such. The people didn't understand her taste. There were only about two people who could read music. The way I did it, it [the choir] was just a bunch of people getting together to sing, and it was fine. People loved it. We sang gospel music, and for some reason the attendance just blossomed.

So then I got accused of having the Preston Johns show, and all these awful things were said. I couldn't understand what that minister meant—he ought to be glad for anything I was doing. I was just doing it to bring the people in. He should have been glad. But he didn't see it that way. So I got real disillusioned with the church. I haven't been back to a regular church since that time.

When I first got here [to Chicago], I was experimenting a whole lot. It was party time for almost five years and it was good for about five years. And then it got too boring. I wasn't feeling well. I just thought "I'd better stop this." So I got my own apartment—*my* apartment—and I got a good job with a major hotel chain. I had insurance, so I felt a little more secure for a while. I did drugs, but I didn't shoot up—but I was popular, I had fun. But then it wasn't good any longer.

When I heard the diagnosis [of AIDS], I knew it meant that I would die. But I didn't know what else I would have to go through or how fearful I would be. At first I was scared to death. I think I must have been in shock because I don't remember a lot. Then I got into a support group for AIDS patients—we just talk: what's going on with us, what we've done to make life a little easier. And we try very hard to make new people comfortable.

I try just to live from day to day. I've had one hospitalization since I was diagnosed. The main thing to face is the fact that I can't work. I don't have any money and I don't see how I'll make my insurance payment each month. I pay my rent and there's not much left over. I can't read because my eyes are so bad, so I watch TV.

I don't think I've ever felt angry. There's nobody to blame.

Some people, even people close to me, are suggesting I should blame myself. But I just don't. Why should I put myself through all that emotional strain? I just try to remain calm and keep myself together.

I *do* get letters from people in Florida suggesting that they are concerned about my soul, my lifestyle. I got a letter from my sister which was supposed to be a letter of encouragement and she just talked about how miserable her life was. So I told my mother: forget it. You've got to accept that I believe I'm saved. I'm not going to change. And I don't think it's fair that she would want me to, because then I wouldn't be honest with myself or with God. And I think that's very important.

I get angry only when "religious" people seem to have this . . . fixed vision of life. My brother agreed to send me fifty dollars a month, for which I was extremely grateful. Then I got a letter with a check and he said he would put me in contact with people in Chicago who could help me. Now these people came to see me, but I didn't really want their help. These were people who wanted to come over to my house and rid me of my sin. I wrote him and said, "Bill, as I told Mother, I believe I'm saved, so lay off." And he has—he hasn't pressed it anymore.

I pray for my family a lot—for my whole family. It's real difficult not having their support. But I figured I would either go crazy worrying about it or just accept it, so that's what I do. But I pray for them all every day.

My one roommate has been wonderful. He does all the housework, fixes meals when I don't even feel like getting up to eat. My second roommate has just been with us for two weeks. He also has AIDS.

My family has always been a great advocate of the straight and narrow path. Whereas I've always been way over here somewhere, off the path. And God, as we see Him in the church, is on the straight and narrow too. But I see Him over here with me, off that path. Is there a way to verbalize *how* God is—*where* God is?

It's just the way I feel—I feel very spiritually close to Him. God is acting through all the people listening to me. I feel it when I speak to people or answer their questions. God is here tonight. I feel sure of that.

Am I afraid of death? No. When my father died, I experienced death close at hand and I had already decided death was just another part of life, another step to whatever is out there. So I am not afraid of dying, especially now that I have my faith. What I worry about is all the hell I must go through before I get to that point.

Why am I still here, going along from day to day? I don't know. I often think about that. My consolation is that I have done a lot of speaking. I'm facilitator for my support group. I'm doing something important with my life, I hope. Our personalities are the ways God works in us and through us. I pray every day that God will use me—that He'll take situations like this one tonight and use me to help people. This is my ministry and I'll do it as long as I can. You don't have to belong to a church to have a ministry, and this is mine, I guess.

DAVID

David is a bright, energetic entrepreneur who, in his late thirties, is president of his own communications firm and an experienced computer analyst. Yet he is deeply committed to his wife (also his business partner and a systems analyst) and infant son. In this interview David talks of his own spiritual pilgrimage from Southern Baptist to atheist to Pentecostal convert to a practicing Roman Catholic.

You have to know as we begin this that I started out as a child as a Southern Baptist. As far as I knew, "joining the church" meant making a profession of faith in Christ and being baptized. And that's what I did, at the standard age—you know, eleven or twelve, whenever. I was the classic good child going to church.

But in college I started to question the whole thing. I was in college in the late Sixties—I graduated in 1967. I was fascinated by intellectual questions, mostly those having to do with historical events and evolution. I was mostly interested in sex, less so in religion! But my real break with the Church came in college. In this environment, everything was called into question. I got into aetheism with real gusto. And in the process, I became kind of isolated. But I felt that I had thrown away my intellectual crutches, for that's what the Church had become to me.

When I got into a more "real working world" type of environment, a lot of the props of my aetheism started falling away. I went into the military service and had lots of emotional problems adjusting to the service—I was then about twenty-two or twenty-three, and I just didn't seem to fit in. So I was drawn to the Pentecostal faith. It was a period of real despair for me. I felt I had pushed aetheism as far as it would go, to its very limits. There was no human good, it was all hypocrisy —and I toyed with the idea of absolute evil as the only end of mankind . . . a very dark period. If I chose evil and total self-fulfillment, life would have no meaning, I believed. Yet somehow I knew that there would be one—would be a meaning somewhere in all this, either with humans or with God.

At that time in my life, I was walking down the street in Virginia Beach, Virginia. There was a sign in a little coffee-shop window that read JESUS DIED, SHEDDING HIS LOVE. And all of a sudden, I felt moved to go in. So I did, and sat down and ordered some coffee. There were some Pentecostal ladies there and we began to talk. They told me that Jesus loved me; that faith was there if I asked for it. That was the first light I had seen in my darkness and despair for many months.

A couple of weeks later, I went to church with them and the minister seemed to be addressing his entire sermon to me . . . I guess everyone has had that experience, but it was new to me and very powerful. So that night I found myself walking down the aisle and having a real conversion experience. That night I *knew* the reality of Christ's existence as I had never known it before. That was a real turning point in my life. All the evil and cynicism just fell away. I've had religious experiences since then, but I have never had more of a sense of the reality of the religious experience. From that day on, I never felt I could deny that there is a God. For the first time, I understood that thing about baptism in the Holy Spirit. I literally felt fire coming into me during this whole Pentecostal experience. It wasn't just a psychological experience, I'm convinced—it was the only way God could get my attention. But one of the Pentecostal ladies I had met kept telling me, "There are things you don't know."

A lot of people had told me, "If you're born again, everything will be rosy." But it wasn't so. I began to have doubts again and eventually started to fall away from the Church.

By now, it was about ten years since my atheistic phase had started. I had first met Roman Catholicism when I was in the service. Now I had a chance to go to Europe, and in those great cathedrals of Europe, I came to recognize the great age and stability—the permanence—of the Roman Catholic tradition as opposed to the doctrinal instability of the Protestant sects and the emotionalism of the Pentecostals. But I didn't deal with Roman Catholicism for awhile.

At that time I was seeing a therapist who was Roman Catholic who was helping me deal with creativity and other spiritual issues—not exactly church membership, but more general issues.

And through the therapist I met a priest whom I liked and began to talk to. And slowly I began to drift toward the Roman Catholic Church.

About this time a couple of amazing things happened. I was driving along the freeway in my car and thinking about this struggle, this ongoing . . . thing that I had had with religion all my life. And I was listening to the car radio, driving along, switching stations, and all I could get was static. And suddenly I found one station that I could tune in loud and clear, and the song that was playing was Billy Joel's "I Love You Just the Way You Are." And I drove along, listening to that song, and started to weep—it seemed just the message that I needed to hear. It was God's way of getting my attention again, of telling me that I was loved and accepted with all my faults.

And also about this time Jennifer, my wife, was trying to get pregnant. We were really trying. We went to fertility experts, the whole thing. And nothing seemed to work. Finally the doctor told us, after months and thousands of dollars worth of tests, he said that the only recourse left was for Jennifer to go on this fertility drug that had these terrible, these absolutely devastating side effects. And we were just reluctant to do that, but we wanted a child so much.

So I decided to pray about it. I made it a kind of test of my faith. I said, "God, let this be a sign to us, give me a sign, tell me what I should do." I don't think I consciously made a bargain with God, but I know I was saying, "If You give me a sign, I'll believe that what You are telling me to do in terms of converting is real." And the next month, we learned that Jennifer was pregnant.

So I made the decision to become a Roman Catholic. I entered a confirmation class and found to my surprise that it wasn't full of kids. People seemed to have a greater maturity than the Pentecostals; the class was full of other adults. I was confirmed when I was about thirty-five.

All this time Jennifer . . . Like me, she was an atheist when we were married. So I put no pressure on her at all. About the time of my confirmation I told her once, just once, "Sometimes I feel sad that here's a part of my life I can't share with you."

So from that one thing she decided to check out Catholicism by talking with a priest. Eventually she took instruction also and just a year and a half ago she was confirmed. She had been baptized as a child, as I had been. She was confirmed at Easter in this very moving liturgy. She says now that when she got pregnant, it put her more in touch with the mystery of life. Our son was baptized when he was about six or seven months old.

We're now going to a small Roman Catholic church in a near north suburb. We started out at a neighborhood church where we were very attracted because of two young priests. But just now the logistics make it more convenient for us to go to St. Nicholas, so that's where we go. We're active, but we could do more. You know, sometimes I think that churches don't ask enough of people. There's so much more, waiting to be done.

CHARLES

We talked to Charles, an architect, at the Cathedral in Little Rock, Arkansas, in a meeting arranged by Dean Pugh. He was modest, but marvelously communicative. He took time out of his busy work schedule to sit down and tell us his story, which begins with a bit of family history.

Well, I suspect my story really isn't unique, but I'm pleased to share this with you. I come from a long line of Episcopalians. My grandfather was a missionary to Arkansas, called by the bishop to establish missions here. My father's family came in the 1920s because my grandfather was in South Carolina and accepted a call here in Christ Church. On both sides we got here because of clergy assignments. I also have an uncle who is the retired dean of the cathedral in Oklahoma City, he's down in Florida. My mother has been particularly active.

I grew up at Christ Church, Little Rock—which is a slowly

dying parish—in the normal sort of family: never faced any crises.

Little Rock, as you know, had an enormous crisis in race relations in the 1950s. It was thought in 1958 the schools would be closed. I was in junior high school, and I and many of my friends were shipped off to Sewanee, a military academy preparatory school. And so I went to an Episcopal high school. I stayed there three years and really liked it. That was not only a break from home, but the chaplain didn't communicate well, and I think that was the beginning of my separation from the church. Religion wasn't presented well and we all hated it, partly my own fault.

Then I went off to a private liberal arts college, Washington University in St. Louis, and was there for six years; that was the Sixties. I graduated from college in 1968 and was very much part of the emotional set of that period, questioning everything; and all my time was filled with other things. I thought I had thought things through very well.

After 1968 we came back to Little Rock and at that time I was married. My wife was in the school of fine arts and her story parallels mine quite a bit. She was raised in the Baptist Church. We came back to Little Rock thinking we would be here for a short time and then strike out for the big city. At that time, architects were very urban-oriented, especially from the big schools, and Little Rock was pretty small potatoes.

We thought we would get off to Chicago, New York, or San Francisco, but we moved downtown and got quite interested. Initially, we moved down here because we wanted to get as far away from home as possible. Then we got interested in the preservation of the old buildings, old neighborhoods, and began to put down roots. Over a period of time our business careers got more involved with Little Rock and we were less and less interested in moving on to the large cities. We didn't want to design bank buildings all our lives; we'd rather do restorations. And so we became very much associated with that and firmly anchored in the downtown area. We felt very much a part of the community.

But during this period the only time we went into church was for funerals and weddings and an occasional Christmas Eve. At this time I would say the person most concerned about my soul was my mother, who kept vigil and applied gentle but constant pressure on me to go back.

Then nine years ago we had our first child, and that begins to complicate the formula because suddenly you feel you're not only acting out your own life, you're responsible for others. And then two years later, we had our second child. So when the second child came, we were also becoming more and more active in our business and other things, and life was getting more and more complicated. And suddenly we began to wonder, were we really in control of things?

Suddenly we were under lots of pressure, and we needed a firmer base to operate from. We began to doubt that we were going in the right direction. We were never making a strong philosophical statement that we were agnostic or whatever, we were just too busy—it didn't fit into our priorities of time. But when our second child was born, in 1977, we—well, when our first child was born he was fine, but our second child was born with severe medical problems, and my mother insisted that he be baptized—"on his deathbed," we thought—and he was baptized and it was most helpful to us. And so was the curate at the cathedral; he was a neighborhood friend and acquaintance.

So that was the first crisis experience, but we made no major change in our lifestyle until our next child was born. She was fine, but we decided we would have her baptized anyway, and that our son would be rebaptized in proper circumstances.

I have to add another aspect to this, and that is that as an architect I had done work for Joel [the dean of the cathedral: *Eds.*] on his house, during the time between the birth of my children. Joel is a really exceptional person, and as I got to know him, he became a role model.

During the construction and post-construction of his house, which probably lasted about a year and a half, we became very good friends. And his example was not wasted. So when we decided to have our children baptized, Joel was the godparent. My uncle baptized them. And it was at Christ Church. And my uncle, who knows us well, really laid it on the line to us in his pre-baptismal instructions. He told us to be serious, and if you aren't really serious about doing this, he said, we shouldn't be doing it, and we took that to heart. By that time, we were both principals in our businesses and under a lot of pressure, increasingly frustrated with some of life's daily activities, and increasingly concerned that some decisions were made without any basis at all, and we decided about three years ago that it was time to start going back to church.

This decision was made because we felt a spiritual vacuum, that spiritually our lives were not providing the reinforcement we needed. So we started coming to church again and we chose to come here because of Joel and because we had a number of friends who were neighbors in this downtown neighborhood who were very much interested in this parish. I think I could name two dozen people in similar situations, all of whom are now here. Joel recently said that when he came here six or seven years ago, only two families lived in the neighborhood. Now all that's changed.

Although I'm sure the majority of our members still live several miles away, the original parish is becoming a definite entity. I think it's because of changes that are happening nationwide, if you believe what you read. But I think it's because of changes that were happening here too.

Our reactivation, if you want to call it that—we didn't get struck by lightning in the middle of the night—was really, is still, a very gradual, planned reactivation. We did it deliberately. It wasn't that we had a religious experience and it changed us, it was more that we decided over a period of time that we were wrong and the way to correct that was to actively start studying issues. I don't give us high marks for philosophy at all.

One of the things about this parish that is excellent, although it's not why we came here, is Christian education. We're coming not only for the fellowship and the spiritual aspect, but also for the Christian education program.

I turned forty this summer and my wife will be forty this week. I think in a very real sense that as you approach that milestone in life you want to re-evaluate, take stock.

I remember well the dean of our school of architecture; he was a strong man, very strong in the professions, and we sought his advice—or rather he gave his advice freely—about the philosophical aspects of architecture. And one of the discussions was about religion: whether there was a God. And he said, "I want you to know, I'm not as sure now as I used to be."

We even got interested in traditional architecture. We didn't start out to return to traditional values or anything like that, we didn't deliberately return to the church and then start to look at traditional architecture because of it. In the beginning we just went where our friends were. We were influenced by some of them on the way. And in Becky's case it meant deciding against her own tradition. She was brought up Baptist.

Becky was confirmed, oh, about six months ago, so we did not make that much a conscious decision for the Church. We didn't make that much a conscious evaluation of the alternatives, but then, that's consistent with us and what we usually do. We came where we were comfortable.

We did, though, make a conscious decision not to go back to my family church even though that was where I was raised, because I felt I should go where my faith would be strongest. I have addressed the possibility that sometime, when my faith is sufficiently strong, I may go back there and help them strengthen their parish too. Right now we're trying to develop some things here, start some programs, but at one time our old family church was the largest parish in the diocese.

This church, the cathedral, is in a neighborhood where people still live, that church, the family church, is in a business district, and it's run-down, not much activity there. And it's a very large building, hard to keep up, not much that can be done there. So we may at some point pick up, feel we're called to go there and help, but right now we're being a little selfish. We need a lot of Christian education and a lot of help for ourselves.

DONNA

Donna, an intense, energetic, and attractive young woman, was one of the persons we talked to after the Garden Mass at the Cathedral in Louisville. She begins her story with a description of the kind of fleeting joy in religion that she always seeks.

Well, for me I guess it was just getting to a certain stage of my life and *needing* something to hang onto. Maybe it involves reaching a point where you have a broader definition of religion, I mean you have the idea religion is really abhorrent, something to rebel against. And then suddenly, I guess I realized I am fundamentally a religious person, and I started searching for some form that would accommodate that urge.

Now frankly, I've tried many, many times going to a service and I find it boring, that it just doesn't do anything for me. It seems that there is a kind of a joy that really speaks to me, a pleasure, but I don't feel it regularly. I mean, this is the first time I've come here in quite a long time. I may come regularly for three or four months, whatever feels right. Or I may stop coming again. It's an up-and-down sort of thing. I come when I either need something or I have something to give.

I don't think it's a return to the "religion of my childhood." I think it's kind of a redefining. In coming back to the Church, I don't think anybody my age or with my educational background has come back to the same thing they left. As people grow up, they either change churches or they change to a different style of church. But maybe what it's a return to is an acknowledgment of a need. And then you look for a package for it. You realize the need and then you start looking around for something that addresses it.

And when you rebelled against it, it may have simply been a natural manifestation of the same urge that sent us away from our parents' homes. There's a certain period of time when you need to be moving out, making the break, pulling up roots, whatever.

But when you're nearly forty, you don't need to do that anymore. Your need is something other than that.

ROBERT

Robert is a Chicago investments salesman. He is also a title-quality bodybuilder and entrepreneur. The impressive physique and dynamic sales persona belie the warmness and utter ingenuousness of this open, friendly, caring man. When Bob walks into a room, he brings the sunshine with him. His story begins with a response to a question about hearing the Lord's call.

You know, everybody has that voice, everybody, and everybody hears it. You think, What's wrong with me, hearing voices? But you've got to listen to it. It hits you right there in your "faith spot," right there, hearing that voice that tells you to go do something. Sometimes you don't even know for sure if you heard it, you don't know that that's what you're meant to be doing. But it always eventually gets you right to where you've got to be. I've found that out.

Well, I had a Christian upbringing from the time I was very young, thanks to my mother and a neighbor lady who made sure that I could attend church and church functions as much as I wanted. This was back in Indiana, in a non-denominational church, fundamentalist, and I had a real good background in church doctrine and faith that allowed me to make a comeback, if you will, to faith in the Christian life. At the time I was probably seventeen or eighteen years old, I talked to Him every day but I didn't do anything about talking to Him. Then I was married when I was about eighteen and I started getting in with a group of guys, drinking, and fell in that trap. You know, the way Satan works is when you feel that you've done something that is against God's will and you don't feel worthy, that's what he, Satan, works on. You feel you might as well go back and do it again because you're not worthy. And I did. At that time I was very susceptible to that kind of suggestion. And he's the master of deception.

But thankfully, I continued to pray, even when I was at my worst and didn't know where to turn. I never got down so far that I lost touch completely with my previous faith. And I got remarried when I was not quite twenty-two to a great girl, but I still had some of my problems, and I—well, for a while I straightened up and flew right. We went to church together and it was at that time that I felt like I was born again. But I started hanging around with some of my old friends again, going out and drinking, playing cards late at night, fooling around, and it didn't take long and we were divorced. My whole world tumbled around me. And I again felt, Gosh, I'm not worthy. Besides, I was over here and He didn't help me, so I thought, Well, I might as well go and do these other, worldly things. This is *fun!* And so I turned my back on Him.

And thank God for my previous faith and the upbringing I had and the attention my parents had given me. Because I had children by that time. And that was my little connection, my one link to God. I guess as you're brought up, so you are with your children oftentimes. So I had all this love and attention when I was young, so I was able through them to still relate to God. And I was thankful, so thankful, to them. You know, it was a very satisfying thing to have their love after having gone through a divorce.

So I remarried to somebody that was not—how do I say it? She and I were not very much alike. After I had been divorced, as I said, I thought I might as well go out and do all these worldly things. And she was very much of that world—you know, going out every night, having a good time, dancing and partying and getting drunk all the time. And that was how we lived.

And then I lost a brother a couple of years back. And he was —you know, I found out that before he died he was reading about religion. I knew he was such a lovely person, but I didn't know much about him. He was reading Hal Lindsay and later, I found some things he wrote that just broke me down. And I know that God had a plan for that. He couldn't have taken any of the rest of my mother's children because we weren't ready. But He was able to take my brother, knowing that he would make it to His side. And it woke me up. My mother in a way, as well as myself, she had kind of fallen away. It woke us both up.

So I started to try to get back to God, and started praying for both me and my wife. And to make what could be a long story very short, I didn't feel like she was willing to come around. And that's the biggest reason we divorced. Although I had had children by her by then, I thought, What are you fighting?

And I tried, tried, to tell her, this is the way people ought to live, and to her I became "Preacher Bob." It was a very uneven yoke. And I thought, if I could suffer through a divorce where I really, really had a good marriage and no one was at fault, then I could suffer through one where there wasn't a good marriage and I didn't feel like I was at fault. And we divorced just this past year. We'd been separated, though, for two years.

I went back in the Church, again to a church in South Bend, I'm usually there every weekend. And two of the children— I have four children now—and my first wife live in South Bend, and my mother's right there, and the other two are in Michigan. Real close by, about forty or fifty miles. One swoop, and you can get them all. And yes, I drive a big van!

But I was able, through so many people and their prayers, to get through a really rough time. And I was able to go back into the Church and a couple of—now it's getting closer to six months—I broke down and again accepted Christ as my Savior and God as my Maker, and tried to turn myself away from worldly things. And realized that my final reward will be my belief and faith in Him.

It's been a tremendous change in me, in my life. Things that used to bother me don't as much. And I've now gotten back into exercising. So many things. I never would even have applied for the job I now hold. I never would have had time for a job like this before, because I was so busy going out at night. Now those things are—they seem like a long time ago, just a memory. I'm, praise God, on my way back to where I should be and who I'm going to be. Personally, I can continue to grow to be a child of faith again and I can continue to help others as I've been helped, maybe bringing some people back into the fold with me.

I've got a young brother who has the same problems I had. He's now living with me and he's reading some passages. He hasn't accepted Christ yet but he will, he will. He hasn't got a chance! And the guy I work out with here in the gym, he went through a divorce and was so bitter about so many things.

And the job that we're employed with, the business is extremely tough. It depends on sales every day. Maybe one out of ten of all sales reps survives in this business. The rest drop by the wayside, it's so tough. It's a difficult business. I sell investments, limited partnerships, mainly in real estate, but some cattle. It's a tough field. And with the President having all this new tax legislation—he's killing all the tax shelters. And I don't know why but I've been making sales hand over fist. I can't even understand why. Well, yes, of course I can. I do know why.

I think that maybe sometimes people should just go ahead and make lots of money so they can give lots of it away, give it to the church, to organizations that have a need for it. I don't have a need for a lot anymore, I really don't. Praise God.

But as I was saying, this friend, he's in the same business, and he was there for about four months and never made a sale. Which is not unusual. Well, actually, he made a contact I ended up selling for him, but unfortunately he had gotten discouraged and so aggravated, feeling that he was unable to perform, that he had left a few weeks earlier. And I followed up on one of his leads and I was able to sell it.

So then he came back for another couple of months and I was just praying so hard: "Please, God, please help this guy. This is my best friend. I want to see him make it. I want to see him make it." And he was starting to read the Bible and pray and read Hal Lindsay, and he bought *The Christ Commission* and it made him—all of a sudden, he got to the point where he's buying books on his own. Then all of a sudden, out of the blue, our boss, the president of the firm, approaches me and says to me, "Joe isn't cutting it." And I was so afraid this was going to happen. But he says, "You know, the guy is very loyal, he's a hard worker, and he tried hard. You know, he's management material."

I'm sales manager but I was not good at it. I can sell because I've got the gift of gab, but to try to teach it to people who can't sell—I never do, because I was never taught. Who can explain it? But the point is that he has to have it laid down one, two, three, step by step. So he's perfect for a sales manager.

So lo and behold, our prayers were answered, and better than I could have hoped. Now he doesn't have to worry about making a sale, he just has to develop a sales strategy. And it's the perfect position for him. He's just pleased as punch, he feels so good about himself. Like I said, I was at this stage: "Hey, I know You answer prayers. What's going on here? Let's get this guy a sale! Come on, God." But the prayers were answered. They really were.

Another example: I was praying for my brother. He's had a real tough time the past two years. He was married and divorced and then he was going with a girl for a couple of years. He took her as his wife, they lived together, and he took her child like his own but they were into the party scene just like I was. I've been through that. And I guess he got into it a little bit deeper and a little harder.

I was praying for him, and said, "Help him, please help him! This is my brother, and he's such a nice young man, and he means so well. He just needs a little of Your help, if you can settle a little of the Spirit on him, and touch his life. I know he can help a lot of people. Lord, we'll make a real showing here. We'll win a lot of ballgames with this kid if You can just help him."

And so He helped him, all right. Now he's ended up on my doorstep and is living with me. Lord, my brother!

But, you know, we're lucky. Our mom has always had an unbelievably giving attitude and a love for us. She wasn't a reader like she is now and she didn't speak of God or Christ like she does now. But she's one of these people who'll make sure all her kids have their glasses.

She never drank alcohol, never smoked, so we had all these good examples set for us. But she never said "We're going to read tonight, we're going to pray." That she had gotten away from. But she was always a good example, was always there, but now—you give her a moment and she'll talk to you about the way it is and the way we should all be: "I want to help you like I've been helped, and let's sit down and we'll speak of the right way and the only way, and why I've accepted Christ as my Savior and why I believe." But that's what I mean by how she got there: she didn't get there like I did.

I see it with friends, you've got people whom you've known for a long time and you notice each other all sharing a faith. I have people I went to church with going back to church and I've looked up sometimes and been surprised: hey, that's my old buddy there! Wow! What are you doing here?

It's truly amazing. In addition to seeing people I haven't seen in a while in church, I have situations where you'll see people and, lo and behold, the Lord has touched their lives too. It's a really good feeling. I don't know, it's like—it's a real joyous feeling. It's not party-party happiness, it's . . . joy. You have certain people that you really loved before and it's a stronger thing, a more joyous type of love now. It's more meaningful than anything you've shared together before, for friends and old acquaintances and loved ones to share this with you.

I'm so thankful that I have gotten to this point and I just pray for continued strength and that blind faith that brings us all to a childlike faith and love and a belief that says, "Hey! It's all in Your hands now. That's why I accepted You. You said You'd take care of me, and I'm going to let You. I need a lot of help and I don't mind admitting it. Just point me in the right direction and, God, I'll try to help everybody I can."

That's what it's all about. It really is like exercise: the more you do it, the stronger you get, and the more you can start helping others.

One thing that's good about this, whether it's sitting down here in this kind of format or just conversing, or any other. It's encouraging to me to listen to the testimony of other people.

The revival of the Church is tremendous. We're involved in taking it back to where it used to be and should be, in all denominations. And I guess we all have our theories, but the end result is: the time isn't far off. The prophecy is unfolding now, and who knows the timetable? I don't think it's too far off when we'll see the triumphant return. I really believe that. And it's so encouraging to me to hear these people. I guess I've got a pretty good opinion of myself, but many of these other people are so well educated. I think that's very encouraging. So many people who are so well educated, as they got further into scientific thinking and got further away from the Church —it's so encouraging to see them coming back. It's a tremendous feeling to talk to people like you; and to not only share my story, but also to hear of others, people I don't know but through you I share a common story with them. It's tremendous: these people really are *smart* because they know where the real education is.

CHARLES

The Episcopal Cathedral in Louisville, Kentucky, has a dynamic group of newcomers who have either returned to or discovered the church during the last few years. We attended a Garden Mass, held in the cathedral courtyard. The mood was informal, and a guitar provided the music. The homily, an interpretation of the meaning of the Cloisters in New York, was given by one of the parish's laymen. This interview is with that layman, who is active in the Integrity movement.

Well, this was not the parish I grew up in. I came here at a time of troubles in my life. And I thought, well, if this parish is like this and there were problems at the other parish basically involving my divorce and a total lack of support toward me (clergy and parishioners—they were very supportive toward my ex-wife but I have yet to get a call from the parish priest), I thought, This is not my idea of Christianity, I can do better alone without the Church than I can with it. And it took me seven years to realize that there was still something there that I needed to come back to.

Also, I think it's important to remember the time when this took place—we're talking about the mid-1960s when I was going through the divorce—lay ministry was not exactly a hot topic at the time. Ministering was done by the priest, that was his job and I think the laity believed that. I don't think we believe that anymore. We can minister to each other and that's part of *our* function and part of *our* job.

There were several other areas I would like to address and did this morning. We don't have a female priest in this diocese. We have one who was ordained at Pentecost as a deacon, and when she finishes her year, she'll be ordained and hopefully stay here. But here we are ten years after the Philadelphia ordinations (the first ordinations of women priests) and we don't have a female priest.

I would be curious to know, in the Church as a whole, how many female rectors do we have? Fifty-four to seventy-four women who are priests? And I think you would find a very, very low number who are rectors of parishes.

Of course, also down here we still have, twenty years, thirty years since the Supreme Court decision on integration, a racial problem. One black priest in the diocese, one black rector, I should say—but he's the rector of a black parish. How many black priests are being called to be rector of a white parish?

But we have involvement at the Cathedral here. It happens in the Garden Mass we have on Sunday mornings. The other place that involvement happens—while people may not be interested in planning it, they may not feel up to it or adequate or whatever—is the participation in the service. There are no acolytes, so someone in the congregation prepares the table. I had to do it this morning but usually someone else does it. There's usually someone to help lead the music. Although we can get through *a capella*. And we sing—sing things that aren't usually sung in other services in this parish. And we read all the lessons; we pass the book around. So there are other things that go on in the service that involve people as well.

I think here you do have people involved with the nine o'clock service, to present the other side, that are on the Chapter [Vestry], which is what we call it here. And they are very much involved and supportive of what's being done—the street ministry, whatever. There's been a shifting of the guard around here.

There's another group that sort of comes into play also, and that's the *Cursillo*. The dean has been very active, and the canon has gone through it. It was an informative experience —it's been going on something like six or seven years in the Episcopal Church. The dean and some others went to a Catholic *Cursillo*. That community goes through all that the *Cursillos* go through—secret sign language and passwords and all that.

And there's the Dignity and Integrity movements [gay activist movements]. Almost every denomination has one, even the Southern Baptist. Now Integrity is something a little unique, because we are part of the ministry of the Episcopal Church.

What you said about other groups re-inventing the wheel: that's always been the case, particularly in any minority movement. Frequently we're our own worst enemy.*

---

*The *cursillo* movement is a cross-denominational movement that started among Roman Catholics in Spain. In the United States, it is largely confined to Lutherans, Episcopalians, and Roman Catholics, although persons of any faith may join. It involves a short course in Christianity, with a strong component of lay witnessing and revitalization of current and potential church leaders. Two major branches of the movement are CHECK (the Episcopal cursillo) and ECHO (the Ecumenical cursillo).

DAVE AND JOSIE

Warm-hearted and completely candid, Dave and Josie are long-time Louisville residents. The house they live in was Dave's parents' house. Dave is an oblate of a Benedictine monastary in Michigan. Our conversation took place first at dinner in their backyard, then continued into the night on their front porch. As it probably is with everybody who visits with Dave and Josie, we didn't want to leave. Dave and Josie were not formally away from the Church for any extended period of time. Yet both have moved parishes within the city several times, mostly over issues of tradition vs. innovation. For them, the traditional Church remains the "real" Church: their stories are laced with nostalgia for the old days before Vatican II. Much of their personal faith and sense of tradition is bound up in their ongoing association with the Abbey. With keen humor and an eye for ironic detail, Dave recounts the story of the enthronement of the last abbot at the monastery. Their conversation begins with a description of two churches they saw on a recent trip to the West Coast.

DAVE: We had a kind of interesting experience. As I said, Josie's young son is in Colorado, just outside of Boulder, so the first Sunday there we found this nice little parish right outside Boulder, and it's close to the university—it is *the* university church—and they have a lot of clergy. So we went there, four years ago, and it seemed like a pretty active place. And when we were there this summer, they had retreated back to the trial service of 1963. The prayer books in the pews were a trial liturgy from 19-something.

We just came back from a trip to the West Coast, and we had played our cards so that we could go to church every Sunday while we were gone, and it was fun.

JOSIE: And it was wonderful, you could feel all these good vibes going on.

DAVE: They had a rather interesting young priest. The next Sunday we went to Grace Cathedral in San Francisco. And you talk about a great big mausoleum—it's a gorgeous church. We didn't go to their big service, just to ten o'clock or nine o'clock or whatever. And then the next Sunday we were in Boulder.

JOSIE: But that little old chapel in that church—that's the oldest Episcopal church in the country—it's old, from way, way back. It's a little tiny building and they've had to replace the roof and all this, but you could feel It there, in that little chapel.

DAVE: And that big mausoleum, that was something else—nothing there.

JOSIE: You know, what Sam was saying this morning [the speaker at the Cathedral that morning: *Eds.*] about the legacy passed on, where that hit me was in Austria. We had been to the opera that night and we were just wandering around, and looking. We walked by this little bitty old church—you had to walk down to get into it—beneath the sidewalk level.

It's all Baroque, all the golden cupids and angels. But the sign on the church—and I don't know what made us look at it—said it was the Feast of Saints Peter and Paul and the church is Saints Peter and Paul. It's the parish church of Vienna and the sign said that at five o'clock or five-fifteen they were going to have a Mass setting by Loti. And Loti was a contemporary of Mozart and I thought, My gosh, we've got to see that.

It was only about fifteen minutes before the service so we went in. They had the Chorus of Vienna as the choir and this gorgeous music, and they did it in Latin, but the service itself was in German, and the fact of being there, in that place, so far away from home, with the same words and the same ritual —it just hit me. Think of all the years, think of all the people, that have done this same thing, and here we are and we're part of it too. It just blew my mind, I couldn't get over it.

DAVE: Well, the first time I went to Europe my whole family went; they're all Protestant now. The records show that in 1520 they sent a letter to Dr. Luther to send them a proper priest. They've been evangelicals ever since.

But when I was in that little Viennese church for the first time, I was by myself and I realized that this was the church where my grandfather was baptized and my great-grandparents were married. The records go back—the present building was built in the twelfth century, but the records go back to the eighth century.

The afternoon when I was there for the first time, I went to church in the morning and that afternoon had a reception and the minister of the church was there. He spoke pretty good English, so we got to talking, and I said, "Is there anything very historic about the church other than the fact that it's so old?"

And he said, "Well, I'll tell you something interesting." He was very cavalier about this, it wasn't anything too remarkable to him. He said, "A few years ago, the people from the museum at Wiesbaden came up and said they wanted to take a look around the church. And I said, "Sure, just don't disturb anything and leave it like you found it."

So of course in their investigation, they came and said, "Reverend, could we take a look at that altar stone?" And in the altar are two pillars of marble and a slab on top of it. And I said, "Sure, take a look." And they said, "Well, we want to turn it over." And they turned it over, made rubbings, and found Runic inscriptions on this stone that indicate that it was a sacrificial stone before we were Christians.

The Germans sacrificed mostly chickens and geese and things like that, because they had gotten over human sacrifice by that time. But this goes back to—maybe the first, second, third century, something like that, and when they needed an altar stone for a Christian church, some monk just flipped it over. But that gives you some idea of continuity too. Then the fact that my ancestors hung the bell in that church in 1453— that made me realize that time is marching on.

DAVE: Of course, if you go to the monastery now, you will see something totally different from 20 years ago. They have taken off all the gold and all the fancy work and it is very, very plain. It is like Gethsemani [the monastery near Bardstown, Kentucky, where Thomas Merton, the great Trappist monk and religious writer, lived: *Eds.*].

And they had strung a net, I don't know, a fishnet or whatever, behind the altar, and they had strung these little votive lights and here was this beautiful, plain, simple altar with all these twinkling lights. But that's all gone now.

There was a lady who lived at the monastery, Mrs. Cross, and Sister Scholastica, and they made some of the most gorgeous things. And some of that stuff has been sold, simply because they don't use it anymore. Or incense. It's all very simple, plain linen vestments, and albs and stoles.

But in the days when they used to do it up—the last jamboree in the old style was the day that Father Abbot was enthroned. That was the most amazing experience of my life. I put on a black cassock and blended in with the monks. I sat in the choir with the monks, and did everything. I had gotten an invitation. I had known Father Abbot before he was even a priest.

When Dom Benedict was appointed abbot, I think I was about the third or fourth person to know it, because Brother Bernard was appointed to call me on the telephone and tell me. At any rate, I had invitation number 3 or 6 or something like that. That was the most elegant party. There were two bishops, one from Western Michigan and one from Minneapolis, and they did the whole thing. They all had red vestments, and it was the most gorgeous sight imaginable.

This must have been about 1970 or 1969. We had this huge reception. I gave the champagne, six cases, that was my gift. And all these little nuns were there from all over the country, there were representatives of every religious order, Holy Cross and all those little orders, St. Anne, the Transfiguration, and then some they call the Tennis Shoe Sisters (I forgot what they are). Then there was this funny little order from Detroit. There were only two nuns from Detroit—there were only two nuns in the order—and they both wore green habits. They were the funniest little ladies.

And there was this order from Canada and one of these little nuns came up to me, 'cause she thought I was a monk—I had on a cassock—and she said, "Can I ask you something?" and I said, "Yes, Sister." And she said, "Who was your caterer?"

We had the most gorgeous hors d'oeuvres, because Brother Bernard can do all that with his left hand. I helped out, slicing bread and opening bottles of wine, and all that. So I said, "Caterer, Sister? We did all of it ourselves." And she said, "You mean you *men* did this all?" I said, "Yes, Ma'am." "Why, we can't fix soup for three," she said.

In the monastery, when you're sitting around the common room and the abbot walks in, everybody hops up. It's like the Army. There were five abbots there, including our own. This was the morning of the installation and we were all sitting in the common room, and we all had coffee and Danish, and one abbot would walk in, and everybody would stand up. And another abbot would walk in, and everybody would stand up.

This fellow from the Black Benedictines, he was the oldest of the abbots there, and he said, "Gentlemen, I want to make a rule. No more getting up when abbots come in the room, because we'll wear ourselves out." So no one did it.

The pictures I have of old Abbot Augustine—from the mother house of the monastery—he came over for the festivities. I can see him yet. Along about four o'clock in the afternoon everybody started winding down a little bit, there was still plenty of champagne left, and so here comes Father Abbot Augustine, with a bottle of champagne under each arm, two glasses in this hand and a cribbage board in the other.

He says, "Gentlemen, I'll see you later!" Nobody ever saw Father Abbot the rest of the day, and nobody knows to this day where he went. Off to play cribbage, I guess. That was one more day! We had a glorious time; and it poured down rain, I'll never forget that. And we had this big tent out on the lawn. It was pouring down rain, and it was in May.

So we all went in the church, and of course the service lasted of course, it was a High Mass, and then the installation and all the bows, and all the monks have to make their obeisance to the new abbot. Even the oblates had to kiss his ring. And when it was all over, we opened the back doors of the church, and the sun was shining brightly. The rain had washed everything away, and it was beautiful.

That was a glorious day. I think I had more fun that day than any other day in my life except my wedding. Of course, I've always been very close to the monks.

DAVE: At Gethsemane, there used to be an elaborate chapel. That used to be the chapel of Our Lady of Victory, but I think it's all gone. St. Meinrad, which is the Black Benedictine community over in southern Indiana—I think it's about sixty miles west—had a beautiful old neo-Gothic church with this glorious, big polychrome altar. And their church was on two levels. The choir and the sanctuary were up about five steps from the nave and the nave was huge; it was not as wide, but as long, as the cathedral nave here. And there were pews—and of course that's a seminary, where all the Roman priests from around here are trained. And so they needed to have that many pews for the seminarians.

And after Vatican II, they took their polychrome altar, and they put it in the basement of the church, and there it is, along with all the statuary. And in the chancel of the church, where there were once high old oak benches, now they have folding chairs.

They sit in a sort of circle and they say their offices up there. And they say the Mass of the Catechumens up there, up to the offertory. And at the offertory, the whole community goes down into the nave of the church and they have a huge wooden table, which I can only describe as an oversized butcher's block. That's their altar, and they all stand in a circle there. And you stand in a big circle—and it doesn't matter how many people are there, whether there are ten or a hundred—you stand in a circle, around the altar, for anything from the offertory on.

JOSIE: Well, you know, even in Europe it's the same way. Since Vatican II—it's just gone.

A while back, I guess it's been thirty years, some governor of this state insisted that his wife be allowed to come along to visit at Gethsemani. And of course they had to give in, and after she left, they went around and dug up the ground that she had walked on, and threw it over the wall. They thought she had contaminated the ground because she was a woman.

DAVE: On my mother's side the family were all Lutheran, all high-church Lutheran. My mother had a first cousin and he had his own business, he traveled, sold paper towels, that sort of stuff. And somewhere along the way, when I was a small child, he discovered he could make money selling laundry supplies, at Gethsemani, no less. He was a very, very staunch Lutheran.

So Albert went to Gethsemani, and he got in with first one brother and then the other. You will read in your books about Merton about Abbot James Fox—he was the abbot who finally received Merton, if I am not mistaken. And Abbot James, whenever he came to Louisville, stayed with my cousins who lived over here about three blocks away, who, as I said, were very staunch Lutherans. I'd go over to Aunt Mary's and there would be Abbot James. And that was my first sight of a monk. I didn't know what a monk was.

Albert spent lots of time there and he is mentioned in *The Seven Storey Mountain.* Albert brought a whole bunch of stuff from the Cloisters and gave it to the monks at Gethsemani and sure enough, he is mentioned.

Mr. Gans, it just says Mr. Gans. But he gave whatever this was and Merton said, "Mr. Gans brought us something from the Cloisters," and it recalled something to Merton. But he had a very fine relationship with the monks out there, and we used to get all their good sausage, and all their good cheese, and they'd just give it to Albert. Albert wasn't quite honest about it either. He'd go out there into the guest house and see a piece of furniture and say, What are you doing with that furniture? It has eight drawers in it, and so on.

And then he'd go downtown and buy an old piece of junk furniture that had eight drawers in it and bring home a cherry chest. And he had a houseful of that stuff when he died—my mother said he stole it from the monks. But they didn't care. They didn't care whether it was an antique or not, all they cared about was whether it had eight drawers.

There's a pretty good relationship now [between the Roman Catholics and Anglo-Catholics]. You noticed this morning we prayed for our companion parish, a Roman parish, and the assumption is that the Romans three blocks away will pray for us. There's been a good relationship back and forth, better than there is in some places.

JOSIE: A lot of parishes in their diocese and our diocese have what they call a covenant in parish, where they meet and exchange ideas once a month.

DAVE: We had an interesting thing with this Roman parish when we were at the Church of the Advent. Of course it was a huge parish, and Advent was very small. They all came to church one Sunday. They said the same thing we did: it seemed like real church. It was just like the old days.

RICHARD

Richard is a layperson who works in the cathedral office of a large southern diocese. We had made an appointment with the dean of the cathedral a month earlier. We made a special trip over three hundred miles off our itinerary just to see him. When we arrived at his office the following morning, we learned that he had left early to play golf with the bishop, and would be gone for the rest of the day. A match obviously made in Heaven. As it turned out, it was probably just as well. All things considered, we can't imagine that he would have been as courteous and helpful as Richard. The interview begins with a response to our question about the enormous growth that the diocese had enjoyed over the last year.

Well, the growth is enormous to us. We can only see it relative to other mainline denominations. It's phenomenal for any non-conservative church in the middle of the Bible Belt. Part of the growth is due to our bishop. That spills over into the way our individual priests operate within their parishes.

Our present bishop has been here for fourteen years. He puts a high priority on shared leadership, he is not autocratic, and he doesn't expect priests to be autocratic in their parishes, in decision-making or at worship. Most of our priests—I know them very well, it's not that large a diocese—recognize themselves as spiritual leaders of a particular parish. But they welcome all the laity to assist in various things. Which, in my memory, even ten years ago, would not have been turned over to laypeople.

Laypeople in this diocese are into everything from decision-making to planning programs, implementing them, then evaluation of those programs. So you can decide where you need to modify them. Another thing, I think we've experienced growth because we've fought a lot of internal battles in the past twenty years, and we're over those battles now. We're no longer fighting the battle of the liturgy, in this diocese at least. And we have fought the battle of the ordination of women.

We have women priests. We have women priests on parochial staffs; we do not yet have a woman rector. We do have deacons and they have visibility. And they are placed—not just because they are women. They are just good priests.

The Bishop tells this story: When he was a young priest he was in this parish and he had come up with this idea that was a marvelous idea, it was theologically correct, propitious for the time, affordable, and he would throw it out to his parish. And they would nod and say okay, and then nothing would ever happen. And he said in the Sixties he discovered that people will not buy into an idea and therefore will not participate in that idea unless they shared in the formation of it. It has to be a collaborative stance in a volunteer system. So that has carried over into our churches.

We use women fully. We have only two parishes that do not yet have women acolytes, layreaders, or chalice-bearers. All the others do. Women in the sanctuary are not a hot issue here. We've already worked through that.

We don't do it by affirmative action necessarily. I travel around a lot and I know that we have full participation of women. Many women senior wardens, many women on vestries. Let me tell you something which may have something to do with young people coming back and with the whole idea of your book. In 1973 the General Convention was the first one where we had ever elected a woman deputy. Recently, in 1984, in preparation for the 1985 General Convention, all four of our lay deputies were women. They were elected not because they were women but because they all are very talented, they all have wonderful minds, minds like steel traps. It makes a statement about where we are today, and I think young people are more sensitive to that statement. They want to participate in a church, in a religious lifestyle, that makes that statement.

Because we in the diocese use this collaborative stance of planning we involve hundreds of people each year. We ask, What do you think our diocese, the collaborative effort of all our parishes, needs to be doing? We check that out. The bishop doesn't say, "Now this is what we're going to be doing." He doesn't impose a structure or a program.

We have just wrapped up an enormous planning apparatus. We brought five reps from every parish, some old, some young, some new members, new converts. And in a very structured forty-eight- or fifty-hour period, we asked questions like, "What should we be doing together as a Christian community?" We synthesized the answers and we are turning all that massive amount of data into programs. It makes us look at all kinds of things: the way we oppress people, the way we treat priests, the way we pay them—all the vicious circles. We said it was a model for the way we want to run this diocese. And parishes are beginning to set that same model.

If these people go back to their own parishes having already participated in this on the diocesan level, they will not tolerate someone coming in and saying, "You *will* do this. We *will* have services at nine and eleven and three-fifteen." They would rather have someone saying, "Why don't you call some of us together and we'll talk about this? Why don't we try this

and this? Which rite shall we use, which hymn shall we sing?"
Now I think that has an attractive point to it, because young
people are more knowledgeable about human dynamics than
we were.

My own thought is we have to recognize the idea of the
relationship to God, and a study of that relationship. And how
can we enhance it. I don't think we enhance it one bit by
setting out a manual and saying, here on page 16, this is it, these
are the *dos* and those are the *don'ts*. I think Scripture provides
us with a lot of flexibility for our own interpretation. And if
this is the way we get on and off the highway or expressway,
or how we watch television—those kinds of things are just as
much part of our Christian life as what we do on Sunday and
what we do in organized religion.

Most systems demand, either verbally or nonverbally, clarification of values, and I think we're making great strides toward
letting Scripture be the basis of our values-clarification system.
I see it in daily life, I see it in my children, I see it in professional people. Values clarification is the heart of our decision-
making.

As for professional people, those people—and I know you
have a great interest in professional people, especially young
professional people—most of those people have been trained in
many areas. But they are not receptive to fundamentalism. I
think that that's the new pattern among young professionals.
They're too sophisticated to be taken in by fundamentalism's
easy answers.

You know, this cathedral has a program in which they bring
in noted people from all over the country. But they organized
themselves, the women and the men, for haute cuisine. It's the
only place in the city where you can walk in daily to business
luncheons and get a Grand Marnier soufflé for lunch.

And they feed three or four hundred people a day, and in
the middle of this damn town, they are—professionally they're

attorneys, brokers, people who came at first only to eat. And never attend a worship service or lecture series. But what we have found is, they have broken the ice of walking into the building. They get familiar with the entrances, the exits, the bathrooms, and they say, Well, let's try going there for public worship.

Young people—of course, I think we attract a lot of young people because we openly acknowledge that we're interested in them. We give young professionals a chance to involve themselves in the Church. Many churches in the South, especially in the Southeast, don't give people that opportunity. In the Southeast especially, often people decide they want to be members of a carriage-trade church.

We've also been on the cutting edge of the hospice movement. We're one of the few denominations that picked up about ten years ago on the dying process, grief, and how to deal with it all. Death is just as natural as birth. Another reason for our growth is our efforts for the recovery of lapsed members. We have good youth programs. Now we have them in this whole area and we have always had a full-time youth adviser and we expect him or her to be involved with young people. And that gives us a springboard to them.

Also, I can't divorce our patterns of growth, just across the board, from the efforts put into teaching. Our plan involves a hundred dioceses, to teach dioceses how to teach their people. It makes a difference in a person's life. The main thing is the difference it makes in a person's life to recognize stewardship. To recognize that there are Scriptural mandates on giving the first fruits that God gave us back to Him. No question about it, that has been very attractive to a lot of people.

Campus ministry has been almost the single largest item in our administration. We learned a lot from John Savage [a popular church workshop leader]. You know, he conducts extensive seminars on listening skills, trains people in what he calls pastoral listening. We have used this plan extensively in our diocese. For two years, we've held these classes, and then the people go back into their own parishes and take what they have learned. It brings back the people who've quit coming. People quit the church many times over trivial things.

People quit over: "They left out the processional one morning," "They had a server I couldn't stand," "They sang a hymn I didn't like," "The minister preached a sermon I didn't like and I never came back." But the Savage training program is for both clergy and laypeople. It is really something. It's about a thousand dollars a person for the week, plus room and board. It's not cheap, and it's hard to organize. But we've done it two years in a row.

When they finish the program, they go back to the parish and find key people like vestrymen and teach them how to talk to parishioners who have dropped out of church: all the eye movements, all the things—how to be a good listener. They let the people talk about why they left the church, and vent all those reasons why they left. There are data available to show that the results are amazing when skilled people are listening. It's really worth it.

MACK

Mack is a research scientist in applied mathematics and computer technology. He is one of the most brilliant thinkers we have ever known. He was a Marine Corp officer, did research on Department of Defense projects for over a decade, and is now doing research at a large Southern university. If you want to understand Mack, imagine the leadership qualities of James T. Kirk, the logical creativity of Commander Spock, and the warm, down-home integrity of Bones McCoy, all rolled into one person. Ralph met Mack in the freshman registration line at Young Harris College in 1955. They have been the closest of friends ever since. One day in 1983,

*Mack called to give us an address change. When Ralph told him
that he had just been confirmed in the Episcopal Church, Mack
laughed and confessed that he and his wife, Susan (a talented
veterinarian), had become members of the Presbyterian Church.
Our conversation begins with a reminiscence of their days at
Emory University in Atlanta.*

Well, Ralph, you probably remember just about as much
about it as I do. We shared so many of the same experiences
at Young Harris and at Emory. The reason for leaving was
simply a total disillusionment with what I found in the church;
and at least initially the leaving was not a protest against religion, but against the organized religion of that day. It appeared
that the issues that were being addressed in the churches—at
least the churches that I had any association with—were social
issues, cosmetic issues, they simply didn't deal with the basic
problems that I think thinking people should be confronting.
I was a Methodist and my father was a Methodist preacher,
with a church in the North Georgia Conference, and of course
that's what led me to Young Harris where I met Ralph, and
later to Emory.

We were out longer than fifteen years—I would say it was
in the mid-Fifties, 1956. At that time we still made some forays
down to Trinity Methodist Church, we were still looking for
something within the Church, and didn't find it. The following year I left Emory and went to the University of Texas in
Austin, and there made one attempt to find a church home, the
Unitarian Church. And they did seem to be addressing what
I considered to be pertinent issues but they did it in such a way
that it seemed to leave all religion out of it. And so that wasn't
satisfying either.

Well, the results of that were, from some point in about
1956, 1957, I simply had nothing to do with the Church. And
that was a situation that remained the same until very, very

recently. Susan's family were Baptists. I wish she were here so she could give you more of her reasons for drifting away from the Church. I know that she was quite involved in the Church in her younger days.

I know that she was quite disillusioned by a political fight that occurred in the Baptist church of which she was a member. She was in Atlanta at the time, I don't know which church. But again, the upshot of it, the Church simply didn't provide answers, whatever the specific reasons might have been, and as a result, she left also. And we were married in a church. I don't think we had any animosity toward the Church; at home, we would attend with parents or family, but not because we felt we were getting anything out of it, we didn't want to hurt them in any way . . . we did it for them. I think that personally I always felt uncomfortable in a church. I always felt uncomfortable in Sunday school.

Now that has turned about and I'm finding Sunday school one of the more enjoyable aspects of it. I had mentioned earlier to you that it seems that the nature of church has changed, to a very large degree. And that change deals with the type of subjects that are discussed and this is particularly true in the Sunday schools of the churches that I have been to in the last two years. It was in April 1982 that we rejoined the Church and started going to the First Presbyterian Church in Americus, Georgia.

When we started going, Susan and I both told the minister, and in fact the procedure within the Presbyterian Church is that you have to go before a session, a board of elders in the church, and state your reasons for becoming a member. And I was very candid with them about the fact that no, I did not have a specific belief, although I had come to believe that it would be better if I did, but that I didn't at this point, but I was looking for something.

And they welcomed us with open arms under those conditions, and we found that there has been no hesitation on anyone's part in church to discuss our reservations with us. And yet no one has tried to force a belief on us, it's been an educational process of showing us things and allowing us to draw our own conclusions from those things that have been shown us. As for the church that I now belong to: the Presbyterians go back for roots to Martin Luther and the Protestant Reformation—the corruption in the Church at that period of time. It was strongly influenced by Knox, the Scottish minister, in Geneva. Also it was influenced very strongly by Martin Luther. The government within the Church is at the local level. One thing that surprised me to learn, because I never picked it up anywhere along the way in my education, was the tremendous impact that the Presbyterian Church had on our government and the writing of the Constitution. A large percentage of the writers of the Constitution were in fact Presbyterians and modelled our Constitution very much on the Presbyterian Church's government.

We have elders and deacons, elders being senior and deacons junior. Each year there is an election of elders and deacons, and anyone can run at any time, except we had a merging—the Presbyterian church split into North and South some time ago in Civil War times, and just in the last two years has come back together again. And there is still some shifting back and forth on some of the rules and methodologies for doing things.

In our church in Americus, the election is made by direct vote simply at a church meeting: we sit down and vote on who will be elders. If they were electing five elders, they would take the ten people who got the most votes and have a run-off between those people to get the five who would be elected. This is contrary to the new order, which calls for a nominating committee.

The old way was strictly nominations from the floor—actually, just a direct vote, you would take the whole roster of church members and vote for whomever you wanted. And our church had to get a dispensation to continue that method. But under the rules of the merger, anybody who wanted that dispensation could automatically have it, just by the formality of asking. The opinion being that this would give you the most open, democratic way of handling it.

Recently, the Presbyterian Church has organized a committee. If a local church wants a new minister, they can get up a search committee and hire one. The Presbytery, however, has the veto power: they can't put one down on you but they can keep one out. Which, from what I have seen, is simply a mechanism for maintaining standards. The Presbyterian Church had an interest in making sure there were educated people in the ministry, not simply someone who had the itch or saw a TV ad.

I went into all this because some of the issues that go into the central issue that we're talking about here—namely, this Force that seems to be motivating so many of us now—seems to be taking hold in some churches more than in others. And the observation that I have made is that centrally governed churches are not doing nearly as well as those churches with government from the bottom up.

Well, we've kind of established that we have more or less agreement on the fundamental issue of Church governance. Let's get the conversation onto what I think we all have a terrible fascination with, and that's a phenomenon that seems to be happening in the world right now in that people like you and me and millions of others, without any volition of their own, and possibly without any will or choice of their own— or often against their will—suddenly are being forced precipitously back into this kind of thinking, this kind of activity.

You know, those of us who practice aikido claim that the concept of the Force in the movie *Star Wars* is the same as the concept of the *ki* in aikido. And it's not unique just to aikido, it's an oriental concept that has general acceptance in Japan and China too, I believe. The idea is that the center of your being is where your soul or your essence resides. It's your center of gravity, a couple of inches below your navel, in the center of your body. And that all activity flows from this point, this center. Remember the ritual suicide, hara-kari? Well, the knife was always thrust into the center, the heart, because that is how you let out this life force.

I find this a particularly interesting subject because as a scientist I have one view: on the other hand, I know with entire certainty that as long as you think of something, in this case this force or *ki*, in certain contexts it allows you to do things that you otherwise could not do. Now, how does that work? I don't know. But it does work. So one possible implication to derive from that would be, that if you just accept the teachings of Jesus, you don't have to understand them, just accept them, and as long as you think in those terms, things will work right for you. Just the act of thinking in those terms sets you up to be in harmony, the way things should be.

The major difference that I would cite now as compared to years ago is the difference in focus now: the de-emphasis on the older rituals and the re-emphasis on what Jesus actually said. And I continue to be astounded, over and over, when I am presented with what is purported to be a good translation and see what the Man really said. These were *not* the kinds of things I was told He said! Or had any understanding that He said, from my early church days.

When I get down to it—and I'm by no means a Greek scholar or have any capability in languages, I think that the translations have improved tremendously over the King James version, as far as accurate renditions go. The meaning of what Jesus was saying is so fundamentally different and because of that difference, so fundamentally important to the way we live today that it just opened up the whole world again to me.

Jesus got behind the scenery of this "world's stage" that we live in. And he shook some of the sets, he irritated some of the local Gestapo so much in the process that they killed Him. And then He came back. That's the crux of the matter. The whole crux is that if indeed He did come back, then all of this has meaning, and if He did not come back, none of it has meaning.

My faith is not strong enough yet for me to categorically say that I believe He came back. I don't know. I don't reject that He came back. I simply don't know. I would like to know. But I don't know how I can find out.

I may never find out. But whether He came back or did not come back to me changes in no way the goodness of what He said, and the importance of what He said. And the worth of following His teachings. In fact, it seems to me that we have missed a tremendous resource, that is, we educated people, we intelligentsia, of the late twentieth century, have missed a tremendous moral resource in the teachings of Jesus because we felt that in order to pay attention to what He said, we had to take all the other interpretations, which is not necessarily true. This is especially ironic when you remember that Jesus always said, "Listen to *me*, and forget all this other stuff."

THOMAS

Thomas, a candidate for the diaconate in a medium-sized Midwestern city, is a dead ringer for John Denver. The wide blue eyes and shock of sun-blond hair and boyish grin make him look younger than his thirty-eight years. He wears a gold wedding band and is flanked by pictures of his small children. We begin the interview by talking about the gradual drift of people from the Church. But we end up talking about his concern for his brother and a friend who are typical of those who are always "in the process of returning" but seem unable to make the commitment.

* * *

I see a lot of people being drawn away from the Church today by the sort of anti-institutional feeling that we haven't overcome from the Sixties and Seventies—the feeling that all institutions, religious and otherwise, are suspect. Also, there's a desire for a really deep, intense sort of religious experience that at least the mainline churches, like the Episcopalian and Lutheran and Roman Catholic, haven't met. And perhaps no church can do that really fully. But people crave this sort of intense peak experience.

Some people find it in monasteries, on retreats, in "fringe religions" like the Moonies . . . in eastern cults. It's a need, a hunger for a deeper participation in the mystery of it all, somehow.

But up against this we have this other strain. There's a counter-movement . . . this kind of anti-religious, materialistic, yuppified world view that is springing up everywhere. These people give lip service to religion, but they are secretly uncomfortable with the message of self-sacrifice, loving others, and living anti-materialistically—you know, "What, me give up my designer jeans and my BMW and my Cuisinart?" That sort of thing. They are really bothered by the fact that they may sooner or later have to rethink or remake their whole lifestyle.

My brother is an example of this. Let me tell you about him because he perfectly illustrates this kind of shift in values we're seeing. He's sort of the classic hippie-turned-yuppie. He was born in 1950, went to college, got very involved in the anti-war movement. He went to Canada, sat on pyramids in Central America, and meditated with all the West Coast gurus. Then he lived on a goat ranch in New Mexico for awhile. And he did drugs, not a lot, but took some LSD, smoked a lot of pot. Then he met his wife and ended the Seventies by going to live with her in a commune.

They came to live in the city near me and the folks, and for a while they really lived the urban hippie lifestyle—you know, very anti-materialistic, simple. They ate bean sprouts and alfalfa and tofu and organic eggs, whatever they are, and wore Indian bedspreads and refused to eat red meat. They were really into vegetarianism.

But they started to change and move up in the world as my brother made more money. It was just little changes at first; he bought a nice car at first, and some nice clothes. And then it was . . . a total change. They started to buy things, lots of nice things: wineglasses and champagne buckets and fish poachers and lacquer trays, and a treadmill and an exercise bike, a VCR, a big television, fifty-dollar running shoes . . . the works. They had to admit they liked it. Their lifestyle had totally changed.

About this time they started going to Unity Church. If you look at its origins, it dates back to Mary Baker Eddy. It's vegetarian, so it allows them to stay in touch with their commune phase. And it's sort of vague—there's no belief in evil. It's against all negative thoughts; the only evil is having negative thoughts. It places no moral demands on them but keeps them feeling spiritual. Oh, they'll come here [to the cathedral where Thomas goes] on Christmas and Easter when there are lots of positive vibes in the air, as they would put it: lots of joy and peace and love and good hymns. But the penitential seasons like Advent and Lent are a bit much for them, they're too *negative*. The only demands the Unity Church places on people are that they have positive thoughts and they like that. It's a way they can keep this spiritual dimension and still embrace this sort of yuppified lifestyle.

I've got other friends who are coming into the church through the back door of psychotherapy or therapeutic experiences—looking for anything that makes them happy and is a reasonably sane cult. Ordinary people on the fringes of the Church or out of it altogether . . . they expect odd reactions from people in the church. I have another friend, a very successful attorney in his late thirties who is a member of a very big law firm here in town. He's divorced, athletic, dating lots of women, successful in a small way. He's sort of a nominal Christian, attends the Cathedral occasionally.

He'll come on Good Friday but not on Easter, which I find a bit odd—but that's his taste. I tell him he should at least try to bring it full circle. But the really odd thing is that this largely secularized young attorney is obsessed with the worship of the Blessed Virgin, says the Rosary regularly, treasures a copy of a book on Mariology that I bought him. He'll party all Saturday night but show up at a convenience Mass on Sunday evening with a copy of *The Scriptural Rosary* cluched in his hands—kind of a funny mix of real secularity and old-style pietism.

Now that I'm into the training program for the diaconate, I talk with a lot of people who are toying with the idea of coming back. And mostly they're afraid of growth, change, being asked to rethink things, maybe having to confront failures in their own lives. People fear being jolted out of a groove. They're comfortable where they are. And they feel the church might free them to think. They fear that freedom. They fear that if they returned to the Church, took their spiritual life seriously, they would have to make new commitments . . . explore, change, grow, perhaps feel pain. And they're unwilling to do this. Some of them will remain stuck forever. I hope not, but I'm afraid they will . . . my brother, my friend the attorney. They may never make the kind of pilgrimage we're talking about.

SOPHIA

Sophia is an attractive woman of great warmth and vitality. Born on the East Coast, she now lives in Chicago but retains close ties with a large, closely knit Italian family. She is married to an ex-Lutheran (her second marriage, his first). Sophia broke off for-

mal connections with the Roman Catholic Church, in which she was brought up, when her first marriage ended in divorce, and for over twenty years had no formal connection with any church. Recently she has been attending another church with friends, going to Inquirers class, and renewing a lively interest in church history. Yet at present she is still uncommitted in any formal way to the Church and remains "in transition." This interview tells the story of her shifting relationship with the church over more than two decades of change.

I was raised as a Roman Catholic by my parents. But there was an ambivalence in this training. Both parents came from a small town in southern Italy and they were very pragmatic Catholics. My father's experiences with the Church were negative. The Church encroached on his property. They needed the land to farm so that they could eat, so they could live. But most of the property in our town was owned by the Church. And so his early remembrances were of hunger and not enough land to farm, yet this land was all taken over by the Church.

My mother was raised in the same town. The women seemed to have a different experience of religion because they had children to raise. They did not negate the church as my father did. This was all in Italy, of course.

They brought this experience of the Church with them to America. My father never went to church, felt it was unimportant. He believed in human beings and in all religions being the same. My mother was a very practical Catholic. Catholicism in Italy is different. They don't revere priests there. The priest is seen as someone like themselves who works to support himself but happens to have this information to help them get to heaven. They don't know what's going to happen with them when they die, so they maintain this connection.

However, she [my mother] believed in the teachings of the Church and she could assist at the Mass and had done so. When she got here to America, if anyone was not assisting properly, she would just go up and take over from the altar boy. She knew the Mass, she knew the teachings, but she had a very practical way of interacting with priests and nuns. Here we esteem them—but this was just a poor little village in southern Italy, I must tell you . . . perhaps it's not typical of all Italy.

So I was raised with this ambivalence. A mother who would say, "It's Sunday morning, get up, you need to go to church," and a father who would say, "If you don't want to, you can stay in bed." A mother who would tell me, when I'd ask why she wasn't going to church, "Well, God knows I must make the spaghetti to feed my family, I have no time." I love it . . . it was unbelievable.

I was baptized as an infant, confirmed, I knew the Sacraments. I was about twelve or thirteen when I was confirmed. And my first Holy Communion took place in about the first or second grade. I went through all these sacraments. I made my first confession before I received my first communion.

I stopped going to church when I was in high school, which in a way was too bad because my early experience was that they never taught the history of the Church or the Gospels, other than what we heard from the altar. My instruction would have come in my high-school years, because then there were Bible classes.

So I didn't learn the history of the Church and began not to attend church regularly. Now I did have an experience in growing up that turned me off religion in a way. It was because of this that I felt I was not loved by God—I couldn't understand it and so I stopped going to church. I had been abused by my godparent, so I felt that this was God saying I was not loved. I felt that I was a sinner and could not go to confession or communion. But somewhere along the line, I met the young man I was to marry. And so again I became connected to the Church, I began to come back to the Church.

He [my fiancé] was a Catholic and there was a Paulist Church in the city, a teaching order of priests, and I would attend lectures there. There was one priest who was especially helpful to me. He taught me how to come to confession, more about the whole religion, about forgiveness. He made me see that I was not unloved, or a bad person because I had been abused, and he encouraged me to get married. I also was having problems with that because in that era women were supposed to be virgins when they were married. So this priest helped me to get married. And we were married in the Roman Catholic Church.

Shortly after that my husband started having problems with alcohol. We were still involved with the Church, so I turned to the Church for help. By then I was in Chicago and they helped me and I found peace. They helped me find the help we needed for his alcoholism, and when there were legal problems, they helped with those. And I found myself going to church every morning. I attended daily Mass and it was a great consolation to me.

I think for the next three to four years, having the Church in my life, having God in my life in this way, having the guidance of the priests—was very comforting. And then at one point it was time for me to go through a divorce, because things were not working with the marriage. It was at the time of the divorce that I turned away from the Church. The Roman Catholic Church was very anti-divorce then. You could go to confession and go to communion as long as you were only separated, as long as you never married again.

I think that's where the Church and I parted company. I already had met so many people from a variety of religions. I was active with the YWCA and met people of many faiths. I became involved with a variety of good people who weren't Catholics, never went to church, but were good people. I cared for them a great deal and I respected their religions. I couldn't believe that I needed to have church . . . that it was the only way I could relate to God.

So I began to develop a personal relationship with God. By that I mean, I began to sit in a park and talk with Him. Or on a bus, or wherever I was, during the day, I would talk with Him. And this was all through the 1960s. It was in 1959 or 1960 that I got my divorce, which started the period when I really got away from the Church.

And so I never really experienced Vatican II. I was completely cut off from the Church. I can hardly remember when I went back into a church again. Until my brother's funeral in 1982, I did not go to Mass. And I really had not been back into a Roman Catholic church for a Mass. All of my brothers and sisters were already married by then, none of my friends were Catholic. When I went home to see the family, I might go to a program in the church and a few times, to a Christmas or Easter service, but I never felt I could make communion with them. I didn't feel I was able to.

I found myself dropping into a Catholic church back here in Chicago. At St. Mary's I would go in occasionally, or to St. Peter's . . . my mother was a big believer in Purgatory, so I would buy those little Mass cards. I felt that I was just outside the Church. I would stop into St. Mary's or St. Peter's and just sit on a bench inside, but I would never go to a Mass. I just went and visited . . . I went to see my Friend. But whenever I really needed to communicate with God, I used to go down to the lake or sit in some other spot in nature. I don't believe I received communion again until 1982.

At my brother's funeral that fall there was to be communion and I thought, my God, what will I do? At that time, my brother had also been out of the Church for years. As it happened, they couldn't find the communion somehow and so we didn't have it. But in the meantime I talked to one of the family members, or somebody, and explained my dilemma. And they told me that things had changed in the Church: that if I just said the act of contrition I could receive communion. So two days later when my sister-in-law died, remembering what had been said, I comfortably went up and received communion . . . twenty-three years later. And when my mother died [in 1983], I did the same thing.

Before that I felt I was outside the Church . . . it was something that was not available to me. And that was all right, because I was leading a very full life without the Church. I felt very close to God through all those years. And I felt that without God's help, I would never have got through all that and been married again. I had God's guidance and protection and the Church really didn't matter. The Church was apart from all that.

I don't think I really got back to the Church in any real way until two friends invited me. On All Souls' Day 1983, my friend had my mother's and brother's names read in the prayers for the dead. Another friend had a Mass said for my mother at Holy Name [Cathedral in Chicago]. She was the one who told me that it was okay to take communion, and she was an ex-nun, and close to God, so I figured she would know. And when I had not blown up or fallen apart or been struck down when I took communion at my sister-in-law's funeral, I did it again for my mother.

I talked to God when I first did it. I was in another church when I received communion again, so I felt I was sinning against the Roman Catholic Church, and I was getting very confused. So I just knelt down and talked to God again. This was all part of my teaching as a Catholic when I was a child. First we were taught that you should never go to another church. And then we were taught, well, you can attend another church but you must never participate in the service because this is a sin. So this teaching must be deeply ingrained in me.

The Paulist father that I knew back East . . . I'll never forget:

I was so upset at the Church one time. We used to go to services at a USO where they had an interdenominational service that was very simple and lovely, on a Sunday afternoon . . . just a few prayers, where we got together with the servicemen. It was so beautiful. But my parish priest would not hear my confession unless I stopped going to a service that was not Catholic, and I began to get turned off—for a variety of reasons. And this Father O'Kelley, this Paulist priest, said, "There are changes taking place in the Church." And that must have been the first I heard of these changes. He was one of the new breed of priests and he said that "[the service] is absolutely beautiful, there's no reason why you couldn't attend that."

When I told him what had happened in my parish church, he said, "Come to me and I will hear your confession." So my first real confession was to him and I told him everything . . . it was as if everything came out, everything about my childhood. It was so wonderful, it was at Easter, and I'll never forget it. It was such a beautiful new way to start over—it was as if my life was opening up. And I got married—and then this problem with the Church again, when I was divorced. Before I was thirty, I was right back where I started from . . . a little sadder, I think.

At the time my marriage fell apart I was fortunate enough to find a great therapist, an analyst who had studied under Jung and who was a Quaker. With her help and love I was able to stretch and grow in my thinking and get through this difficult divorce. Even though the Church had said I would have to stay in this terrible marriage the rest of my life. The Church did help in some ways. . . . I had lost my child by that time too; my son died when he was less than a year old, and the church suggested I go to this place for orphan children and volunteer there because they thought it would help me. And I would have done it, except I had to work at three jobs at that time just to pay the legal fees.

So my therapist helped me and that was the luckiest thing,

that she did. I was having a breakdown, I think, and didn't know it. She gave me good advice. My family also wanted me to get the divorce . . . but I just could not do it. I was so Catholic. If you're married once, you're married for life, I thought. I could have separated and remained married to him, and that would have been all right, and then I could have had communion . . . if I had never had a relationship with a man again. The intent not to have any other life than this would have to have been there. But I couldn't lie to myself—although a lot of my friends did. I remember when I was growing up. The Pope had said that rhythm is the only birth control. At sixteen, a girl I was very close to in high school was married and was now practicing birth control. I was shocked. I said, "How can you do this? You're sinning!" And she said, "The Pope has to live his life and I have to live mine."

I didn't like going back to the Roman Church at first, with all the changes. I loved the ritual, the Latin Mass. There was a beauty to it. But I thought, if that's the Mass they're now doing, I will learn it. But I didn't like all the new things they were doing. It didn't feel like church to me. It wasn't special anymore. But when I went to the other church, I felt at home. I didn't feel I was in a Protestant church at all because of the liturgy.

I'm really not sure. When I am going to Inquirers' Class at this church and going to services, I find a community of people who seem to feel as I do. Yet I also fear organized religion. I really am uncomfortable with it, because I just don't like what happens with organized religion, with groups of people in the Church. I don't like the way they set themselves up above and apart from the rest of society. I walk down the street and see somebody writing on the wall "Trust Jesus," and in my head I think, "I trust Jesus will be as offended as I am." It bothers me.

I love what I feel at the church where my friends go, what

the priest there does, what the people are experiencing together. But you know . . . there's a friend of mine who's also
searching for religion, who's been searching for a while, and
I kind of like what she tells me. I don't like being caught up
with too many of the trappings of religion. I like just living it.
I like just going out and *being*. She says to me; "Sophia, why
do we have to be inside a church? If we just come together in
the name of Christ, why isn't that enough?"

A lot of people I love and respect, who wouldn't harm a fly
if they could help it, are people like this woman—and I like
that. Whereas many of the people I meet who go to church,
who get all caught up in church, really aren't very Christian.
It bothers me. I'm so afraid I'll get so caught up going to
church, attending all the services, that I'm not going to have
time just to go out among people and just *be* and *experience* and
become. I don't know why I feel that so strongly but I do. And
it's my hesitancy to get lost in all the ritual and communal life
of religion . . . I am happier this way, just floating, I feel this
is more my calling.

Yet I'm also at a period when I feel it's time for me to learn
—not to say anymore, this is what I *think* or *feel*, but to learn
the history of religion, all religions. I'm feeling, if I can be
anything, I'd prefer to be a Roman Catholic again. I'm feeling,
strangely, that I'm getting more in touch with that again. Yet
I don't want to get so caught up in anything that I can't feel
empathy with a Moslem, a Buddhist. I can't believe that we're
not all one, no matter what we believe. Even the non-believers
. . . somehow, by interacting one with the other, we come to
terms with our own individual selves. He [God] knows about
this, and I can't believe He could condemn all this, having
created it. I trust Him and love Him enough to believe that,
whatever it is, it's going to be all right. I don't want to feel I'm
part of a special group.

I have been thinking of going back to the Roman Catholic

Church. But I don't want to come back in under Phoenix [a re-entry group for divorced and remarried Catholics] or any special group. I'm me, I'm Sophia. I'm a human being created by God, to take part in His love, His church, and if they can't take me back, I'm not interested in them. I don't feel I need to be accepted again. I could walk into any Catholic church today and feel part of it. I don't know how they would feel, they may have all these rules that I don't believe in anymore. But I've lived long enough to see that rules change. What is really important is my relationship to God.

III · In Transition

One Person's Story of a Pilgrimage From Laity to Priesthood

There was a transitional moment of delicious uneasiness, and then —instantaneously—the long inhibition was over, the dry desert lay behind, I was off once more into the land of longing, my heart at once broken and exalted as it had never been since the old days at Bookham. There was nothing whatever to do about it; no question of returning to the desert.

—C. S. Lewis, *Surprised by Joy*

RALPH'S STORY

Imagine a perfectly *ordinary* dull day: a morning with overcast, featureless skies, neither too warm nor too cold, too damp nor too dry, too noisy nor too quiet. A day with no defining shadows, no contrast between darks and lights. Nothing in the air; too early in the year for flowers, too late for snow. The streets are dingy with the dirt and oil of winter. Your skin feels grimy under clinging clothes, your hair is lank, and your spirit is as pallid as the day around you.

Now imagine that suddenly, without warning, to your utter astonishment, the clouds part and the warmth of the sun streams down, bringing with it a crisp breath of air that evaporates the dullness and drabness around you. And imagine that with the rays of the sun—miraculously, as if time were tele-

scoped—the flowers spring from the ground and trees begin
to bud.

If you can imagine these things, then you have a glimmer
of what happened to me on Easter Sunday, 1983, when, for the
first time in twenty-five years, I sat in a church pew, in the
Church of the Ascension in Chicago, listening to Rector
Edwin Norris quietly and lovingly talk about the miracle of
Easter.

As the wave of warmth swept over me, I felt my eyes brimming with tears. I reached for Valerie's hand and discovered
that she was already reaching for mine. We sat there together,
astonished by what was happening to both of us, stunned by
the miracle that had come upon us unawares, certain for the
first time in our lives that the Grace of God was a real and
tangible force, and that the Holy Spirit was indeed spreading
light where once there had been only a dull gray.

How had I come to be sitting there in that church on Easter
Sunday morning? And why had it been twenty-five years since
I had sat in a church for any reason other than weddings and
funerals? Why had I left the Church if it now, suddenly, meant
so much to me? Why was it that at this juncture in my life I
was suddenly to change irrevocably, to change the way that I
looked at the world, the way that I understood myself and
everyone around me?

I am still searching for answers. This book is one of the ways
that I am searching.

My earliest recollections of church are of the First Methodist
Church of Tallapoosa, Georgia, the little west Georgia town
in which I was born. The church had white columns in the
front and a double door in the center of the columns. Inside,
a proscenium arch spread over the pulpit. The carpet was a
deep wine color, and the muted light played over the dark
wood of the pews.

The pastor of the church was the Reverend Frederick L.

Glisson, with whom I was to work years later as the assistant chaplain at Emory University Hospital. But in 1939, I was eight years old, in school, and a year into my battle with rheumatic fever.

"Brother" Glisson (as he liked to be called) visited the school one day, and introduced himself to all of us. He was of medium height, wore a dark suit, and clasped his hands in front of him when he talked. He told us a funny story about how he had never known what to do with his hands when he was a boy. He said that he had finally decided simply to hold them in front of himself, fingers intertwined, so that if he made too big a fool of himself, he would already have his hands in position to pray.

When I became so ill that I had to be taken to a hospital in Atlanta, it was Brother Glisson who made the arrangements and came to our home to baptize me before I left. When my mother called home with the news that the doctor said I was dying, it was Brother Glisson who held the all-night prayer vigil for my recovery. And when I survived and returned home to be bedridden for a year, it was Brother Glisson who arranged for hot food to be left on our doorstep every morning.

Many years later, he was the pastor of Trinity Methodist Church in Atlanta. My mother was married to my beloved stepfather in that church in 1948. I gave the bride away, and Brother Glisson performed the ceremony.

We attended church sporadically. Occasionally, I went to other churches. I was not really "attached" to any church. My mother's marriage to my father had ended in a bitter divorce. I felt the inevitable alienation that accompanies a broken home, but I did not even think of looking to the Church for guidance.

Instead, I went to school, eventually bought my first automobile, rode motorcycles, went camping and fishing, lifted weights, dated girls, and mostly read—hundreds and hundreds of books, ranging from science fiction to the entire 1910 edition of the *Encyclopedia Britannica*. But I was neither in nor *of* the Church.

* * *

One week, in the spring of 1951, I attended (with my then girlfriend) four "tent meetings" at a Baptist church in East Point, Georgia. A large canvas tent had been erected in the church's back yard. It was filled with wooden benches, and the grass was covered with sawdust.

The evangelist was a man whom I will call Jesse Crumley, who was from Birmingham, Alabama. He was lean, of medium height, red-faced, and dressed in a light, cream-colored, gabardine suit. Around his neck, he wore a red tie with a crucifix stick-pin. The Reverend Crumley started his first sermon with a joke.

He asked the congregation if anyone there had ever told a lie—". . . white lie, gray lie, black lie, any ole kind of lie."

When everybody admitted to telling lies at one time or another, he asked if anybody had ever stolen anything— ". . . a book of matches, a bar of soap, a towel from a hotel room, any little ole thing." Again, everybody nodded yes. He then smiled broadly, and said, "This is just the kind of congregation I like to talk to: full of thieves and liars!"

I had never been to a tent meeting before. I was alternately attracted and repelled. Crumley's story was simple. It went something like this:

In the beginning, God made the world in six days, got tired of creating, and rested on the seventh. He made the Garden of Eden, and when he got through, he made Adam to live in it. He made Eve out of one of Adam's ribs, to keep Adam company.

Now, the Devil went down to the Garden and tempted Eve with an apple ("Now we all know what that apple represents—what really went on in that Garden"). Ole Eve, she was vain and easily tempted, and after the Devil got through with her she took the "apple" to ole Adam and tempted him with it. And when both of them had eaten all the apples they could take, they saw everything in a different light.

So one day, God came looking for them and when he found them, they had made some clothes out of leaves, to hide their shame. God knew very well what they had been up to, and he got them to confess that they had "eaten" of the forbidden fruit. He put a curse on both of them, and had some of his angels drive them from the Garden, to spend their days in toil and suffering.

By this time, people had begun to squirm in their seats and dig their toes in the sawdust. They (but not I) knew what was coming next: the exciting part they had all been waiting to hear!

Crumley said that we were all born in sin—the Original Sin of Adam and Eve—and that we were all doomed to burn in hellfire for all eternity. He said that no matter how hard we tried, there was no way that we could escape sin on our own. We were all thieves and liars, with lust in our hearts. And because we were tainted with original sin, no human being could resist the temptation to sin. We were covered with sin, permeated with sin, shot through and through with sin. The story continued:

God knows all about this, knows how sinful we are, but He loves us in spite of how bad we are. The first time the world got in this shape, God sent a flood; but he saved Noah and his family, along with two of all the animals. We are all descendants of Noah, but, even so, we are still all born in sin because of Adam and Eve.

And the world has now turned rotten again, and the time of judgment is at hand. Fortunately for us, God so loved us that almost two thousand years ago, he sent his only begotten son to die on the cross for our sins. We are born in sin, and we are all sinners, and we are all doomed to Hellfire and damnation.

Except.

Except that if we recognize Jesus as our personal savior, give our life to Jesus as He gave His life for us, He will intercede with God on our behalf and our sins will be washed away, we can lay down our burden, find the peace that passeth all understanding, lie in the bosom of Abraham, live in one of the many mansions of God's house, have life everlasting, become angels with golden wings, walk the golden streets, and shout hallelujah for all eternity.

And the marvelous thing about this is: all you have to do is walk down to the front of the tent, declare that you have accepted Jesus as your personal savior, get down on your knees and pray, and Jesus will save your evil soul from Hell.

On the other hand:

If you hang back, if you procrastinate, if you don't give your life to Jesus, if you leave the tent without making a decision for Christ —what if you have a wreck in your car tonight? What if a snake bites you as you walk across your yard tonight? What if a black widow spider bites you while you're sleeping tonight? What if you develop cancer or have a stroke or have a heart attack? If you haven't gotten right with God, you will be lost to Hellfire and damnation for all eternity!

"Now!" The Reverend Jesse Crumley pulled himself up to his full stature, braced his shoulders back, and pierced the congregation with a fiery stare. "Which one is it going to be?"

People streamed down to the front of the tent in droves, pushing and shoving each other until they could fall to their knees in front of the makeshift pulpit, screaming, waving their hands in the air, and giving themselves to Christ Jesus.

I did not go down to the front. I did not give myself to Christ Jesus. I wanted to run—not from any religious fervor, but from sheer revulsion.

I was appalled at what I saw: people shrieking and rolling in the sawdust, flailing their arms and pulling at their clothes and hair; the rest of the congregation droning "Just as I Am" over and over again; the grotesque oversimplification of the scriptural reconciliation of God's ways to man. The arrogance of the preacher, the slickness of the pitch, the forced decision, the bait and switch, the closing of the deal.

My girlfriend was enraptured. The next night I returned, this time not so much to be with the girl, but because of a kind of morbid fascination with what Crumley was doing to the audience. I eventually realized that there was a structure to the pitches, a distinct pattern to all that was being said:

Tell a few jokes and warm up the crowd. Get 'em on your side.

Tell the story of original sin.

Explain how we are all doomed to hellfire, both because of original sin and our inability not to sin.

Lace the story with scriptural references.

Scare the hell out of them: make them worry about what would happen if they died tonight.

When they've just about given up hope, tell them how Jesus Saves.

Give the invitation and bring them down to the front.

Years later, I attended a huge Crusade for Christ rally at the Atlanta Municipal auditorium. On the same stage where years before I had played bass drum for the West End Elementary Band, and where I had seen the Atlanta Symphony Orchestra play and José Greco and his Spanish dancers perform, now an internationally known evangelist stood behind a pulpit, thumped his Bible against the lectern, and shouted the same questions about thieves and liars I had heard from the Reverend Crumley. The rest of the evening followed a predictable pattern.

The thing that repelled me the most about all of this was that nowhere was there the gentle, loving concern that marked

Brother Glisson's way of being a Christian. And there seemed to be nothing of the gentle firmness with which Christ himself taught His lessons about God, man, and the world. Instead, there was a kind of brutish, surly, bullying undercurrent to the whole thing. It reeked of a hatred of enlightenment and of the arrogance of power.

Adam and Eve brought down the wrath of God for all time. It doesn't make any difference how good you try to be, you'll burn with all the rest unless you accept Jesus as your saviour.

Death will bring down the rich and the powerful, and it will throw them into Hell. Nobody with money will get into Heaven. Only the poor have a right to eternal life.

You don't have to know anything to get into heaven. Better that you stay ignorant. There are things we aren't meant to know. Knowledge confuses and takes you away from Christ.

All you need to know is this: accept Jesus. Take it or leave it, buddy, because time's a-wasting. Accept Jesus *now*, because if you don't, I'll see you burn in Hell.

I didn't go back. And I broke up with the girl, partly because of her enrapturement with the Reverend Crumley's world.

Except for occasional visits to Trinity Methodist with my parents, I avoided church like the plague. To me, the kind of Christianity that Crumley represented *was* a kind of plague.

Trinity, on the other hand, seemed just as bad in its own way: it had a new minister, the vapid opposite of the Reverend Crumley, and its services seemed little more than social gatherings where people had coffee, chatted about trivia, and showed off their clothes. Far from being obsessed with sin, neither the minister nor the congregation seemed to be obsessed with anything—especially with the problem of justifying God's ways to man.

Catholicism was not an available alternative in my neighborhood: "Catholic? You mean the Pope? All they're after is your money. Confess on Saturday, go to Mass on Sunday, and do anything you want to for the rest of the week. How can an Eye-talyun be descended from the Apostle Peter?"

Episcopalians: "Aren't they the snobbish ones who can't make up their minds whether they want to be Protestants or Catholics?"

Presbyterians: "They think it's all predestined, so they do whatever they want to and think they'll get into heaven just like the rest of us."

Lutherans: "They're Germans, aren't they? We were at war with the Germans! How could anything German be Christian?"

Judaism? "The Jews! They're the ones that killed Jesus!"

I came to be repelled by all of them, as they seemed to be repelled by each other. I hated the crudeness and brutality of the evangelists, and I was horrified by the stories of Torquemada and the Spanish Inquisition. I knew only one nominal Episcopalian, a Nova Scotian named Henschelwood, who had little time for a curious teenager. I knew only one Lutheran, an uncommunicative man who lived in the next block. My friends were either Methodists or Baptists. I had little use for either denomination. I admired Brother Glisson the man, but I had no interest in his church. When I wanted my imagination to soar, I didn't go to church, I read science fiction: Ray Bradbury, Arthur C. Clarke, Isaac Asimov, Robert Heinlein, and Frederik Pohl. In short, for all of my intellectual pretensions, I was much like most boys my age.

I finished high school in 1950 and started to work. Pickings were poor for an uneducated former country boy, and I wound up working as a warehouse tractor operator for the U.S. Government. By 1952, I had learned how to do data processing, and by 1955, I was the assistant head of the data processing department at the Trust Company of Georgia.

That really meant that I was a tabulating machine operator, responsible for the day-to-day data processing operations. It was a tiresome, detail-ridden job, in which I stood all day, every day, over a clanking tabulator, watching numbers spread across pages of paper at a steady, numbing rate of one line per second.

My science-fiction reading continued unabated—two or three books a week. However, it served only to underline how abysmally in need of education I was. I wanted to go to college, but I could not see my way clear financially to do so.

I had been giving a lot of thought to doing something different—anything—to escape from the basement of the bank and my supercilious boss. But I had no real career plans, and simply could not decide what I should do with my life. The absence of one eye and the presence of a heart murmur limited my job flexibility.

Except for a semester at the Atlanta Art Institute, I had no education past high school. I had always read voraciously, on a wide range of topics, and I knew from my reading that there was a vast, marvelous universe out there, and that there were people who devoted their lives to things other than numbers on printouts. But I also knew that I had no part of their universe. No member of my family had ever attended college.

I was at such loose ends, I actually began to attend church again. I shopped around from one church to another, looking for somebody who would talk to me about the religious topics I had recently become interested in. I wasn't the least bit enthusiastic in singing in the choir, taking part in the Wednesday night socials, or going to Sunday school. But I was intensely interested in talking to the minister about the nature of God, immortality, the creation of the universe, and all the other things with which I naively thought all ministers would, by definition, be equally fascinated.

Unfortunately, the ministers I talked to had no interest in these things at all. Most of them had done little reading in theology since their last set of exams in seminary. To the average pastor, these things that intrigued me the most were irrelevant subjects.

The ministers I met were immersed in the chores of their ministries: marriages, baptisms, funerals, communions, sermons, public prayers, counseling, visiting the sick, organizing Sunday-school lesson plans, working on church committees, keeping the doors open, keeping the mortgage paid. There was no time and little inclination for reflection on theological subjects.

I eventually realized that the topics I had become interested in were explored and discussed in theological seminaries. But one had to be "called to the ministry" and have a bachelor's degree. Somewhere, deep down in the recesses of my mind, I must have begun to formulate the proposition that if I wanted to learn about God, freedom, and immortality beyond the Sunday-school lesson plan, I would have to go to college and then to theology school to do it.

From the vantage point of 1985, the amusing and annoying thing to me is how naive I was about it all. I was interested in metaphysical questions, but I had neither the education nor the language to know it. I thought that since churches were "houses of God," they would (naturally) be places where one could go to learn about the nature of God, His relation to the world, and man's obligations to Him.

The truth was that the Southern Protestant churches with which I was familiar seemed to be places where sermons were orated, prayers were spoken, rules for conduct were prescribed, and advice was given. And the advice offered was simple and, to me, wholly unsatisfying: go to church, fear God, love Jesus, repent your sins, stay out of trouble. Be nice.

I was caught in an ironic situation: I was fascinated by religious questions and the existence of God was something that it had never occurred to me to doubt. On the other hand, I could not stand either version of the Church I had experienced, because the ministers seemed to have no interest in the very concepts that made religion so fascinating to me.

One set of ministers seemed interested only in preaching what I called "Hellfire and Damnation" sermons; the other set seemed interested only in maintaining the social structure of the Church community. I couldn't bring myself to make a commitment to a particular denomination; but I also couldn't shake the feeling that somehow the things that I was after were there in the church.

I hated my job, but I had few skills and no money other than what the job brought to me. I couldn't get the answers I was after from the churches I visited, but I continued to visit them. I knew I needed what college had to offer. I knew I needed an education, but I didn't have the nerve to seek a scholarship or state aid to get it.

Then, one day, as I walked up the steps to my apartment, I was literally stunned by the sudden emergence into my consciousness of a truth that my subconscious had probably known for some time: I had to resign my job at the bank, find money for tuition, go to college and prepare myself for theology school. But the realization did not present itself as a conclusion drawn from a string of propositions. Instead, it struck me as an imperative, something that I *had* to do.

I was suddenly weak in the knees, and had to sit down on the stairs to keep from falling. I immediately thought of St. Paul on the road to Damascus—and I immediately interpreted what had happened as a Call from God.

With all the confidence of the newly converted, the next morning, I resigned my job and visited the offices of the State Department of Vocational Rehabilitation. I remembered that I might be able to get a tuition grant if I could meet the aptitude requirements. I was given a battery of intellectual and psychological tests. In less than a week I had qualified for four years of college tuition and an allotment for books.

I next sought out Brother Glisson, who was by then the chaplain at Emory University Hospital. I felt that I had had a Call from God, but I didn't know how to respond to it. I knew I had to go to school, and I had successfully jumped through the qualification hoops for state tuition aid. I felt that I had to serve God in some way, but I did not know what to do or how to do it.

My old friend and counselor first advised me to study for the Methodist Lay Minister's License, the first step toward ordination in the Methodist Church. I read several prescribed books, including a biography of John Wesley, and pored over the *Methodist Discipline,* the nearest Methodist counterpart to the Anglican *Book of Common Prayer.* I took the required examinations, was interviewed by a committee on Lay Ministry, then by the district superintendent, and given my license.

I was also advised to spend a few quarters at a junior college before taking on a full load at Emory University in Atlanta. It was good advice: I had been out of high school a long time, and I had a lot of catching up to do. By March 15, 1955, I was enrolled in Young Harris College, a small Methodist school in North Georgia.

I preached my first sermon on Easter Sunday morning, 1955, in a little country church nestled in the mountains. We had "Chicken Dinner on the Ground," as church picnic lunches were called. I talked clumsily but earnestly about Jesus as a kind and loving man who was willing to die for those he loved.

Although the school in the mountains was an idyllic setting for my first quarter in college, by the fall of 1955, I had matriculated at Emory. It was time to get down to business.

Emory University's tree-lined, acorn-strewn campus was like the promised land. I had spent five years on meaningless jobs since graduating from high school, and I couldn't wait to learn all the things that were now open to me. I was starved for knowledge. When I walked up and down the corridors in the stacks of the Candler Library, I would become dizzy with anticipation of all the things I would soon have the opportunity to learn.

Although I was only a second-quarter freshman, and knew that I had four years of hard work ahead of me, my plans were already made to enter Emory's Candler Theological Seminary after I earned my Bachelor's degree. For all of my naive planning, however, I had no idea what courses I should take, much less how to construct a program that would give me the requirements I needed.

I learned during freshman orientation that all students who had not declared a major should meet with an assistant dean in order to plan a curriculum. Since I was not even sure what "declaring a major" meant, I walked over to the white-marble administration building and made my way to the undergraduate advising offices on the second floor.

There I met an assistant dean, and asked for help in planning my program for the fall. Fifteen short minutes later, I emerged with a schedule for my entire freshman year. Each term, I would take five quarter hours of biology, five hours of English, and five hours of Greek language. I was told by the assistant dean that all pre-theologs had to take Greek, and that I might as well get it over with.

This, of course, was simply not true. I could have earned any number of Ph.D. degrees at Emory without ever having to take Greek, and I certainly didn't have to have Greek to get into (or out of) seminary. Obviously, the assistant dean wanted to fill up the Greek classes, and he didn't mind bending the truth to do it. Having been out of high school so long, the last thing I needed was a course in Greek. I took it, nevertheless.

We translated bits and pieces of everything from lyric poetry to Xenophon's *Anabasis*, from Herodotus' *Persian Wars* to

Thucydides' *Peloponnesian War,* from Plato's *Republic* to Aristotle's *Nichomachean Ethics,* from the *Old* to the *New Testament.* When we began in the fall of 1955, there were thirty-six in the class. By the beginning of winter quarter, the number had dropped to sixteen. Six of us finished the three-quarter sequence.

I have never regretted the misinformation that the assistant dean gave me. That year of Greek did three things for me: it taught me how to discipline my study habits, it introduced me to the glories of ancient philosophy and literature, and it relieved me forever of the naive notion that the King James Bible (or any other version, for that matter) was the one true, unchanged, unadulterated, and literal word of God.

My tour of biology had similar effects. It was not so much that I was unfamiliar with anatomy and physiology; I had read enough medical literature to know what was going on inside our skins. What I had not considered were the larger issues: if we can explain what goes on in our bodies in terms of genetics, metabolism, and biophysics, where is there room for God in the biological equation?

The theory of evolution didn't bother me: I could see how evolution might simply be the method God used to bring us into existence. But I could not see why he also had predisposed us to malaria by making us a host for the Anopheles mosquito. And these issues seemed like pretty small potatoes compared to the more fundamental problem: how was I to deal with the fact that the introduction of religion into scientific discourse seemed totally irrelevant, either to understanding the physical universe or simply to curing a case of skin rash? And what, on the other hand, was I to make of the fact that the introduction of the scientific method into religious discourse seemed to reveal it as nothing more than myth?

Most of my friends at the time were students at Emory's medical school. I spent hours as an observer in surgery, watching everything from the reconstruction of a mangled hand to an aortic graft. I spent long hours in the pathology department, watching autopsies of patients who had died of everything from the loss of blood after simple tonsillectomies to complications following ectopic pregnancies. I was later to spend three years working in a local funeral home, piecing together people who had died in car wrecks, flaming buildings, and seedy nursing homes. At times, I seemed surrounded by the dead and the dying; nowhere did I see the hand of God. It was God's apparent *absence* that impressed me more.

Paradoxically enough, during this same period, I served as assistant chaplain at Emory University Hospital, working with my old friend Brother Glisson. I made rounds every week, and saw every patient in the hospital every Saturday. I was on call every night, and spent many a night counseling people who were about to go into surgery, or who were dying of incurable diseases, or who were perched on the fourth-floor window ledge trying to find a reason not to jump. During the summers, when the chaplain was on vacation, I ran the office by myself for two weeks.

Over the next four years, I watched hundreds of people die horrible deaths from a wide variety of causes. I prayed for them, each and every one. I tried to comfort them and their families. I prayed a great deal, both for those people and for my fading faith.

I lived three lives at once. I went to school full time, because the state tuition grant money was offered only for full-time students. I had no money and there was no money forthcoming from my parents, so I worked full time at night and served as assistant chaplain during the afternoons and on weekends.

I lied to the school about the number of hours I worked, otherwise they would not have allowed me to continue full time. I found difficulty seeing God's hand in all this. If this was one of His tests of my faith, I failed miserably. But like Boethius, I found consolation in philosophy.

My introduction to philosophy eventually led me to declare a major in philosophy, in a department in which almost all the light emanated from one person: Charles Hartshorne, the great Whiteheadian, philosopher of religion, and process theologian. Hartshorne was to become one of the two greatest influences in my intellectual life.

I had at last found the place and people I had been looking for. I loved my classes, my professors and my books. Each day was a new beginning, a *vita nuova* for me. I was enraptured, swept away by knowledge itself. Every evening, I sifted what I had known before through what I was learning now. The word "philosophy" (the Greek *philos* and *sophos*) means "the love of knowledge." I had become a philosopher in the truest sense.

Philosophy was heady stuff. Over the next four years, I took courses in logic, the history of philosophy, philosophical problems, metaphysics, ethics, aesthetics, political philosophy, epistemology, and the philosophy of religion. Most importantly, I learned how to think, and I learned how to string concepts together into beautiful intellectual constructs.

In the history of philosophy, I started with Thales and went all the way to Bertrand Russell. There were marvelous pitfalls at every step along the way. Socrates had died an intellectual hero, had died for Truth, with no assurance of a reward from God.

Honest thinkers had been persecuted and burned by the church. Time and time again, it seemed to be the Church that stood in the way of progress, stifled inquiry, and rewarded intellectual integrity with the stake or the rack.

When I encountered David Hume's *Dialogues Concerning Natural Religion* and *The Natural History of Religion*, my religious faith was devastated. I had always looked to the universe itself as the best proof for the existence of God. The very existence of the universe, the apparent evidence of design everywhere one looked, seemed to my untutored mind the most obvious proof of the existence of God.

This view, as I was just then beginning to learn, was a form of what is called "natural theology," that is, the position that there is evidence in the natural world for the existence of God. This evidence supposedly presents itself in the grand design of the world around us: observations of nature show that these patterns in the physical and biological world fit together into a vast, orderly, intricate, overarching natural system. Design implies a designer; and in the same way that human designs are a product of human thought and intelligence, the design of the universe itself implies the existence of thought and intelligence.

What intelligent agent would be capable of designing the vastness of the universe? Only God could do such a thing.

All well and good, but Hume showed that even if the design indicated the presence of a Deity, it might be only a lesser Deity, or several Deities, or maybe a Deity who made the universe and then abandoned it. In short, the presence of design in the universe may imply the work of an intelligence, but we don't know what kind or even if He is still around.

The point is: confining yourself to effects is a poor way of getting at the cause of things.

But it got worse: What we perceive as design may be only the random collecting together of particles. We may be in a process of development, and what we call "design" is simply what the universe happens to look like *right now*. Or maybe the world generates its own order, simply by developing or growing.

To compound the problem, Hume had already demonstrated, to the consternation of empiricists everywhere, that our knowledge of the natural world is not direct, but restricted to perceptions and ideas gained from sense impressions. What we perceive to be causal relations between objects or events may be only habits of the mind concerning the supposed relations between our perceptions. We can't demonstrate causal relations. We can only infer them. Indeed, what could the mind itself be but a "bundle of perceptions"?

Kant's *Critique of Pure Reason* left my faith equally chilled. If we can know only phenomena and God is not a phenomenon, how can we know God? It was not for nothing that Kant's *Critique* was called by some "The Doomsday Book" of western philosophy. No wonder also that Hume was known by many of his contemporaries as "The Great Infidel" for his critiques of religious knowledge.

It remained for Nietzsche to give me the news: "God is Dead . . . and we have killed him, you and I." Later elaborations of this theme by Professor Thomas J. J. Altizer seemed delicious in their daring, courageous in their devotion to the truth.

If natural theology was out, I was left with revealed theology: evidence of God's existence as revealed to us by God Himself in what are called "religious experiences." Here, I ran afoul of William James's *Varieties of Religious Experience,* in which the ineffability of the religious experience—the impossibility of demonstrating the validity of the experience to those who have not had it—left me out in the cold altogether.

I could not prove the existence of God through evidence in the universe. Neither could I prove His existence by the religious experiences of others. By this time, I had come to doubt that my "Call" on the apartment steps had really been a religious experience. So, never having had a religious experience, I could not honestly attest to their validity.

A reading of the transcript of Bertrand Russell's and Father Frederick Copleston's BBC debates showed me what seemed the only logical and ethical position to take: philosophical agnosticism.

I was certainly no atheist, for two reasons: first, as with Russell, it seemed to me that atheism was a contradictory position. To be an atheist is to say that God does not exist because his existence cannot be proved. But if you cannot prove God's existence, you must also admit that you cannot *disprove* God's existence. Ergo, you should make no statements about the existence of God at all.

Second, for all of my inability to *prove* the existence of God, to me His existence was still intuitively certain. I may not have had a mystical experience, but I simply had never doubted the existence of God. My problem now, however, was that my insights concerning the existence of God did not carry any convictions about what God wanted me to do—if, indeed, He wanted me to do anything.

I was lost. All of us were lost, it seemed: doomed to use our freedom to become whomever we would become. There was no essential human nature, only the existential becoming of who and what we are. And in this thing of being lost, there was a certain appeal, a certain romanticism, a certain *frisson*, a quickening of the blood. We were only reeds in the wind—but thinking reeds, nevertheless! We would all go down into death, but at least we could lead lives of intellectual honesty.

After Hume, Kant, Nietzsche, and Altizer came the great host of social scientists who, although notoriously inarticulate, nevertheless convinced me the God of the Christian Church was a God that man had invented. In the face of overwhelming evidence against God's continuing presence or concern, to persist in taking religion seriously seemed to me to be a symptom of intellectual cowardice.

While I believed in the existence of God, I could not believe that the God I believed in would have anything to do with Christianity. I did not think that any denomination of Christianity had a corner on God; nor did any other religion, for that matter. The Church's explanation of the universe seemed to me to typify the inability of religious thinkers to face the historical, psychological, biological, and philosophical realities. The history of philosophy and the triumph of the natural and social sciences, on the other hand, seemed to me to be man's great soaring flight toward the Truth.

The most important thing about this flight seemed to be that it was made largely without (indeed, in many instances, in spite of) the Church. In fact, of the many contributions of the ancient Greeks, the greatest appeared to be that they had been the first to develop ways of explaining the universe *without* having to resort to the gods as causes. It was a *virtue* not to have to haul God into the picture to explain what was going on.

Despite my double-full-time schedule, I took enough courses in sociology for it to constitute a minor. There were also courses in history, geology, mathematics, and every other subject I could cram into my program. I sought out the tough professors. I tried to broaden my horizons. A year of the Humanities Colloquium introduced me to readings and discussions of the great works of drama, philosophy, poetry, and literature: the plays of Aeschylus, Sophocles, and Euripides, Jonson, Shakespeare, Sheridan, Shaw, O'Neill, Anouilh; Augustine's *City of God,* More's *Utopia,* Huxley's *Brave New World, Aucassin and Nicolette, Tristan und Iseult, Romeo and Juliet, The Nibelungenlied, Beowulf, The Elder Eddas,* Nietzsche's *Twilight of the Idols,* Kafka's *Metamorphosis,* Sartre's *No Exit.*

I even took a year of astronomy at Agnes Scott College's Bradley Observatory with Dr. William Calder, a pioneer in brightness measurements of the moon's surface. My classmates asked me if I intended to become a philosophical astronomer. In my best Isaac Asimov persona, I informed them that I would become an astronomical philosopher!

I developed a whole new attitude toward human knowledge. The attitude had little to do with religion. It wasn't that I was anti-religion. I still worried over the same metaphysical questions that had brought me to college. But now I knew that they were, indeed, *metaphysical* questions, not questions that concerned the Church. I was not losing religion, but I was becoming totally indifferent to organized religion, to the Church. I adopted the attitudes I thought were appropriate responses to the "truths" demonstrated by the subjects I had studied. And in my simple-minded way of looking at what I was learning, these truths seemed to condense into a few propositions for each field:

The Physical and Biological Sciences

1. It's all either particles or waves.

2. The earth is a small planet, orbiting a middle-sized sun, way out at the edge of a galaxy that is only one of billions of galaxies.

3. *All* events can and should be explained in terms of *natural* causes.

4. If it can't be measured, it doesn't exist. At best, it has no meaning.

5. When you die, you die dead. There is no immortality.

6. The highest virtue is to explain the universe without resorting to a *deus ex machina*.

7. Causality is the basic principle of the macro-universe; indeterminacy is the basic principle of the micro-universe.

The Social Sciences

1. There is no soul, there are only mental processes, or:

2. There is no soul or mind, just behavior.

3. Human values are simply needs and desires. The fundamental axes on which the human race operates are money and power.

4. Religion is a projection of human needs, the opiate of the masses.

5. Morality is relative to the situation or the culture. There is no absolute right or wrong.

6. Religion belongs to humanity's childhood; the human race has grown up now, and no longer needs religion.

7. Free will is an illusion.

ART AND LITERATURE

1. The noblest sacrifice a man can make is to sacrifice himself for his art.

2. Beauty carries its own truth.

3. Religious art is not real art because it is morally didactic. Real art must be free of ideological constraints.

4. Biblical prose has a certain primitive beauty, but should be taken as mythology, not fact.

5. The organized church is the enemy: it always tries to censor the artist or writer.

6. There simply is no comparison between medieval art and literature and the glories of Greek art and literature.

7. The only true religion is Art.

At length, all organized religion seemed to me nothing more than myth: a primitive attempt to explain the universe in anthropomorphic terms. There seemed no virtue in bringing God into the picture every time we hit some new level of discovery. Science seemed to be doing quite well without the Deity. Scientific progress must be divorced from religious considerations and celebrated for its own sake.

I made rounds at the hospital, but I had little awareness of the depth of the ministry that was available to me. Eventually, the time came to choose between seminary and graduate school. I choose the latter, and drifted further away from a future in the Church.

The final incident, the final deciding factor, was an interview with the pastor of the campus church. I had been serving as assistant chaplain for four years. Now, for the first time, I was called in by the campus pastor for a conference about my ministry.

I was upbraided for not preaching more sermons and for not being active in the campus church. When I replied that I had worked full time at night on an off-campus job, had taken a full load in college, and had served as assistant chaplain at the hospital for four years, I was told that it was my lack of commitment to saving souls in the hospital that had precipitated the conference.

A nurse had complained that I had not tried to convert a Buddhist who had been in the hospital. I remembered the man well. He was devout, and we had spent many afternoons talking about Buddhism and Christianity. I was looking toward a future in philosophy; he was looking toward an early death.

We confessed our doubts to each other, but decided that we were on different paths up the same mountain. The man became my friend before he died, and I mourned his loss. I prayed for him, to Whoever might be listening.

Now I was told in no uncertain terms that because of my lack of commitment to my calling, the man was now condemned to Hell, and that it was all my fault. For me, this was the last straw.

As I sat there in front of the pastor's desk, everything seemed to be held in a balance. On the one side was the majestic sweep of Western civilization, with its art, literature, philosophy, science, history, and intellectual virtue. On the other side, in some ways personified by the preacher sitting before me, was a narrow, guilt-ridden meanness of spirit, a blind worship of ancient myths, a slavish adherence to a single version of religion, to God as Jailer, Judge, and Executioner.

On the one side, there was truth, beauty, and all that was admirable about the human spirit. On the other side, there seemed to be brutal ignorance, censorship, and the death of everything true and beautiful. I walked out of the pastor's office and out of my association with the Church.

I repeated my conversation with the campus minister to some of my pre-theolog classmates: people who only a week before had not had the wit to grasp the simplest of Hume's arguments, but who now readily agreed with the campus pastor's argument that perhaps I was not really cut out for the ministry.

I decided that they were right. Given what the Church had proved to be, and given my still-persistent belief in a God who would have nothing to do with the kind of meanness I saw in organized religion, I left the Church for what proved to be a quarter of a century.

My decision to leave hadn't come to me in a flash, the way that the "Call" had come. My leave-taking had been coming for a long time. It began the first day that I really took a good long look back down the corridor of human history. What I saw down that corridor was a gradual uphill fight on the part of philosophers, artists, and scientists against the forces of darkness and superstition—in other words, against the organized church, the Christian establishment.

But now I was free. Free to do anything I wanted to do, to think any thoughts I wanted to think. When I started graduate school in the fall of 1959, it was with the same sense of joy and wonder that I had started college as a freshman four years earlier. I embraced philosophy with the zeal of a starstruck lover. I was free to explore the whole universe. I embarked on a quest that was to last for twenty-five years.

The irony is that although I taught philosophy in five universities, published widely, and eventually became dean of arts and sciences in a Chicago university, the nagging feeling never left me that I would someday go back to pick up where I had left off. The feeling never left that God was somehow still with me; neither did the feeling leave that the life I was living had turned out the way it had for a purpose. But this feeling was buried beneath an intellectual hardness that precluded taking seriously any explanation of reality that was not the product either of science or philosophy.

At the time, I thought that my intellectual awakening was unique. It wasn't—which is why I'm telling you about it now. I want to let all the others who had similar experiences know that they were not alone. What I didn't know at that time was that my quest would eventually lead me back to the Church— but not back to the version of religion I had left.

I eventually finished graduate school and began my teaching career. My first full-time job was at Oglethorpe University, where I met the person who would have an even greater influence on my life than Hartshorne. I met Professor Harry Dobson, a music historian in his late sixties, who—how can I say it better—seemed to understand everything there was to know.

We all called him "Papa." He was an eccentric. He had been born to wealth, but his parents had died young. He studied at the University of London, the Sorbonne, and at Bayreuth, but he never entered a degree program. In his teens he traveled all over the U.S. in a private railway coach. He grew up in a suite of rooms in New York's Plaza Hotel. He bought his first Rolls Royce from Rachmaninoff. He saw Kirsten Flagstad's debut at the Met. He also had read every book that I had read in my eight years of university courses, but understood them all better than I did.

Papa was short (around five feet four), was portly, and looked like the wise owl he was. He was a bachelor. His one true love, a ballerina, had been killed years before. She had no family, and he had buried her, had played the love theme from Tchaikovsky's *Romeo and Juliet* and the "Liebestod" from Wagner's *Tristan und Isolde* at her funeral, and had never allowed himself to become serious about a woman again.

When his wealth was lost in the 1929 stock market crash, he held a party for his servants, gave them the little money he had in his pockets, and left the Plaza. He got a job playing string bass for Walter Damrosch and the New York City Symphony Orchestra, but had to quit when a taxicab accident injured his left hand and ended his ability to play the instrument. He dropped out of sight for nine years, then emerged at Florida State University, where he got a job teaching music history. After seven years, he moved on to Oglethorpe University in Atlanta.

Papa was a perfect product of late nineteenth-century romanticism. But his profound historical perspective made his intellectual life an ironic amalgam of romanticism and aestheticism on the one hand, balanced, on the other hand, by philosophical agnosticism and an acute critical and analytical ability. I doubt that anyone since Ernest Newman knew more about Wagner and his music dramas than Papa. He knew the physical and social sciences almost as well as he knew music and art. He respected the achievements of the physical sciences, but he had little use for the social sciences.

At his invitation, as a fellow faculty member, I sat in on a year of his music history courses. It was a year that opened my eyes to a dimension of human achievement and understanding which, for all of my courses at Emory, I never knew existed.

In our 1972 book, *The New Humanities*, I said that Papa clothed with flesh the bare bones of the knowledge I had gained at Emory. It was true. We would talk for hours on end. He became my mentor, my confessor, my All-father. No one has ever loved another human being more than I loved him.

One day, when he was in his seventies and only a few years from death, we met in a downtown Atlanta restaurant for some of our treasured conversation. He had with him a battered, dog-eared, leatherbound copy of the 1928 edition of the Anglican *Book of Common Prayer*. I didn't know what it was, and Papa explained to me that it was the codification of the Anglican worship services.

He turned to what I now know to be the post-communion prayer and read:

Almighty and everliving God, we most heartily thank thee, for that thou dost vouchsafe to feed us who have duly received these holy mysteries, with the spiritual food of the most precious Body and Blood of thy Son our Saviour Jesus Christ; and dost assure us thereby of thy favour and goodness towards us; and that we are very members incorporate in the mystical body of thy Son, who is the blessed company of all faithful people; and are also heirs through hope, of thy everlasting kingdom, by the merits of his most precious death and passion. And we humbly beseech thee, O heavenly Father, so to assist us with thy grace, that we may continue in the holy fellowship, and do all such good works as thou has prepared for us to walk in; through Jesus Christ our Lord, to whom, with thee and the Holy Ghost, be all honor and glory, world without end. *Amen.*

When he finished, he looked up at me, his eyes brimming with tears, and said, "God, isn't that beautiful? It's so beautiful. How I wish I could believe that. Oh! I would love to be able to believe in that."

Then he put the book in his coat pocket and we spoke of other things.

Papa was a magical person, a man clothed in mystery, as

anyone who knew him in those days will tell you. I tell you about Papa for two reasons. So that you may know him, too, and also that you may know of the miracle we shared with Papa—the miracle that started both Valerie and me on the path that eventually led us to back to the Church.

The miracle wasn't Papa's reading from the *Book of Common Prayer*. It was something else, something that Valerie and I have told only to a handful of people since it happened twelve years ago. But we tell it to all of you now, out of a sense of obligation to you as well as to Papa.

I am not embarrassed to tell about it, although a few of the people we have told were embarrassed for our sake when they heard it. Some people are prepared to believe in miracles, others are not. Once, years ago, sitting in Papa's crowded classroom, I was moved to tears at the death of Siegmund in *Die Walküre*. I later apologized to Papa for weeping in public. He put his arm around me and admonished me never to be ashamed of understanding.

And so, now, I tell you the story of Papa's miracle so that you may understand what he meant to us. Keep in mind that you, too, need not be ashamed of understanding.

Harry Dobson died in July 1973. He was seventy-seven years old. He had had two heart attacks, but he died suddenly one night, as two nurses were walking him to his hospital bed. One second he was with them, smiling and talking, and the next second he was gone.

We heard about his death through my secretary who, coincidentally, had a friend who was taking a course with him in Atlanta (we were living in Chicago). The funeral was over by the time we heard. My secretary gave me a copy of the letter the friend had written to her:

. . . I'm sure Dean Carnes will want to know that "Papa" died Saturday. His service—a most unimpressive one—was held today, and he will be flown to Florida tomorrow in order to be buried in a plot with his parents. I didn't cry at all until this afternoon, when I peered into his classroom. I think I semi-collapsed against the door at that point.

It was only two weeks ago, if not less, that Papa was again speaking lovingly of Dean Carnes and his wife. He obviously thought the world of them both—which is no small tribute.

He died quickly, and in good spirits, I understand.

We went to Atlanta in November of that year, to visit my parents. On November 19, Valerie's birthday, we drove out to Oglethorpe and talked to some of the people who had seen Papa during the last days. We drove by his little faculty cottage, got out, and gathered up a few pine cones to take back home with us.

That evening, we had a quiet dinner and then drove around Atlanta. Papa was on both our minds, and eventually we realized with a start that we were driving down the street on which he had lived. We pulled up in the driveway and parked around back, where we used to wait for Papa when we came to visit. The yard was grown up with weeds and grass, and the house had been padlocked since the week he had died four months earlier.

We sat there in the darkness until almost midnight, talking about Papa and all that he meant to us and to the others who knew him. We missed him so much, we could almost feel his presence. I remembered his longing to believe in the prayer of thanksgiving in the *Book of Common Prayer*. I also remembered the soaring leitmotif of Redemption Through Love at the end of Wagner's *Götterdämmerung*.

Distraught, I called out to him in the darkness: "Papa, I love you, I really do."

I turned to Valerie and she was crying. I said, "Let's get out of here," and started the car. We backed up, turned, and pulled out of the driveway. It was midnight, and we both looked back one last time through the branches of the pine trees at the dark, empty, padlocked cottage.

We called softly, "Good-bye, Papa." And then, as if to answer us, *every light in the house went on!*

A completely unexpected feeling of warmth and love swept over us like a rolling wave. We could almost hear him laughing. We knew, with an ineffable conviction, that Papa was all right, that somehow, somewhere, he was alive, was well, was happy, was still busy learning all that there was to know.

We sat there for a few minutes, too stunned to move. Then we called out again, this time to thank Papa, and to thank God for giving us this assurance that Papa was not gone after all. As we drove slowly away, the lights went out as suddenly as they had come on.

We went over to the campus and walked around until early morning under the trees outside the building that held his classroom. The feeling of warmth and love never left us. We still feel it, even to this day.

> . . . *We pray for all who have died,*
> *that they may have a place in your eternal*
> *kingdom.*

> . . . *Give to the departed eternal rest, O Lord;*
> *Let light perpetual shine upon them.*

> . . . *May the souls of the faithful departed*
> *through the mercy of God rest in peace.*

I know now what I did not know then: if he really had not believed that passage he read from the *Book of Common Prayer*, he would never have read it to me, would never have told me how much he wanted to believe it—believe *in* it—would never have cried as we sat there in a small restaurant drinking Cointreau on a summer afternoon.

Had the lights not come on that night as we sat in the car in front of Papa's cottage, we would not have felt compelled to go back over the religious territory we had long since left behind us. And I think we would not eventually have found our way to the Church of the Ascension on Easter morning in 1983.

Valerie and I left the academic world in 1977, to help develop a humanistically oriented training program for a nationwide Health Maintenance Organization whose headquarters were to be located in Houston. The HMO chain was to be fully computerized, and management was concerned that the patients might get lost in the machine. The head of the corporation's computer department was a former student of mine, who had done his M.A. degree under me. I took the job with the firm resolve to stay on it three years, then resign and devote my time to research and writing.

At first, it seemed like a dream come true. My job expanded, Valerie took over the task of writing the curriculum, and I was made vice president and CEO of the development arm of the company. My immediate assignment was to hire the architects and get the building designed. I hired one of the top architects and troubleshooters from Harrison and Abramowitz Architects in New York. Every day brought a new challenge, and every day I was refreshed by the prospect of working at my full creative capacity.

What I did not know at the time (and neither did anyone else) was the extent to which all of our efforts to create a quality-care facility were anathema to the president of the company. Although our assignment was to develop a top-flight system that would deliver health care to the maximum number of people for the minimum cost, the actual plans behind the company were to deliver whatever the federal, state, and local regulatory agencies forced the company to deliver, at the greatest realizable profit, and the patients be damned.

The problem was simple: the president and chairman of the board was the most consummately evil man I have ever known. I don't say this lightly, simply because I didn't agree with his policies. He was evil not in a trivial sense, but in a fundamental way. He was a source of toxicity: he poisoned every environment in which he moved.

He was also a Harvard graduate, a former Naval officer, and a financial genius. He operated smoothly, suavely, and without fear. He was lean, handsome, poised, born to money, and he dressed like an ad for *Gentleman's Quarterly*. He was also as deadly as a viper.

His plan was to open 110 HMOs across the country, and to rake in the money that was presently being spent on hospitalization policies. The humanistically based training program that Valerie and I developed was nothing more than window-dressing, a ruse to convince the Securities and Exchange Commission that his private investment offerings were for serious research and development.

We left the company for good on a sultry spring day. The feasibility study was finished, and it looked as if the president would not be able to clear the million-plus per year from each HMO if projected standards of patient care were maintained. His reaction? "Well, I guess more people will just have to die. I *will* make that margin."

It gave us little satisfaction that both the SEC and the IRS eventually nailed him, that the company was dismantled, that he had to leave the country to avoid prosecution. Our lives had become brutalized, and every day was simply another scramble for food. At the end of summer, we wound up at the Houston flea market, selling the art objects we had collected over the years in order to get money to buy groceries. We sold our Mercedes and bought a Ford truck.

It was as if we had become hunters and gatherers. Each day, we got up, got into our truck, and drove down through the sweltering humidity to make another raid on Houston. We bought a typewriter on the installment plan and started a writing company. During the next few months, we did writing for a real-estate company, a modeling agency, and a jewelry store. Our literary agent sold a book to Simon and Schuster, and we lived on the small advance.

The real-estate company welched on payment and we had to take them to court. The modeling agency owners got in trouble with their investors and their creditors and defaulted on their account. The friend who had gotten the jewelry store job for us cheated us on our percentage. The book was published, immediately became a best-seller, then was pushed aside to make way for a celebrity book on the same subject. We felt surrounded by evil presences. Every day, some fresh disaster came in the morning mail.

In desperation for cash, we sold our home and moved into a townhouse. We lived upstairs and ran the business out of the ground floor. One day, while we were seeing a client, someone backed a van up to our townhouse and cleaned us out. The only things left were a few clothes, a typewriter they'd overlooked, several pieces of furniture, and our books. They even stole my seventeen-year-old Gibson classical guitar I had once played for Papa. We resolved to move back to Chicago.

We rented a Ryder truck, hitched our truck to the back, and loaded what was left of our possessions. One hundred miles from Houston, we discovered that the compression springs on the truck hitch were broken. We had to get out every fifty miles and tighten up the wingnuts with a sledgehammer. We ran into dense fog just east of Baton Rouge, and drove all the way to Jackson, Mississippi, with visibility under one hundred feet.

Two days later, when we arrived in Chicago, the people who were to unload the truck for us didn't show up. Also, the universal joint had fallen off my truck. This necessitated a cab ride to Warshawsky's auto parts store to buy a new one. I ended the day lying in a puddle of freezing water, installing the new universal joint.

We leased loft space, and put the nest egg we had made on a Texas Instruments writing contract into building a darkroom and a sleeping loft. We bought thirty-five metal shelving units for our reference library, as well as a water heater, a stove, a refrigerator, and two sinks.

The furnace went out, and all the plants we had brought from Houston died. A water seepage problem overhead ruined most of our clothes and the furniture we had salvaged from the Houston burglary. And the day after we unpacked all the books and threw all the boxes away, the city inspectors condemned the building. The owners had not brought it up to code. We had ten days to get out. We had left only shelves, books, a few clothes, a dining table, a mattress, and our typewriters. Everything else was either lost, stolen, or ruined. We felt that we had been abandoned by whatever force was in charge of the universe, or by luck, or by whatever made things go right.

But one night, a few days before we moved out, I woke up suddenly and felt the same wave of warmth and love I had felt years before when the lights had gone on in Papa's house. I awakened Valerie. In the midst of the wreck that our lives had become, I was filled with inexplicable joy. I told Valerie not to worry about things anymore. Something had happened in the middle of the night. I didn't know what it was. But everything would be all right.

Something had happened during the night, something marvelous and ineffable, and despite our losses, the world suddenly looked bright and hopeful again.

I was right about the feeling I had. We weathered the storm, got our business off the ground, and wrote eight more books for ourselves and (to date) forty-two policy, procedures, sales, training, and computer manuals for our clients. We had lost almost everything in Houston. But by April 3, 1983, when we discovered the Church of the Ascension, we were doing very well.

We were members of the Independent Writers of Chicago, had a display ad in the Yellow Pages, had become minor celebrities with our four exercise books, and, more important, were developing a reputation for high-quality computer documentation. We had money in our pockets and we were almost completely out of debt. Things had never looked brighter.

It was under these circumstances that we delayed Sunday brunch and our usual perusal of *The New York Times* for a visit to the Church of the Ascension. I had never heard a sung Mass, and Valerie thought I would enjoy hearing one. It was just a lark, something different to do on Easter morning. It was just one of the multitude of pleasant surprises that Valerie is always giving me.

It was the first time I had been in a church in twenty-five years. The architecture was (is) beautiful, and the music, played by renowned organist David Schrader, was superb. I sat in the pew looking forward to the sung Mass. It was interesting to be in a church again. Especially to be in an Anglo-Catholic church, although at the time I didn't know that's what it was.

The altar at Ascension is made of white marble, and large alabaster angels stand at either side. Above the rood screen are figures of Christ, the Virgin and the Apostle John. The vaulted ceiling is dark, and the wood is figured in red and gold. Stained-glass windows line the two sides of the nave, and the choir loft and organ rise above the narthex.

As I sat there, waiting for the service to begin, I felt ill at ease, as if the church had been there waiting for me for a long time, as if the wheel of my personal history was once again about to turn. The organ prelude began, and was followed by the entrance of the priests and acolytes. The greeting, the Collect, and the scripture lessons followed. By the time the rector, Father Edwin Norris, crossed the sanctuary to give the sermon, I had become drawn into the ceremony.

Suddenly, strangely, I felt the warm love of Papa's presence there with us. I could not resist looking around: if he had been sitting in the next pew, I would not have been surprised at all. Father Norris stepped down to the bottom step of the chancel, smiled, and looked at Valerie and me. "Why are we here?" he said.

Why, indeed?

By the end of the sermon, I was in tears and I didn't know why. I didn't believe in Christianity, but I felt Christ's Presence right there on the chancel steps with Father Norris. I knew all the philosophical arguments against the story I was hearing; and I knew all the psychological explanations for what I was feeling. But none of them carried any weight in the light of the Presence that I felt.

A question called out in my mind, so clearly I had to look around to see if anyone else heard it. Like a tiny light, the question seemed to grow and grow until it illuminated everything around me, a question whose answer I knew but which I did not want to face. I would fight the answer daily for the next two years. I would pray about it. I would talk to Valerie about it. I would weep about it. But I would eventually come to grips with it and seek Father Norris's counsel about it. It would eventually lead me to seminary, to my present journey toward the priesthood.

For at the end of the sermon, when I felt the Presence of Christ so close I could almost touch Him, the question that I heard in my mind was, "Why are you out there? Why are you not here, with Me, doing the work that I have given you to do?"

And what of Hume, and the arguments that were so convincing so long ago? All of the carefully couched arguments seemed to dissipate in a mist. I had known for two decades

the problems inherent in empiricism; it ultimately led to sub-
jectivity, to solipcism. There were no iron-clad arguments
against the existence of God, nor were there any compelling
arguments *for* His existence. I couldn't find God in the same
sense that I found the front door in the morning (that is,
empirically: through the senses), but now, sitting in the third
pew at the Church of the Ascension, I had found God in the
form of a Presence so overwhelming that I could not deny
His existence.

I remembered ruefully how I had laughed at theologians
over the years, especially those who said that you have
to *experience* God in order to understand His reality. And
that once you *do* experience God, you can never deny Him
again.

But it was not that I had not believed in God before. I had
never doubted the existence of God. Instead, I had not believed
in the Church. And now I, the arch-empiricist, the logic professor, the village skeptic, had experienced God in a church!
The revelation was not lost on me this time. I realized with
compelling force that I was no longer trapped by arguments.
I was free to know God. I realized for the first time in my life
that the freedom I thought I had found when I left the Church
was illusory. The *only* freedom that is real is the freedom found
in the Church, in the Body of Christ.

Hume? Kant? Russell? My task now was not to refute old
arguments, but to explain the devastating experience I had had.
I spent the next two years rereading all of my philosophy
books in an attempt to do just that.

I didn't trust my motives. I was afraid that I had grown
muddy-minded in the years I had spent away from the academic world. I re-examined every argument I had once believed in, and found none of them as convincing as the experience that I had had on Easter Sunday 1983.

I shared my doubts and my newfound convictions with

Valerie. Together, we prayed for guidance and understanding. We felt like utter fools at first. (Me pray? Surely you jest!) But pray we did, for weeks, for months—as it turned out, for two years.

The problem was simple: I had had a call. I had heard God asking me why I was not with Him, doing the work that he had given me to do. But my reaction was not to answer the call, but to fight it, to fight it with every bit of philosophical sophistication I could muster.

I lost the fight. In due time, I was confirmed in the Episcopal Church. But I waited a year before going to Father Norris to ask advice about the call. We had a long conversation, in which he listened carefully to my story, then advised caution and diligent prayer. I took to heart the things he said. I gave myself another year before committing myself.

During that year, we made the trip out of which this book has grown. Although I had already heard the call, the trip, in a real sense, was my journey back to Jerusalem. As I talked to the people on the road, in city after city, church after church, my conviction grew. God had come into the lives of each one of these people. And he had done it in the same way that he had come into mine. We all shared that common element: we had all, in one way or another, heard that Voice calling to us. I was gratified to learn that most of the people who had heard that Voice were just as astonished to hear it as I had been.

We were caught unawares, day after day. We visited churches all over the country, and in most of them, we felt the Presence as soon as we walked through the doors. We felt that God was with us on the road, as a kind of quiet strength, guiding us, causing things to happen that we never expected. We were never alone.

We will never be alone again.

* * *

At the end of the journey, I am ashamed to say, I still wanted a sign, some assurance that I was on the right path toward finding the work that God has given me to do. Of the many ways in which one can serve God, ministering to the sick is one of the most difficult, but, to me, one of the most appealing.

I felt drawn to the hospital chaplaincy that I had left over two decades before. I wasn't sure that my vocation lay in that direction, but it seemed to me the logical choice. But I wondered if, after all those years, I would still be able to help the sick, to reach out and touch their minds and spirits.

I received my assurance in an unexpected way that I cannot begin to talk about without feeling the tears welling up in my eyes. I have shared it with only a handful of people since it happened, but I feel that if I am to be honest about my own spiritual journey I must share it.

My mother was a victim of Alzheimer's disease. She died on December 4, 1985, after years of suffering. Valerie and I visited my mother and my beloved stepfather, Robert, at their home in Atlanta. When I entered her room, she did not recognize me, did not even look up. She simply stared at the wall and mumbled gibberish. I learned that she had not uttered a sentence in six months. She could speak only nonsense words, strings of sounds with no meaning. Her eyes were glazed and unfocused.

Valerie and Robert stood by as I leaned down over her and kissed her on the top of the head. She did not respond. I put my arms around her and placed my cheek next to hers. I did not speak, but instead thought as hard as I could, "Mama, I really do love you."

Suddenly, she turned her head and looked me straight in the eye. She smiled and said softly: "I know that."

She smiled for a moment longer, then turned and lapsed back into a silence from which she never returned. The three of us stood over her, weeping at the miracle we had just witnessed. We thanked God for the gift He had given us.

And through my tears, I thanked God for giving me the work that He has given me to do.

IV · The Good Shepherds

Clergy From Many Denominations Tell Stories of Their Churches and Congregations

You must picture me alone in that room in Magdalen, night after night, feeling, whenever my mind lifted even for a second from my work, the steady unrelenting approach of Him whom I so earnestly desired not to meet. That which I greatly feared had at last come upon me. In the Trinity Term of 1929 I gave in, and admitted that God was God, and knelt and prayed: perhaps that night, the most dejected and reluctant convert in all England. I did not then see what is now the most shining and obvious thing: the Divine humility which will accept a convert even on such terms. The Prodigal Son at least walked home on his own feet. But who can duly adore that Love which will open the high gates to a prodigal who is brought in kicking, struggling, resentful and darting his eyes in every direction for a chance of escape? The words *compelle intrare*, compel them to come in, have been so abused by wicked men that we shudder at them; but properly understood, they plumb the depth of the Divine mercy. The hardness of God is kinder than the softness of men, and His compulsion is our liberation.

—C. S. Lewis, *Surprised by Joy*

JIM

This story was told us by an Episcopal canon at a large neighbor-hood church in a small midwestern city. An energetic, athletic man in his early sixties who had just come in from his early-morning jog, he has been at the same church for over thirty years. Jim's son graduated from Seabury-Western Theological Seminary in June 1985.

Well, if you want to talk about renewal in the Church, you came to the right place. We're on fire here.

It's thrilling, just thrilling. I've been very fortunate and blessed here. We came out here thirty-three years ago, my wife and I, and I've been here ever since. We started with about forty people, about six families, and we mushroomed in the fifties with the baby boom and the war veterans. And we leveled off in the Sixties. And we just hung on, because the kids who were bucking the Vietnam war were going to Canada in protest of the war, hanging college presidents in effigy—you know the story.

We had one boy who just disappeared. Tom went to Canada and his parents died in terrible pain because they never knew what happened to him, whether he was murdered or what. And we started picking up again in the middle Seventies. Many of these young people who rebelled went to Canada. We didn't have actual conscientious objectors here, but many who had rejected the Church or didn't believe in families, or getting married, or even if they did get married, in having children—have now come back and see the value of this institution.

I was thinking of this as I was jogging this morning. I was trying to think through some of these things. I was in the Navy during the war. I wasn't a pilot but I was on carriers; basically, I was in the Marines. But the Church represents to me, in a sense, an aircraft carrier. The pilots are symbolic to me: they would go out on strikes, they did the bombing, they did the strafing, but they had to have a base from which to operate. But they would protect that carrier with aircraft guns and destroyers against submarine attacks.

Anyway, the big thing to me now is the return and the number of young children. I experienced this, my wife and I. I went to seminary right after the war as a naval officer from the Pacific. I had two years in the FBI before I went into the Navy. So I got in at the tail end of that time. And then I came home and got married and went to seminary in the early Fifties. We had a baby boom. We had three children, other people had five or six, a lot of children. Then we had a void period, at least a slack, and now another boom. And it's thrilling to me. You know, people say to me, When are you going to retire? I say, I'll retire when the Lord says, You're too old to work and you're no longer effective. (And we do have to retire at seventy-two.)

I went over some names of people for you. Joe and Margie. They are in their mid to late fifties. They both work and Joe is suffering from a heart condition. She was an Aussie, and he met her, brought her back to the U.S. They have two sons who live out here in our area, about two miles south. He was a Methodist from southern Iowa and she was a dedicated, church-oriented person.

Their boys were baptized here. I counseled their oldest boy. He got into a lot of problems with the police. Joe at one time was a city manager. Bobby, their boy, has been divorced a couple of times, he was living with people, had babies, that sort of thing; just embarrassed them to pieces. And their other son Bill, who was their pride and joy, was a good athlete, is divorced. Now, I tried not to neglect Joe and Margie, maybe I did and it was my fault, I have to live with that. The mistakes I make I say, Lord, you'll have to forgive me, and He does. So I live in the freedom of forgiveness.

But anyway, my analysis is: they left the church over being disillusioned at their boy. "How could God do this to me?" they wondered.

You've read the rabbi's book *When Bad Things Happen to Good People*? I don't buy him all the way, but there's a lot of good in the book and it appeals to a lot of people. So many people ask this question, Job and all. His conclusion, of course, as I read it, is that either God is all-loving or all-powerful, but He can't be both, because if He were all-loving and all-powerful, He would not permit this to happen. So he says God is not all-powerful.

Now in orthodox Christian teaching, we say He *is* all-powerful. He is all-loving, but we just can't understand. Ultimately we can't understand. *I* can't understand why I am sitting here talking to you. I saw men killed around me all during the war. I had a terrible illness and I came through it. I came through and these other fellows didn't and they were better than I, much more perceptive than I. So I don't understand it. I can't explain it.

Getting back to Joe and Margie again: they were disillusioned, I think, over the child, that's the basic thing, and just the disappointment of life. He had had some knocks being city manager. In that position, you're not the most popular man on the block. If the garbage isn't picked up and the street lights go off and dogs are running loose, and all that sort of thing, it's your fault. I continued my calling on them and this sort of thing, but they were cool to me. And they wouldn't come to church. But I continued with their son. And I kept praying for them all.

And then all of a sudden, they came back about three or four years ago. She was in the Altar Guild and everything. And now they're there every Sunday at eight o'clock.

And this is the lovely, the thrilling, thing about being in a place for thirty-three years: you see the whole cycle. I am baptizing children whose parents I baptized and I am marrying some children whose parents I married. And I love it! It's a good ego trip for me, I see it and I feel it's worthwhile, and I have rapport with these people.

Now here is a case that is very interesting. A big factor in these cases is children. Here's a girl who was on drugs and her mother and father were active. She grew up here. She's small in stature, just a beautiful little thing, but she was on hard drugs and had an illegitimate baby and they sent her down to relatives in New Mexico so most people didn't know it. I talked to her during this time and she was "in love with" a "bad character" here in town who was peddling drugs, this sort of thing. She was married here and the boy to whom she was married did not have a church background and they were divorced, and now she has two children.

She has been very active with youth work, she taught in Sunday school. At one time she aspired to the priesthood and I really felt that would have been a difficult thing with two small children. So that didn't pan out, but she is here, recently remarried. She has come back. Now to me that's a life that's been saved. When I see where she was and where she is now. . . .

Here's another case. We have a lot of split marriages here where maybe the man was a Methodist or Presbyterian and she was a Roman Catholic: ours is a "bridge" church. We allow and advocate family planning. And this is a big thing with the Romans. Eighty percent are practicing birth control but they feel guilty and that sort of thing. The remarriage issue is also important.

Here's another couple. He was a teacher in the schools for quite a few years, he had two of our boys. And he had been married twice. One was a very young marriage and he had a very crazy fundamentalist background as far as the Bible was concerned. He was educated in college and got his Master's degree and so he dumped his religion, he dumped the Church. He's a very thoughtful, loving person. And his wife was from a very strict Roman Catholic family in Cartertown.

Cartertown is about 90 percent Roman Catholic. A "mixed marriage" in Cartertown is not a marriage between say, a Baptist and Roman Catholic, or RC and Episcopalian, or Baptist and Methodist. A mixed marriage there is a marriage between Roman Catholics in which one is from the German Church and the other is from the Irish Church. That's how strong the Roman community is there. So Krissy was born there in this strict tradition, and she is a very supportive and lovely person. She's a teacher, she's younger than he by ten or twelve years. And they were married and they came to this church because I had known Don through our boys and she had an aunt who had violated the Roman Church's rules on remarriage. It's really a poignant story.

I could almost write a book on *that*. They came here, they were married here, they have two small children. One is about four and one is two and they are very active and she is head of the Women's Guild and a choir directress, and he is junior warden—well, they were married here about seven years ago. This is such a common story line.

We have many young people like this, coming back to church. Take the case of Tim and Marie. She was received in the Roman Catholic Church and he was confirmed here in 1979 and they were married a couple of years ago, and have two sons. They have come, I think for her need *and* his need to come back to God and have a rooted relationship rather than just looking at stars. They also want the best for their children. Many of our young people are that way.

Once they get married, I could almost predict a pattern. Say a couple gets married here. They disappear for a while. Then they reappear when the baby's born. Or better yet, they go through high school here and they drop out during college, and come to please Mom and Dad, at Christmas and Easter and during the summertime. And then they disappear. Then one day I get a phone call from her, saying, "Father, I'd like to have a conference." Which I interpret as her saying, "I'm going to get married." And then after the wedding is over they disappear.

Then there's a baby born and they want the baby baptized. They don't come around for maybe a year, but when it's time to get the baby going, they're back and we try and integrate them. We've got lots of other people like them, and they take their turn in the nursery, and it's wonderful. They're young, they've got vitality. They don't have any money and they're head over heels in debt, but we've got, thank the Lord, some older people here who were like this back thirty years ago. They were tithers and they'll pick up the tab and we can keep the ship—keep that aircraft carrier—afloat. Everybody's necessary.

Let's see; another family would be Lem and Tina. Lem is probably thirty-eight and Tina is thirty-six. He was married before. He had a Congregational background, in southern Indiana. He brushed with the Episcopal Church at the state university but it ended when he was there so he was not confirmed. Tina was a die-hard Roman Catholic. Her mother teaches in a parochial school in a nearby city. They have two children. Lem Jr. must be about nine and the little girl is about four. They dropped in one Sunday, because they live in the area, and we seemed to hit it off. I'm a jogger, very interested in athletics, and a Braves fan. And Lem is a Braves fan and Lem is a jogger and on the vestry now. They are so concerned about their children, they are responsible people. Lem was confirmed and he asked me, "Should I force Tina—should I insist that Tina be confirmed?"

Tina has had guilt about this as far as her mother is concerned and so I said, "By all means, Lem, do *not* put pressure on her. When she's ready, she'll come." And so he did not, and she has thanked me several times for this. She's very active, in church every Sunday, and feels at home here, and they're really a part of a team. They're one of the younger, thirty-year-old couples.

I served for a year in an interesting program. We had a clergy exchange in 1965–68 and three of us were chosen out of three hundred applicants. I got it because our bishop was on the national council at that time and he kept pushing my name. I think he took my name and put it on top of the file every time! We lived in Lincoln, England, 120 miles north of London, for a year. And we lived in the shadow of the cathedral there. We had a parish of ten thousand very, very poor people. Old people, retired people, and steel factory workers just a few miles from the cathedral. That was an experience—we're a middle-class, typical WASP parish here—for us to work with really poor people.

It was a good experience for our children. We tried to live the way our parish did. We lived on our income. Because the boys in the parish would have one pair of shoes, our boys had one pair of shoes. And when they needed to be repaired you went down and sat and waited for them to be repaired. And the same way with food. We thought, we cannot live with these people if we supplement our income with American money. We can't identify with them unless we live on an income equal to theirs. It's like trying to identify with the poor or the blacks and not living in their section: they say, *you're not one of us.* And they're right.

You see, we are a family. Or we should be. But some people don't want a family. They want a country club, with the rector as their private chaplain. They want to own him, body and soul. And that can't be. They're really saying to all the outsiders, *We don't want to grow, we don't want to meet new people, we don't want these strangers coming in.*

These same people will not tithe, they will not give, even in proportion to what they have received from God themselves. However, if you have a special drive for a new building or a new organ or something, they will—some of them will—come up with a large amount. But they have to *see* it, get their names in print. But if you're going to send it to Sister Teresa in India, you couldn't get a penny for that.

I read in an article in the paper this morning, just before I came here, that a couple of women in this town were raped. And they had nightmares and trauma. Well, the two of them got together and formed an association of support, the same as we have in this church for alcoholics, and divorced people, this sort of thing. They're helping each other. And *you* can help others, too, others who have fallen away from the church. This book gives them support for coming back and knowing it's okay to come back.

It's an exciting time to be in the Church, an exciting place to be. I can't imagine having lived my life another way.

EMMETT

This interview took place with a young rector of a small church in a distant suburb of Indianapolis. We were referred to the young priest by his bishop, who designated him as someone who had been active in the evangelism and renewal movements in the area. It was a humid, foggy morning in late August and Father Emmett arrived at his interview in his clerical collar, highly polished lizard cowboy boots, and neatly pressed designer jeans. We came to stay a half hour and ended up spending three hours in conversation on renewal in the Church. We wished that we could have stayed longer. You'll see why when you've read his story.

Well, if this is the third from your last stop before you head back to Chicago, you must be all "churched out" by now.

Well, to get down to business: I am chairman of the Evange-lism Commission in this diocese. A couple of things have been happening. I don't know whether or not you have run across the Alban Institute thing in Washington—it's Gribbon who did a book on people in their thirties who are coming back to church. And then they also did a study funded partly by St. Paul's Church, here in the city, on what kinds of corporate experiences people do have when they decide to darken the door of a church, and why they choose to stay or not to stay.

Our evangelism commission has been involved in a project. I guess it is technically called the Springfield Model, named after the diocese in Springfield. But we're calling it the Parish Evangelism Project. The basic premise is that in the Episcopal Church, at least, the parish is the evangelistic unit and not the individual. For example, in the Church of the Nazarene there's a lot of emphasis on making a quick and penetrating evangelis-tic encounter. And on leading a person directly to faith.

But our experience is that, at least with the kinds of people who tend to come to the Episcopal Church and the people who come out to welcome them, something less direct and less threatening is best. People enter the institution *before* they come to a faith. And all that is something we use in our teach-ing. This is a little diagram we use in our teaching, this would be called the acceptance line and this the faith line. And this is the world. Well over half the population is functionally here —about 70 percent of the population claims a church affilia-tion, but well over half the population is functionally outside the Church and is not living with a faith and a transcendent God. Everyone has a God, but maybe it's a job, an employer, or a family.

That's Scott Peck's point, you know—that we all worship something but it's not always what we *should* worship. [*Draws a diagram on a piece of paper, starting with a circle.*] This would be the position of faith. And what the Nazarenes try to do is to isolate the person who is in a period of transition, a person who is open to the evangelistic encounter, and take him directly to a position of faith. In the Episcopal Church—and I think most churches tend to work this way—the person comes out of the world, into the church, and then at some point crosses over the faith line into an active, converted faith: a phase. It is possible—and I think our church's history has shown us—that many people will spend their lifetimes very happily in the church without coming to a personal faith. You've probably talked to them: the ones who have come back and are happy, very busy, and active and involved. But they haven't crossed over that line and perhaps never will.

You see, that's what our Evangelism Commission is concerned with, this particular transaction. Is the barrier here an obstacle? Is it open? How do people come from the world into the church? And then the renewal, there's concern about that: cursillo, Faith Alive, movements like that. Now the diocese used to call our commission the Commission on Evangelism and Renewal, which meant that we were trying to focus on both things at the same time. But that wasn't working, and the reason it wasn't working was that we would go to a parish and do a presentation and say to them, "These are your opportunities and this is what the Lord wants of you, and people will not linger at a dry well."—you know, the great line—and no matter what we *said*, what they *heard* was: *You're not okay!* Your parish has got to change and be different from what it is in order to bring people into it. And who in the world wants to receive a message that says you're not okay?

So we have separated the two tasks, and there's a whole new group worrying about renewal, and we're focusing on evangelism. Now we go to parishes and say, You're fine. And in the process of becoming different: you are okay and you *can* evangelize, you *can* draw people. That's been the focus of our mission.

We are training parish evangelism teams to take an honest

look at their physical parish facilities, the hidden entrances the churches seem to have, how do you find the johns, how do you find Sunday school? Is it possible to walk into the church and walk back out again without ever crossing anyone's path? All those physical things. And then there is the personal. You walk through the door of the church. What hits you? When you walk through the door of a department store, a very carefully constructed display. But in a church? People running helter-skelter!

You come out of the world looking for peace. You walk into a frenetic environment. And that isn't what the church should be.

Another thing to notice: Do people speak to you? One thing we find is that during the first six months of a newcomer's journey into a parish, he or she doesn't hear a word that the rector says. They don't listen to sermons. They don't listen to church music. Their experience is one of asking, "Am I welcome here?" And the signs, the signals they get come from the parishioners. Are they spoken to, are they made to feel welcome? Does anyone come up and ask them who they are? Do they say "Where are you from and how do you feel about not being there anymore?"

As for the evangelism teams: working at the parish level, we have four pilot parishes. Pastoral-sized parishes, the terminology of Arlin Rothange's book *Sizing Up Your Congregation*. It includes some definitions of how parishes respond to newcomers, a phenomenon that varies entirely by size. Has nothing to do with demographics, racial mixture, facilities, style of the liturgy. It has to do with *size*. That's his premise.

So the four pilot parishes each created a team, ranging in size from six to twelve parishioners, with a lay chairman and an outside lay consultant assigned to work with them. All four of their parishes and their clergy and their consultant were taken off for a weekend at our church camp and trained by a man from Cleveland who's our regional associate in evangelism.

That took place in March and those four parishes are now back to acting out their plans, each one of them quite differently, because the plan was tailor-made for the parish.

We're one of the four, so I can tell you what it was like for us here. We're now preparing for the second phase with six parishes, and I will be doing the training—same idea, create your team, do some self-study. You're asked to interview the last six families to join the parish and to ask them "Why did you stay? What did you find when you came here?"

Two reasons for the questions: one is that their information tends to be reasonably objective because it's still fresh, and also, it's good news if they *did* choose to stay. You can also go out and interview the people who chose *not* to stay and get the bad news, but . . .

And then there will be a third phase, starting, I hope, next year, trying to get some of our larger congregations to under-take this same sort of thing.

"Pastoral-size" means 50 to 150 on a Sunday. Family size is zero to fifty. The next size is program size, 150 to 350 on Sunday, and that's as large as we need for our purposes.

The training is done according to the trickle-down idea. I walked through the process with Ernie Durass [a popular workshop leader] and he told me at every step of the way what he was doing and why he was doing it. And now I am going in and training my successor and working along with him.

Although it's early in the study, we had already drawn con-clusions about the results at St. Martin's Church even before this project came along. We did a study of the families who had joined St. Martin's and we found that they didn't have a strong sense of my presence. In some ways, I was neutral. If anything, their perception was that I was okay and friendly. But almost to a person they could name the individual who greeted them at the coffee hour. And that became their significant reason for staying.

We doubled our facilities just two years ago and we deliberately incorporated evangelistic strategy into our design, so that, for example, you cannot walk into the nave without coming into the greeting area first. That was part of the design. And as far as we can tell from our answers, it seems to be working. They liked the fact that I called on them. It was unusual in their experience to have a priest call on them.

That surprises me. I thought it was standard. And in some cases, we have laity making calls. Under our new process, as a result of this training, all newcomers will have a lay call. Which builds on some research; I think it was Durass that did it. It's the *lay* call that makes the difference, not the clergy's.

Maybe that's not surprising, in view of the fact that the real renewal movement, the grass-roots movement as you call it, is a lay movement. In fact, I've experienced considerable resistance to my making calls. And I've learned that parishioners may need to come three or four Sundays before they talk to me. They need that kind of anonymity, without pressure to come back.

Another thing that we have learned: people are coming to church now into a very different environment than in the Fifties in a similar surge of churchgoing. I talked with a friend of mine who is a priest in Providence, Rhode Island, serving one of the big downtown parishes. He says in the Forties and Fifties the president of the company was in the pew and he looked around every Sunday to make sure that all his vice-presidents were in their pews. And they in turn looked around. So that the pews were full, but out of a sense of obligation. Kind of a business-world variant on the Roman idea of the Mass of obligation. That broke down in the Sixties, when the president stopped having kids in Sunday school. And he stopped coming himself and the VPs stopped coming and their families stopped coming.

And eventually only those came who wanted to be there,

and that number turned out to be small. What we're experiencing now is that people are coming here out of no sense of obligation. There is no cultural imperative in the Church, no social imperative, no family breathing down their necks to go to church. It is entirely their decision. And they are coming, *really*, to make a commitment. They may not know what that entails. But they are not coming just to hang out here, there being so many other things they can do to hang out.

What we've done is to pull a page from the Methodist Church. We've started new member orientation classes. It's very vague—"membership" is vague. At no point are you ever "enrolled" as a member. What we've done here is: five Sundays a year at the baptismal feasts we have a time when new people formally stand up before the congregation and say, I want to belong here. And we prepare for that with a series of classes that help them understand why they come to church, what change in their lives suddenly brought them to church? And the answers are astonishing. They're all different. For one person, it was not only the move to a new town, but she was in the aftermath of a divorce and looking for some sense of meaning. New town, no husband, no job. Another was a couple about to launch a marriage, and the only person who had made any human contact with them back where they had lived had been the chaplain at the university where they worked. Even though they were not churchgoers, the chaplain at the time had been kind to them, and had agreed to marry them. So when they came here they thought, Well, that means something, and so we'll have it be part of our marriage.

In another case, it was also a new marriage. They had just bought their first house. They were in their twenties, about to have a first child. The wife had had a strong church tradition in the Presbyterian Church, and they were looking for a church that they could share. He, I think, was Lutheran.

Another was a woman who had come here for a Senior

Citizens program that we had. She liked being here and wanted to continue her life with the church. Another was a woman whose husband had left her. In every new town they had moved to, she had tried a church. She was always trying a church. But this time, she stayed. When her husband had left her, she was in the final stages of a Ph.D. thesis. And to try to get some sense of stability, she came to church and deliberately sought out the pastoral kind of church where she would be known as a *person*. She did not want to go to a big church where she would be invisible.

None of these are adult baptisms. They all have had somewhere in their past an ostensible Christian experience, usually in their childhood. Only one of them was Episcopalian. One was a Roman who had married a non-Roman and they were looking for a common ground. And the others were all from other Protestant denominations.

It's hard to detect a single pattern. They're from mainline churchs. They're not from the fringe groups. We've had one person come here from the Assembly of God, but all of them come from other mainline Protestant denominations. We did have a Southern Baptist join us a while back. When they come, you get the impression they're not coming because we are a specific church. They're coming because when they walk through the doors of this building, they encounter a certain set of people and worship experiences that touch them.

What we're hearing is that among the special things that they liked was the emphasis on human contact, the participation, the Peace—the way we receive communion, all of us kneeling together at the rail rather than seated in pews. And we work hard here, at both the sermon and the announcement time, to build community. I preach informally from the crossing. And I use announcement time to share softball scores and marriage news and prayer requests. We have a ministry of healing here. Twice a month on a week night, plus a Sunday

morning, we offer, when the people come to receive communion, the opportunity to receive the laying on of hands for
healing, in a low-key way. And that seems to touch people, that
acceptance of woundedness and a desire to minister to the
human person.

Now this summer, another shift occurred, and I think this
is a kind of cutting edge. We have over the past few years
attracted more and more singles, which is surprising, because
Zionsville's community is very family-oriented in its other
services. This community revolves around its children. But
singles were coming here, and as we talked to them, we found
that they came here because it was *not* a singles ministry. It was
not the big melting pot of singles where people were kind of
eyeing each other. There was a nice mixture of civility and
vulnerability here. And they could be known for who they
were rather than that laundry-list of characteristics that some
singles seem to need as contact points.

This summer we offered a series of talks by a female priest.
I was on vacation and for five weeks she had a nine o'clock
discussion time on issues like "Forgiveness," "Guilt," "Addictive Relationships," "How to Deal with Anger."

She thought it would be a ministry to single women, to
professional women. But people are coming from all over the
metropolitan area. The first talk, she had ten, the last one she
had fifty-five. Fifty-five people in a church on Sunday to talk
about addictive relationships tells you where people are hurt-
ing.

I don't know if you have looked at any of the work on
church growth by Wynn Arendt of the Fuller Institute for
Church Growth, but his premise is that churches grow when
they are homogeneous. They don't grow when they are het-
erogeneous, which is a real challenge to the Episcopal Church
because we really value heterogeneity. But it also makes it hard
for us to grow. We have that situation right here. For the last

three weeks, we have been scrambling around, trying to get an outstanding Sunday school program going with 90 percent of the emphasis on the children. There are forty families that have children and there are forty families that don't have children.

Sunday is church time, that is one thing that is very clear. The image is this: people who are in church today have probably four or five major commitments in their lives, and each one has an assigned time value and an assigned time slot. And people are trying in good faith to honor all five commitments. A key part of their lives is keeping those things in balance.

We find a growing interest in networking among the women and men. Carrying it out is difficult, because women no longer have a consistent time when they are free.

The men probably are ready for a once-every-other-month commitment. At painting parties to paint the buildings and grounds, which is the way men functioned in the church twenty and thirty years ago, we get two men in attendance. People are hungry and they don't have time for things that don't touch them. They are *not* looking for additional work.

And they are willing to pay. This church has a paid secretary. We pay to have the grass mowed. And parishioners are content with that. They don't want to do these things.

The trick—and it's not so much a trick at St. Martin's because nearly everyone here is new—but some of the other congregations with older members are having a hard time receiving this new body of people, because their sense of churchmanship is so different. They come across as money-oriented, even though all they're saying is, "Let's pay for this thing so that we can have the things that really matter to us." The older church members who found fellowship in church projects don't understand that. There's a conflict.

As to the age of the people coming back: the community itself selects to a certain extent, because the houses, those houses across the street start at about $120,000 and go up to

$200,000. There are two other developments like that in town.
So the people living across the street are in their thirties, tend
to be middle management, reasonably transient. Where we're
drawing people, aside from that, are late twenties, city dwell-
ers, they don't live in the area. Or if they do, they're living in
apartments here.

They're just breaking into the housing market, they're just
getting their careers off the ground, often they're having their
first children. But they are *not* coming to find a Sunday school
for the child, which is the way it was in the Fifties. They are
coming for their own reasons. Some elderly, but not much.
The community does not have a large elderly population. But
I think if we did, they would be here. I know the church in
Florida is just going great guns—they can't find enough seats.
The elderly *want* to be in the church.

My luncheon appointment must be canceled . . . that person
never called back, which I must say is typical of the way it goes.
He is a well-intentioned man who is being interviewed for a
new job. And he really wants to talk with me, he really wants
to get counsel and get some suggestions for getting God's
guidance in making a responsible job decision. But he just
doesn't have the time. So it looks to the old-timers as if it's
noncommitment.

Someone asked me the other day, Why don't you get angry
at these people when they don't show up for meetings and
don't honor their commitments? And my answer was, Well,
I don't get angry because I understand it. I know that the guy
didn't do this deliberately. His life is a shambles, his marriage
is falling apart, he can't function. Priorities isn't the right word,
but he's pinching. And there may be some security in that,
knowing that I will understand. And that God will wait, God
will be there. And I don't see that as faithlessness. In a sense
there's a kind of *faith* being expressed in that.

We preached about returning to the church on Sunday. Two members of our parish evangelism commission shared the preaching with me and one talked about his own personal journey, why he came and why he stayed, and what it has meant to him.

I understand what you're doing: anyone can just gather statistics. But people and their stories, that's a different thing.

That's the success of Charles Kuralt's book, and Least Heat Moon's. The statistics don't matter; the *stories* do. Who was it that said, "Just tell stories?" That's the secret to this whole movement back to church: the people and their stories. And we're only seeing the beginning.

MARLOWE

This speaker is the Episcopal bishop of a large, rural, midwestern diocese. The diocesan offices, however, are quite modern, and are located in a large city in the heart of the nation's "breadbasket." The day we interviewed him, it was 105 degrees outside. Inside, the air conditioning was working only in his office. We started with the story of how we had come to make our journey, and related several anecdotes about conversations with people about religion. The bishop spoke with the easy assurance of a person who had been in charge for a long time.

Well, around here you're likely to find people who'll talk your arm off about religion. All you have to do is to mention the subject and they'll have at it.

We have an "institutional stance." As we talk among ourselves about our lack of evangelism and our real desire to be evangelistic, we are aware of the fact that our most fertile field for evangelism is among the *lapsed* rather than among the unexposed. So there's a great desire on the part of the Church to welcome people back and quite to the contrary, not to fuss at them for having gone away but to say "Welcome," to be very receptive.

We have a national department for evangelism, and even after all this emphasis in the national Church, the "official" stance of the national Church is that the evangelistic unit is the parish rather than the individual.

Now that gives us a distinct character. But after you've said it, what precisely does it mean? Perhaps that the community itself is to be evangelistic and that we receive people into a community, into a congregation, into a parish, into a diocese, rather than just handing them a book and saying, okay, this is your manual, now read this. Just study this book and that's all you need. But that would mean that the community would have to be receptive to new people to give them a positive reception from the parish.

Of course, as you say, many people who come back find that their friends, especially academic friends, are appalled when they hear they've returned to the Church. Others are baffled by it, and want to make an appointment with the rector for themselves to see what's going on.

You know, people who come back are the ones who often make the most engaged Christians.

I think the only faith worth having is an examined faith and a questioned faith, and as with so many people, this is what distresses me: many people *don't* have trouble with faith, don't have *any* trouble in their religious practice. This has to breed reaction and rebellion, as one rebels against anything that is not worthy of the name. If it means for the first time that someone is beginning to examine his or her faith, and then come back, why, that has got to be a new authenticity.

As I said, I've never left the Church, but I've never left the church or religion *because* I've always had problems with it. I had a philosophy background, I taught in college, and I've always had problems, and that's why I never found it necessary to leave the Church. I tried to tell my students, years ago, that Christians ought to be people who share the same problems instead of people who go around claiming to have answers to questions.

In answer to your question about the kinds of patterns I'm seeing with people returning to the Church—mine will be a rather generic type of answer, because of the type of pastoral relationship I have with people in congregations. I have been kind of stratified. My work is primarily with other bishops and with the diocese.

With candidates for the ministry, sometimes people come back and even offer themselves for ordination because religion was just a family exercise with them and never had spoken to their real problems. Other people never had any real-life problems, and having had no problems, they needed no real answers. When they *had* big problems, got into real trouble and needed help which transcended the casual, they began to get to the level of the transcendent, and that brought them back.

But what we had to do with that kind of person—they always felt they had to offer themselves completely to God, they had to become an ordained minister—what we had to point out was that this was not an adequate response to the stimulus. That one *should* feel this way and this should be the nature of every Christian, but does not distinguish the clerical order from the lay order.

One's self-evaluation is not always accurate. I count it as a medal on my chest that I kept a professor of high-energy physics from being ordained priest because he had this kind of experience and felt there was no way in the world he was going to go on teaching, given what he felt. I think he had a lot of inadequate biblical exegesis on this. Difference in preparation should not be the difference between ordained people and lay people.

The people that I know who have come back have never indicated that they did it with fear or trembling. They anticipated a welcome reception and they found it. And they really rather exult in the fact that they came back and feel good about it.

One reason people who haven't come back feel hostility toward people in the Church, I think, is because the image projected by religion has been that we're the people who have all the answers and that the answers make us "saved." And that means that the person who takes the role of believer says, "I am saved, God is my answer." But when people observe their lifestyles, they don't see anything different about them that would merit salvation. And then they see no difference about them, other than their superiority, which is offensive.

I really think the Church should be made up of people who share problems for which God gives the answer. And the answer is always beyond us instead of being in our hip pocket. Which makes it an answer that we can tell others.

I know of some instances where people fell away from the church, and—"fell away" is not the word, "walked away," or "ran away" because of the engagement of the Church with the world that was characteristic of the 1960s. That was not their conception. For these people, religion exists to make their lives comfortable, and this involvement made them uneasy, so they left. You can always devise a religion of your own that will do what you need. You're writing your own prescription. And when a prophetic, normative role is played by the Church, these people found it abrasive and uncomfortable. And after things had calmed down long enough so they were sure they were not being tricked, when they could come back on their own terms, then they came back.

Some come back to a different version of the Church. For example, I was having my annual teeth-cleaning the other day and the dental hygienist was in the Unity Church, and she was asking me about it. They have these thirty-second radio spots. That movement is centered here. And it did start out, I think in the Thirties, as an additive to other religions and was never supposed to be a denomination in itself. It was supposed to stimulate your activity in the church to which you belonged. But not to be a separate denomination.

People are attracted to these sects sometimes because they don't really require change. It's the same type of thing as television evangelism. They build motels and an occasional hospital here and there. But they have none of the liabilities of religion. All they do is a form of self-deceptive positivism in the name of Jesus Christ. Just love Jesus (or yourself) and all your problems will evaporate.

I taught for twenty-three years in philosophy, and when I was elected bishop, I was meditating and praying whether to accept it or not. But I felt I really had to because I really had the suspicion, which has been confirmed many times, that I am basically a coward. And there's no place where it's easier to be brave than in the classroom.

I was reluctant to get out into the world, because I knew there would be a lot of problems and I knew also that I would be the one who couldn't pass the buck on to someone else.

And so, shortly after I got down here, I established a system of diocesan themes. I wrote and printed a little summary of the New Testament and I told everybody to keep it, that it would be our theological road map.

So here are our themes.

The first theme is *God's Presence Changes the Status Quo.* If you're a religious participant, you recognize the need for God's presence in our lives. And if you recognize God's presence in your life, the first thing you realize is that God is different from us. And because God is different from us, his presence always makes a difference to us, so God's presence changes the status quo. If a person can claim to be in God's presence and use that presence for a proof that things should remain the way they are, that's proof positive that he doesn't know what the presence of God is like. God's presence is always beyond us. That's why we know that if we are in the presence of God, He'll change the status quo.

The second theme is *The Church is Community.* God is personal presence. We're in His presence and we're in each other's presence, and that makes the Church a community, a community of people who are really interested each other. If the church is interested only in itself, it's not really a community. The community must also be interested in the world beyond itself.

And the third theme—and it's the one that hooks people the quickest—is *We're Set Free in Christ.* Everyone in the world wants to be more free than he or she is. The kind of freedom people want in the world is freedom for themselves. But the thing about Christian freedom is, it's freedom *from* one's self. As a matter of fact, it's because it's freedom *from* ourselves that it works.

We're a Christian community in the presence of God, and because we're set free *from* ourselves, that makes us available to God for other people in His name. That's the basis of our participation. I'm fighting a battle against great odds with the national Church because I'm trying to keep people from using the terminology of the "ministry of the laity" or "the priesthood of the laity." Everybody is supposed to be "for" the laity, but nobody is. In our usage, "laity" is a denigrating term and I can't understand that.

We have this stance here that we, the priests, are the pros, the professionals, and we really make a professional/lay distinction. In England it's just the opposite. The amateur was the real historian, or theologian, the "pro" was the term of denigration, because a gentleman wouldn't have to make his living that way.

I think the key to this in the Bible is—(in Genesis and in the first letter of Peter)—the key term is, *I will make you a nation of priests.* The royal priests . . . the fact is, when you're baptized, you're a member of the priesthood.

Everybody, then, by virtue of his baptism and confirmation, is meant to be a priest in the world. We are a community of priests. Now that's a communal priesthood and the ordained priesthood is not a separation, just a functional derivative. It exists only to enable the royal priesthood to be itself. And you get right to the kind of thing Teilhard de Chardin was talking about: you consecrate something by saying a prayer of thanksgiving over it; that's how it's made holy.

Christians consecrate the world to God by being thankful and that's the consecration of the world. That's how the Kingdom comes to the world.

I've spent all of my life reading philosophy, and I still say Christianity is historical. If God is love, a person can live in love only in reaction to an historical act or event. In the last little book I did on the "Jesus prayer" ("Lord Jesus Christ, have mercy on me, a sinner"), I was trying to make the point that a Christian has to absolutize, has to accept that as a revelation of the absolute, based on something that actually happened. It's true because it happened, it didn't happen because it's true.

In terms of mass movements, I don't see any great movement one way or another, nationally. We have about bottomed out. This part of the country is rather atypical. Actually, this is a religious part of the United States, so we didn't have much falling away. Those [movements] we had happened because of social involvement. And we certainly have, over a generation, a decrease in confirmations, but that's primarily because of a shortage of youngsters to be confirmed. The constitution of the classes is much more adult now.

When I was doing work at the University of Chicago, it was right after the war and I majored in philosophy and Hartshorne was there. I can remember this one young fellow who sat next to me in class was taking philosophy "to help the world solve its problems." Rational analysis, he thought, would do the trick.

Given the failure of rationality in the world—well, it doesn't take as much faith to believe in God nowadays as it does to believe in the efficacy of rational analysis.

HAUGH

Haugh is a "late vocation" priest: a person who realized his call to the priesthood late in life. Once called, he wasted no time in becoming one of the most active persons in the Oklahoma City diocese. He is a wiry, intense, and thoroughly lovable man. Haugh begins his story with an account of his own return to the church.

I am one of those late-vocation persons. I went to seminary in my forties, and in the process of seeking ordination you are asked about three million times, "What makes you think you are called to be a priest?" If you're asked the same question often enough, you try to figure out what answer to give. My stock answer was, "Well, I was *not* struck blind on the road to Owaso"—which is a suburb of Tulsa.

I went back to church in midlife, when I took my child to church. We felt it was time to expose our child. And that led to this, this career change for me. I was ordained just three years ago. Most of my adult life, I worked with my brother in a small manufacturing business. And before I went to seminary I was part owner in a small art gallery and paint shop with my wife; she was my employer. We're not such a rare breed. I think there is something in the Church that attracts late vocations.

An experience that I am having I know is not unique, but I wonder if it's a kind of untapped or undeveloped resource for the people in the Church. I work quite a bit with Alcoholics Anonymous people and I am discovering that a number of people get led into a church career from there.

AA is a spiritual program, but it cannot serve the purposes of the Church. And vice versa. A number of people I have worked with—two of our last confirmation classes were heavy on AA people. Almost a full class in each case. Six, eight people per class, at least.

Four individuals in our last confirmation classes at Easter; one was Roman Catholic, one was nothing, one was Church of Christ, and one was a Methodist. That's typical of classes today. Also, they're more heavily adult than, say, ten years ago: people well into their thirties.

We are experiencing a renaissance in adults, families with young children. Two or three years ago the nursery and pre-school area was not much larger than this office and now it's three times as large and bursting at the seams.

So I'm sure some of these newcomers, in lots of cities, are part of the urban renewal: people moving back into the cities. Your situation in Chicago is very similar to our situation. Downtown, just north of us, an old prestigious neighborhood, and on both sides, it's a pretty rough area.

As for my own story, well, I had been in this church for years, and served as a lay reader and vestryman and senior warden, and all along people would say, "You ought to be a priest." And finally one Lent I decided to make that my Lenten discipline, and pray about it seriously and investigate that question.

After Easter I went to the rector, and—it was Charles W— I caught him in the hall of the church, and I said, "Father, you think I ever might be priest material?" And he took me by the arm and steered me into his study. It was piled high with books and papers because he never filed anything. He went to the desk and pulled out the middle drawer and there he pulled out a packet of materials with my name on it and pitched it out at me and said, "What in the *hell* took you so long?"

And it was all the forms, the applications to theology seminary. This was right after Easter, and next August, I was in seminary. My head is still spinning!

I went for the initial required interview with the bishop and about forty-five minutes into the conversation he said, "If you had your druthers, where would you want to go to seminary?" I said, Damned if I know, I don't even know what seminary is. He picked up the phone and called someone and said, "Barney, I reckon it's a little late, but how do we get a guy into seminary?" I was his first postulant from the cathedral.

Maybe it's self-serving, but I really believe I have quite an advantage over younger men in the church. I remember my first summer here, I was wearing a short-sleeved shirt and a fellow wandered in and he was obviously indulging in some kind of drugs or alcohol. I took him out of the office and we sat outside in the courtyard on the bench. And in retrospect I am quite convinced that my tattoo saved me from a beating.

As I said, I had on short sleeves and the man wanted to know when I was in prison. In his mind I had experienced the same sort of life he had. People want to feel you know about the world out there. The world that they have to deal with every day.

REED

Reed is the rector of a large, suburban church north of Oklahoma City, Oklahoma. More than eight hundred people attended the eleven o'clock Mass the Sunday we visited the church. Although we were total strangers, we were greeted by smiles and handshakes from dozens of people. Reed himself gave us over an hour of his busy Sunday-morning time to tell us about his church and the people in it. He begins his story with an account of the current renewal of interest in the church.

* * *

Yes, we *have* had a revival. People have been inactive and have been coming back into the life of the Church. And we've had a lot of adults who have been in other denominations, so we've been running probably an average of sixty adult confirmations a year. And then probably about forty children that have grown up in the natural course of training classes. It's been very gratifying.

I teach the adults personally. Others teach the young people's classes. And actually there are only two full-time men on our staff, which for a congregation of two thousand is a lot of work. Two are ordained. But we do have a full-time youth minister and I do have an almost full-time director of communication.

As far as what they are looking for is concerned: well, I think people are looking for stability in the world in which we live. Of course, the time I started in the ministry was forty-one years ago, in the middle of World War II. Ever since then, we've been going through a transition. In the Fifties we had a revival of those who had been through the war; and then in the Sixties, the youth of America had their upset times, and all the things that went with it. They wanted to go away on their own.

Then in the Seventies things began to change. For the last ten years I've felt a very strong sense of a return to the Church. Of course I'm a traditionalist by nature and choice—people want the kind of stability that's found in the Church. And that's one of the things: we are traditionalists in our approach to religion. We try to meet everyone in the parish. I think that's one of the things that's led people back to the Church.

The second factor that we've found to be so important is that we've tried to reach out to the community as a whole. We're open to anybody who'd like to hear our story. That's basically what I'm doing with two classes a year. I welcome anybody who wants to come. Whether they've been attending a church somewhere else, or whatever. Let them come here and let me tell them the story. You just let 'em come in the first couple of times. If I don't get them into the church, it's my fault.

We just sent out a questionnaire. Every summer we send out this questionnaire and we ask the people what they think about what we're doing. Our services, our organization, et cetera. One question is, Do you believe our church is meeting the spiritual needs of the congregation? And if your answer is different from last year (the answer's yes or no). If the answer is no, please tell us why, tell us what we can do. We send it out to everyone in the congregation and then we re-evaluate our whole program on the basis of the questionnaire.

For example, last year the big thing was that they wanted to have an adult group class on Sunday morning. Now we had Bible study during the week and two or three things on Sunday morning. So we revamped our Sunday mornings, so we have some coming in at eight o'clock. (I call that my "Golfer's Special," so that by eight-thirty they could be on the way to the golf course.) Nine o'clock, that we call the "Family Service," when the whole family comes together to worship. And they worship from nine to ten together. Everybody. And we try to keep the service moving and short.

We also sent out at the same time a share-your-time-or-talent questionnaire in which we asked them to sign up where they'd like to share their time or talent with us. That gives us a good chance to get volunteers to work in all kinds of categories. The old story may be true, you know: the more people you get involved, the more successful your church life is going to be. We tried to find something for everybody.

We try to make them feel welcome. Every Sunday when I invite everyone to come back for a cup of coffee, tea and punch, my grandchild says "Granddad, why do you always say 'Coffee, tea, and punch'?" Well, I want to get the message across. You know, you get tired of saying that, but it has to be said. It's a place for conversation, for people to meet people. Yes, once you get back into the fold . . . This is happening more and more, and it's really very exciting. It makes me anxious to get to work every day. I've been a minister for forty-one years, and it's been more exciting every year. It's interesting to notice trends—revival trends.

I would say that the present trend started when we finally got through the Sixties. In about the middle Seventies. A large part of it is simply our enthusiasm and challenge. And perhaps because other people weren't finding what they were looking for where they were. Now the Bible study has been a big thing here. In fact, we're getting ready to launch the Bethel series.

We have about two or three Roman Catholics in every Inquirers' class. Each class is about thirty. So you could say about 10 percent are from the Roman church. And there is a very heavy filtering of Methodists, which is where I came from. I would say about 20 to 30 percent Methodist. And 20 or 30 percent Baptist. Some Presbyterians and Church of Christ and a few others.

They come because church is the only place where they can have a worship experience. This is what most of the people I've talked to say, "I don't want to be patted on the back, I want a worship experience."

When I first came here, the budget was $75,000 a year and we were struggling to make ends meet. In fact, when I came, I had been the dean of a cathedral back East, and I told them what my present salary was. They told me, "Why, that's more than we pay the bishop." And I told them, "Well, maybe the bishop needs a raise." And I said, I can't come for any less. I had been in Buffalo for seven years, I loved my work there, but I wanted to get out of that climate. When the wind comes off the lake and the snow piles up, you know . . . I said I was going someplace where it's a little warmer.

So I said, I'd love to come, but I can't come for any less, so they decided to take the leap of faith and they did meet my salary, plus a little more, and the next year the bishop got a raise. He said to me, "Thank you for getting me the raise!"

Now, twenty-two years later, our budget is nearly $600,000, compared to $75,000. And we have a very low-key campaign. My philosophy is I spend fifty-one Sundays a year preaching the Gospel. And if I'm doing my job, when I talk to them on the fifty-second Sunday of the year about money, just once a year, they're going to respond.

But the real thing that brings people to the church is—well, I think that phrase I gave you, "a worship experience," is the key. They won't come just to hear a great preacher—which is fine—but they come here to have a worship experience, and that's why the altar is the center of the church and not the preacher.

It's endlessly fascinating to me. When I was in the Methodist Church, the pulpit was the center, the preacher was the center, and everything revolved around him. If the preacher gave you a lousy sermon, the whole day was lost. I gained no real feeling of worship.

This isn't true in our church. You come here to worship the Lord and to receive the sacraments. The altar is the center, worship is the center, and if the preacher gives a lousy sermon, well, the poor guy had an off day, his kids kept him up all night, but that has nothing to do with the experience of worship I have here at this church. So that when you move the center of the church away from the Lord and the altar and the experience of sharing in the sacraments, you're turning everything around, you'll lose it all.

One of my goals when I go into a church is not to build a ministry for myself, but to get as many people involved in the ministry as possible, so that if and when I do move on, the church can go on. Instead of saying, "Well, we had him but he's gone, and here we go," the church just goes on. When you start building up a personality cult in a church, you're on dangerous ground.

And now I've reached the point where the vestry says, Well, we'd like to have you work past retirement, as long as you can work twelve hours a day. [He laughs.] But I don't worry about the church when I'm gone, I know they can handle it. If I go away, when I come back, things are going to be maybe a little better than when I left because they're trying harder to show the old man up. Show him: we can run the show without you, you know!

Which is great! That's how my philosophy works, because sometime in the next five years, I *am* going to retire. The canons of the Church say you can't be rector after seventy-two. You can work but you can't be bishop and you can't be rector of a parish, which I think is a good rule. But they are prepared to get along without me. I've put twenty-two years of my life into this place and I sure don't want it to quit when I walk out the door.

WILLIAM

William is the minister in a lovely suburban church near one of the largest cities in Tennessee. His story begins with the occasion of his return to the parish where he is now rector: a parish that collectively has experienced a kind of renewal.

I myself left the parish and returned. I had a church in Knoxville for five years—and I felt that the church needed to clean up its act. I was given a choice that wasn't very pleasant, so I chose to start this new church rather than to go to a little rural town. I stayed with that for four and half years. That was during the civil rights movement and the new prayer book furor.

Then a congregation of people went there expecting to get away from all of those issues, and it was really tumultuous. We had terrible leadership problems. Finally we got things together. And I got out of there. I just wanted to stay until the war was won. Then I went into secondary school chaplaincy. I went to Emory to work on an advanced degree and to work in a school in Atlanta for seven years.

So ten years after I left the parish, I was ready to come back to parish work. It took me that long to regroup after five years. Now I've been here five years and I'm quite sure I'll stay here for the rest of my ministry. But it's hard for me to answer your question about people returning to the church without talking about my own experience, and also what's happened to this parish.

I was so ready to come back into the parish, but I wasn't fully conscious of just how much. I just knew, vocationally, I was ready for a change. I was looking at headmaster jobs in parochial schools and I looked at a number of those. And all of a sudden this parish came up, and this parish has a school. I was still in Atlanta, but I was in touch with the bishop here, and I immediately made the decision to come here.

The former rector had been physically ill for a number of years.

He had had quite a remarkable ministry here during the Sixties, a very unpopular ministry. His ministry had been primarily to individuals under stress, so that this institution suffered badly. I am very much a community person and my concept of the parish is as a worshipping, caring community.

When I came here, immediately, I guess as an offshoot of how I function, a lot of activity was generated. People began to become active again. I don't know what happened, but things started happening. And all of this community life started to happen, in addition to this tremendous ministry to Alcoholics Anonymous groups that the parish already had.

We've got at least eight AA groups meeting here, ALA-NON, and small groups of women, people addicted to pre-scription drugs, and women who have alcoholics in their families. Closed meetings, open meetings—a wonderful ministry that people in the community know about.

But there was no appeal being made to families with young children. There was no Christian Education program. People weren't being asked to give, there had been no stewardship program for a number of years, people weren't asked to make pledges. Confirmation classes and Inquirers' classes had been discontinued, so people were confirmed after only individual conferences with the clergy.

There had been a Christian Education director hired before I came, because they knew there was a problem with Christian Education, but there was very little offered for adults. The choirmaster was a professor at the university, and most of the choir consisted of his voice students. We had some very good quality voices in it, but it wasn't a parish choir.

Underneath all this was the fact that there had been about five men who held the church together. They were fairly young people and they and their wives formed the core of the church and it was a very tight core. They really wanted the church to grow. They weren't trying to be exclusive, but they were. They really had control and the vestry didn't negotiate or discuss or plan or pray. Being on the vestry meant that you didn't do anything unless you were in this group of four or five who did everything.

They were exhausted. They were absolutely worn out. And I talked to one of them who lives in Houston now, and when his daughter got married a few months ago, he left here saying he was going to become a chalice bearer. But he never was. That was five years ago and he never will, he was so burnt out.

The people cared a lot. But the bishop told me after I ac-cepted the call here, that there had never been the opportunity or the training for any lay leadership in this parish. I thought at the time that was an extreme statement. So now there is a tremendous amount of vitality here. And a lot of it has just been having somebody at the helm—namely me—who was really open to making decisions and doing things.

If you walked down the halls, you probably saw that there is an art exhibit. That was the sort of thing that just started completely out of a groundswell. Now we're spending over $100,000 renovating our parish hall and that's going to be an art gallery, with lighting and carpeted walls.

So yes, a lot is happening here. I have really seen a lot of people coming back into the Church. But I think it's because we have a damn good parish. It's alive. We value little children, we think there's nothing more important than how the nursery is run. We've got a growing number of babies. A growing number of pregnant women. And I think there is a belief here, a guiding belief, that every stage of life is important.

One thing that existed before I came that was very good is a retirees club, and it has really picked up. They have done a better job than any in the church in incorporating new members. I can always depend on them to bring in older members who have come back to the church.

Now the people who had left and then came back are either people who left in the late Sixties because they were mad at the rector and some of his stands, or they just lost interest and left. There's a young man who's thirty-two and he's just come back into the Church. He was very active in the Sixties, ran a coffeehouse. So that was fifteen years or so that he was out of the Church.

Thinking about one particular individual, he just returned this year but he's already gone again. He was engaged to a girl in the parish but she rejected him, and he's not back this summer and I haven't reached out to him. What brought him back was that his father was Jewish and had been in the Unitarian Church for a long time. When he came into the service for the first time, he was overwhelmed by the power of the liturgy.

I think that's one thing that's happening. People are finding the liturgy to be symbolic of their lives and to add the mystery and meaning they didn't think was possible, and to find it in the Church. Whatever else is going on here, and whatever programs we have, the most important thing is the worship.

We have sacrificed the quality of professional music for having music that really belongs to the congregation. It's now a parish choir and it has ups and downs. They take August off and start again in September, but over the summer a lot of people have joined the choir. So it's now to the point where people have decided to spend over two thousand dollars on a new organ.

With all this AA work that's going on during the week, we have decided to bring the subject out of the closet and put it into the Sunday services. So in the spring we had a series on chemical addiction where members of the parish actually got up and told their own stories. It was very powerful. My goal is to have AA meetings on Sunday morning here in the church building, to bring it from the dark recesses of the church up into the light of Sunday morning.

Now I'd like to say something about these people coming in with children. I discovered something three years ago in my children's confirmation class, which had six children in it at the time. Three were from single-parent homes and the other three from two-parent homes. The next year we had eight in the class and I made a point of finding out and noticing that four were from single-parent homes.

This year I have eight in the class and six are from single-parent homes. The church is acknowledging the single-parent adult, the single adult generally. I wrote something on the cover of our newsletter this year on the single adult and it got more responses than anything in any previous newsletter. Single people are beginning to feel that they have a place.

I think we have a parish family, we *are* a parish family. We

have covered-dish suppers that really aren't covered-dish because many people work and come directly after work. And
many of the people with children come; for them it's an extended family if there is only one parent at home. I really see
the parish as an extended family that nurtures its children and
single people, gives them a lot of support.

We've been trying to get into this program where people in
the parish are trained—there's this program, it's by LEAD
consultants with John Savage. Our parish has implemented it.
I'm a trainer. We meet tonight with the group that's been
trained as a pastoral care team. They don't just reach out to
people who have left, they reach out to all kinds of people,
including people who were in the parish and are moving out
of town. I know it's made a difference. It's meant some of the
people who would have dropped out otherwise haven't
dropped out.

CANTRELL

*Cantrell is a Canon of a cathedral in a large southern city. Al-
though he has all of the administrative duties one might expect from
a man in his position, he is also a deeply spiritual person with a
profound understanding of the needs of the diocese and of the church
at large. He is keenly interested in renewal and was a charter
member of the National Commission on Evangelism. His interview
begins as he talks with us about some possible resources for our book.*

Are you familiar with John Savage, his studies on the apa-
thetic and bored churchman? You might want to look at his
book on why people leave and why they have come back.
. . . He makes the point that lapsed people are often lapsed
because they felt guilty about something they didn't do, or that
someone did or didn't do to them, and they were hurt. Most
of the time they don't go to another church. He was trying to

get to them . . . by listening to them and saying a little more than "It's all right to come back." He was saying, "I love you, I hear your pain, I'm equipped to listen and hear the pain, whatever it was." So they do not feel threatened.

When we first formed the National Commission on Evangelism, we discovered, as we got into it more and more, that evangelism is so broad that just about anything you do can be evangelism.

But we decided that evangelism had to be intentional. [We also learned] that there was a lot of prejudice against it. I used to start off every session with the question "What has been your bad experience with evangelism?" I'd share all my bad experiences with them and try to get to the essence of it.

Somehow it was as if nobody down the line had presented Jesus as Savior and Lord and given people the opportunity to say yes to that and to respond in a way that they knew about. All the pressures were there to accept Jesus as Savior, and people were answering, but a year and a half later they didn't even remember or know why they had said that.

One guy helped us clarify that. He said, "It's as if you went out there and said to the people, 'How many of you are married? How many know if you're married or not? I didn't ask you if you had a good or bad marriage, just are you in the process?' " Similarly, everybody ought to know if they're in that process, if they're a Christian. Not just if they go to church but if they have said *yes* to the Lord in a way that is concrete to them and is moving them step by step in a new direction.

Anyway, we found that as we were trying to do that, there were more and more people coming in. The more we prayed about it, the more came back. They weren't prepared for it, there hadn't been a new face in that congregation for years. And when we prayed about it and started a group together who were willing to deal with new people—I think the first Sunday there were five new people. And once we started to do what the Lord wanted us to do, people came—for all those other reasons you're talking about.

We saw it a little differently because we were ready to do something with all the people who came. But then we saw that we needed to do more, that if we would bring people to a congregation, the congregation itself didn't necessarily know that they had made a commitment to their Savior and Lord and sometimes they weren't sure what they were doing there, either.

The thing I like about this parish is that people come in here and stay in. They're always asked why they stay. And they say that there's something "special" that they have discovered, there's a spirit here. They hear the Gospel from the pulpit. There's something about the people, the whole atmosphere here that is drawing them in.

I think that's a part of it, a part of why people are coming back. People know that God is real. In the church you meet people who say that God is real, and that He loves you and cares about you.

I think the real reason is that, well, God is once again— the Holy Spirit is once again—revealing Himself in the world. That's the cause of the renewal. That's the real cause of what's happening around us now.

JOEL

Joel is a handsome, softspoken man, who looks enough like Phil Donahue to be a twin. He was one of the most knowledgeable and energetic priests we met on our trip, and was up to date not only on his parish and the diocese of Little Rock but on the national and international religious scene as well. The cathedral in Little Rock, where he is Dean, sits on a small rise, nestled among a grove of hardwoods. The diocesan offices are immediately to the left of the cathedral. They are guarded by a three-colored cat named Trinity.

* * *

It's always difficult to generalize. But I think what you perceive is accurate, that there is apparently both a return to the Church and a rediscovery of churches like ours. Maybe this is going on all the time, and one just perceives it happening in one's own generation. I think what we have going on here, looking back to the period of growth in the Fifties and Sixties, is an influx of a lot of people who came because their friends were there. They were upper-middle-class people and churches like ours represented the kind of social class they wanted to be in.

One of the characteristics of our church is that it's a very small church. We often tend to become a sect instead of a church. We do tend to draw very strong lines, unlike the Church of God or the Romans. The difference is that the ones coming into the church now are not necessarily *of* that class, or even aware of that class. They are better educated, so social life and class are not as important to them.

The reasons for the renewal have to do with the Gospel and the desire to learn and be aware of it. I once met a man who was the Bishop of Tanganyika, whose assistant bishop is Alfred Muhammad—Bishop Medina—and he reminds me of your topic. I asked him why Christianity was on the upsurge, since they have no connection with European Christianity. He said, Well, you see, Christianity is *true.*

One of the things that is important here is we really get behind preaching. It's not just off-the-cuff remarks or what we read in *Time* magazine, but really Christ-centered preaching. There are lots of reasons for doing this, [for example], the sacredness of the altar. I think people respond to it.

I had a friend, a priest in Pennsylvania, who grew up in Shreveport, Louisiana, and he said, "You know I went down to Shreveport to visit my family, and I decided I would just go visit all these other churches. So on Sunday night I went to the biggest Baptist church in Shreveport, and I assumed that what they were doing was the Gospel, but what I discovered was a kind of mixture of patriotism, motherhood, and religious anecdotes. They weren't really proclaiming the Good News, the Gospel at all." I think there's a lot of bad preaching in our church, but there's also a real response to good preaching on people's part.

Also there's a real response to the kind of worship we have. There's a sense of the importance of it all: the prayers aren't just rattled off, the lessons aren't read with the assumption that nobody is listening. There's a real sense of importance that catches on. But that doesn't have a lot to do with churchmanship. Both Anglo-Catholics and evangelicals—churches where that's done—people respond to it. It's just a heightened sense that maybe this really *is* the most important thing in the world. It's all new to them, at least they tell me that.

One of the things I always ask them [converts transferring from other denominations] is "What brought you here? How did you get here? Did somebody bring you, or did you just read the sign outside the door, or what? And why did you come back? Why did you stay?" The answer is nearly always the same, to that second question: the sense of having a spiritual brush, an encounter.

On the other hand, I think it's very interesting, the assumptions of some people who are very close to the workings of the Church. They emphasize such things as not having any indebtedness; they believe that people don't want to belong to a church that's in debt. That you must have a kind of a whirlwind program. But the interesting thing is that, with the people I talk to, I have yet to have an adult who will come to me about the Church and say, Do you have a debt? They don't ever ask that; they don't care. They'll cope with that when they get in. They don't care when they're joining.

I think what people are really looking for in programs is

sound teaching. Both for their children and for themselves. They are serious about that one. The evidence is that it's not only *how* you attract people but how you hold them as well.

Adult education is important. We've really said to people: Sunday school's for children. But *we've* graduated from all that —adults just don't do that. Even with the long history of Sunday school, adults respond to more serious issues.

Going back to what attracts people to the Church, I find that time and time again, one of the most powerful evangelistic tools we have in the Church is the funeral service. Last week a man passed away and one of his friends came who had never had occasion to be in this church before. And when it was over, he drew me aside and said, "This was just unlike anything I've ever heard or seen before." I've had occasion lately to go to one or two services in other churches that were billed as a "memorial service." In my own mind, I always thought that a funeral was where the body was present and before actual burial whereas a memorial service was done at a later time and featured an address on the life of the deceased.

This one was billed as a memorial service, and I realized with a start that yes, that was what was done most of the time in other churches, talking about the merits of the deceased and so on. And that's all right, but it's different, different from what we do. It centers on the person, his life and his contribution. But it seems to me that in the face of death you want something more substantial.

A funeral is a very low-pressure occasion, like a confirmation or wedding, and it brings in people who would never think of coming on Sunday. Really, you know your first task is just getting them through the door.

And what is the appropriate degree of "evangelism" to be expressed? Where do you draw the line between pressuring people on the one hand and making them feel welcome, a part of the Church, on the other?

I think that's one of the advantages of a place like this, that it has a very large congregation and it allows a certain degree of anonymity. You can slip in the door and be invisible and slip out if you want. We have about six hundred active in attendance; on the books we have fifteen hundred at least. The larger a church is, the larger percentage of inactive people you have. Some people just want a church to sort of nominally belong to.

We were one of those churches that just automatically prepared the children for confirmation at about age twelve, and now we no longer do that. That's one of the reasons we started this Christian Education thing. We think of confirmation more now as a mature affirmation of the faith, a rediscovery of faith, and a twelve-year-old just can't do that. If parents don't want to go to church, there's not really much he [the twelve-year-old] can do, but a sixteen-year-old can do it.

Our program really suffered because of the assumption on the part of some people in the parish that all high-school students *are* going to drop out. If you say that enough, it's self-defeating: they will drop out. Whereas the *facts* are that some of our most active people are high-school students. I was confirmed when I was about twelve, and the whole thing was a disaster. I was embarrassed, it was just disastrous.

When adults come in to this church, either to be baptized for the first time or to transfer from another church, we have increasingly presented the instruction as "Inquirers' classes," not necessarily leading to confirmation but as kind of an option that a person has, something he or she might be interested in pursuing. If you have Christian education on a weekly basis and good sermons, that can supplement the classes that prepare people for membership in the Church.

CLIFFORD

Clifford is pastor of a large Lutheran Church and school in Tennessee. He is a warm, friendly man, who has put a tremendous amount of effort in making his church a place where people can find Christian education as well as an opportunity to worship. Pastor Heard begins his story with a few statistics on people who drift away from the church.

Well, I guess we're a little bit similar to you Episcopalians in our traditions. For Lutherans there is a mass exodus at about ninth grade. We confirm at the end of the eighth grade. Statistics have shown that about 50 percent of the kids presently drift away.

I've quoted this statistic in the past thirty years and it's shocked people, because we had our largest confirmation class this past June 26. But in the next year, thirteen or so of them will drift away from the church. I think we do fairly well with high school. But the big hit comes at about nineteen, I would say. Kids go off to college, kids entering various vocations.

We have tried to start—actually made four attempts—to get a Sunday school started. And each time for one reason or another it's gone down the tubes. We do have a singles Bible class, but that's one where a divorced person can come. They usually pick up at about age thirty or thirty-five. So we're talking about a gap of ten or so years.

I don't know how familiar you are with Chattanooga churches, but there are two churches that I know of that have really good singles programs—150 members each. There is a potential there, if you just hit the right combination. That group does seem to respond to something. Whatever it is, we haven't found it.

We have an interesting history in this congregation here. The congregation grew out of this school: we operate the

school in partnership with another congregation, First Lutheran. And this congregation came out of the school, with a core
of good solid Lutheran people. But the real growth of the
congregation came with children who were at the school and
tasted of the Gospel and it infiltrated into the homes.

We have brought in parents who are probably in their late
twenties and they became members of the congregation in
their late twenties or early thirties, and they became very committed. What has attracted people, particularly in this area, is
that if you want to be a teaching church you've got to be well
organized, and Lutheranism is doctrinally well organized. This
appealed to people in this area.

Our emphasis on education, our emphasis on people understanding—well, these people stayed and saw their children
through school. I think their children went through that period of dropout. But it wasn't as long as usual. A lot of these
kids settled here, came back to the congregation. Now their
kids are the grandchildren of the first generation.

When I got here, a good number of these second-generation
people were ready to move out. And they were now about
twenty-five to twenty-eight years old, settling down, and
we've got a number of these young families in pretty active
roles because the children are in school and they feel a real
commitment to the congregation.

The school dates back to 1886 or '87. They're going to
celebrate their hundredth anniversary in three years. We became a partner in the school about five years ago. But it's the
school that has provided the continuity between what the children experience and the world of their parents and grandparents.

Here in our own congregation we have a very strong adult
Christian education program, and I think that's a key. I don't
know how to say this without being critical but it's Bible-
centered, person-centered. It's not "Let's hit them over the

head with the Bible," but "Let's go in and explore the Bible." It's not "We will go in and tell you what this means" but "Let's learn and explore together."

I don't know if you've heard of the Bethel Bible series. We have a course similar to that one. And generally it's taught by a pastor, but here in this congregation it's taught by two lay-people who went through the training themselves. We have two laypeople teaching that by themselves.

I'm not involved in that at all. And the first reaction was, well, if the pastor isn't teaching it, I'm not going to it. I finally got through that and finally people are beginning to see the point. That laypeople can teach the Scriptures, can teach the faith, that well-organized material and dedicated people work with the Spirit in an adult education program. To me, that's a key.

To use theological terms, so much of religion gets tied up with righteousness, gets tied up with the guilt and the fear and all that. And people put the stereotypes on Christianity, often rightly so, because we just fail to communicate the very basics of what Christianity is. It's relational—a relationship with God that is based on belief.

I think those churches that are emphasizing the relationship aspects of Christianity in the long run will tune in better to the needs of people. Because as you said, in more philosophical terms, humanism has become about bankrupt and people realize that. And many religions are built on works, righteousness, self-fulfillment, all that. You can track all the way with self-righteous approaches and there is nothing left.

As you say, sometimes the language of sociology texts and religious text is so similar, you can't tell the difference. Some of it can be beneficial, I think, but without the relationship itself, concepts really become empty.

So much depends on the area. If you're out in the Midwest, you're going to have a lot of "cradle Lutherans," "born-and-raised Lutherans." If you go out in the Midwest, the rate of congregations with cradle Lutherans is probably very high, 85 or 90 percent. In rural areas, there it might be 95 percent.

The real missionaries for the Lutheran church were the saltwater states. From New England around the coast and over on the other coast in California. We tended to be very suspicious of other people, clannish. We didn't have an evangelism department on the national level until something like 1955.

We have about sixty to seventy percent of converts and that's because of the school. Our highest number comes from the Baptists. That's the stereotype of legalism, our Baptist friends. I admire their zeal and I know there's an honest commitment to Our Lord. But oh! what gets perceived and what gets taken home is a legalistic model of Christianity: "Do this, don't do that."

Next probably is Methodist, and what appeals to them is the organization. I don't know what happened to the Methodist Church in terms of its teaching. Methodism got into that social action bag, and really lost its educational component.

As for ourselves, we've often joked in the Missouri Synod that "We're more Roman than the Roman Church." While there are many in the Lutheran Church working for justice and civil change, this is where the Lutheran Church in America has had some real ferment at home. They've been much more involved in taking a stand on denominational issues, whereas in the Missouri Synod, our tradition has been that we seldom take a position churchwide. We will lead our people to the Scriptures and encourage them to make their own positions and take their own stand. The one exception has been abortion. We encompass many different views and recognize the validity of all of them.

We've experienced a real growth in this church and last year —no, in 1982—we took in twenty-nine adults. We were tied in our district, which is Tennessee and Arkansas, then last year it was twenty-six. But we weren't prepared for the continuing influx of people.

It was like the awkward teenager who has these growing spurts and is stumbling over himself. We started stumbling all over ourselves because we didn't realize the growth we are experiencing. And so I spent a good deal of my time putting out fires. When you do that you don't have a great deal of time for planning and for evangelism.

We're reaching thirty-five-year-old people—families, husbands and wives. Divorce is causing a disruption in our society. It hit me last year when I realized only half the kids were living with both parents. We have to minister to these people. And that's where the Gospel overrides the rules, getting people back into relationships, into the relation with God, into relational thinking.

Maybe that's one of our own designs. *We* built the walls, and God is there knocking them down. As you say, we tend to build up more and more complex structures. That's been Judaism's problem: how exclusive shall we become? The Scriptures say, "You, the nation of Israel, are to light the way to the Gentiles."

The area I'm really working toward in the Church is in family life. In teaching couples how to live together, generally the Lutheran Church has been strong in that area. Here we are back to relational concepts, back to relationships—that whole area is an untapped strength.

DON

Don is the rector of an inner-city parish in Chattanooga, Tennessee. He was a treasure trove of information, not only about religious renewal but about every aspect of the parish ministry as well. As we transcribed the tapes, we were struck by the depth of his own religious feeling. Father Johnson begins with a wry de-

scription of the efforts of the local Roman Catholic church to bring in members.

Yes, they're doing door-to-door handouts, nicely printed, well-done handouts, that say basically, what Catholicism is and inviting people to open houses in the parishes, inviting people to come and find out what it means to be Roman Catholic. It's low-key but very effective.

They've done a rather good job. I think the Romans have done a very good job advertising the new openness of the Roman Church in dealing with some of the realities of American life: the marriage issue, the divorce and remarriage issue.

I do not find that most people come back to church initially to hear the Gospel. I think they come back out of, often, that sense of something missing but also because they are lonely and alienated. A lot of younger couples come back to the Church because they've already done the bar-hopping routine. And you can only do that for so long, until you see the futility of it. Or else you *really* get into it, and then you finally come back to church because you're looking for an AA meeting.

Christ Church is growing. When I came here six years ago, it was an inner-city parish, and the total attendance on Sunday morning was between twenty-five and forty. It's a marvelous place, and my predecessor, Father Morley, was marvelous, a real sweetheart.

While my style is very different from Father Morley's in many ways, I think we agree on more things than we disagree on, especially concerning the sacramental nature of religion, and I think maybe that's the missing element for people. If there isn't an underlying purpose behind all these various activities that the Church does, they're just activities, just busy-work. I find that from time to time I as a priest have to stop and ask myself why I am doing all these things. The credibility of the Church depends more, in my opinion, on the *why* of what we do than on the *how* or the *how many*. You know, you can stay awfully busy and never meet God.

Now Christ Church has grown to about 180 total membership in the course of a year. The average attendance at Sunday masses is about 110 per Sunday. Because it is a small church, it has certain characteristics that a big church really cannot have, except by intentional planning.

The big church has to create "small church cells" within itself, a sense of community. Christ Church in its own way is more organic, has more a sense of community. But that's a stress on us too, because as the church begins to grow, we have to look consciously for ways to maintain the closeness while at the same time making new disciples.

A lot of people who grew up in the South come from fundamentalist backgrounds and are living with the tension that comes from knowing that they need a relationship with God but that the old ways of approaching it aren't working for them anymore. I grew up Baptist myself so I was really shocked to find that you could talk about God in language other than "Southern Baptistspeak." I just didn't know there was another language there. And when it came along, it was a surprise.

Some couples are returning because of their children, and some of the old values begin to surface again as they begin to realize the responsibility that comes with the nurturing aspect of raising children. So there are some good side effects. I'm pleased to see that people are being fruitful and multiplying if it will get them back to church. There are extremes of that— I don't know if that should be quoted—but you know what I mean.

There's an interesting aspect to education that I ran across just the other day. The person reports that it's an old saying, but true, nevertheless. The story is that if we look at Jesus in the Bible, he played with the children and taught the adults and we do just the opposite. I think there's a really interesting implication there, [the idea] that education classes are a lifetime thing. One of our emerging strengths is that more and more people are seeing the lifelong side of this: that you don't stop being educated at thirteen along with confirmation.

One of the reasons people are coming back to church is that they are going through different stages in their lives. One of the reasons the Church focuses, has focused, so much on salvation theology—and here I am thinking more of our fundamentalist brothers and sisters—is that in a tradition like that, they invoke that salvation, over and over again, and many of them never move beyond it.

Backsliding is important to that scheme. That's the reason why they have to motivate people out of guilt and fear. They're either going to scare the hell *into* you or scare it *out* of you, one or the other. I mean this in a loving way, because it's done with the best of intentions—with the intentions of the cure of that soul.

Why? Because of our nature and our sinfulness, we will continue to falter along the way. The problem is, they don't have the sacramental means of grace built into their system and so they have to keep hitting you with fear and scaring you.

It's very important to realize that the Church holds out for people a promise of contentment. And in the sacramental churches—especially to people who have come into it from a fundamentalist background—they see this as a sort of fantasy land where you pick what you want to believe, and you don't have to take any responsibility. They want contentment but they don't want any *content*.

You know, that's the problem: people begin to bounce up against some things that sound to their ears like that fundamentalist background and then they rebel. They begin to rebel against the new situation because it's playing an old tape. It's a call to respond to God out of love rather than out of fear, but if you're not listening right to it, it sounds like, "Well, my gosh, I thought I got away from all that: now I'm being called to enter into it."

What happens after they come back? It comes close to a movement back to the original concept of a parish as a geographical center, sort of a community, a center of activity. But we have to cast it in twentieth-century terms, so we have fish fries and bake sales.

But fundamentally it's a coming together into a society. A lot of times, for these folks, it's the only time they ever see each other. So it's a way to draw people together. You can tire people to death with it. But it does give an important chance for people to come together.

And that brings me back to what I started to say at first. When people come back to church, they don't come to hear the Gospel, I think. They're looking for an experience where they will feel at least some love, even if at that point they don't feel acceptance. At least they don't feel condemned. Sometimes it's one of the best things that's happened that week, if they can come back into that environment and see if there's anything else there.

We have a community kitchen here, and we feed about 120 a day, and it seems to me that those people [who are fed] would be much more open to hearing from those who are over there with them every day, feeding them, meeting those basic needs every day. They are more open to hearing something that's a little challenging to their souls, more so than if we were downtown and they were hungry, and we just told them they need to "get right with God."

First you need to experience the love—"while we were yet sinners Christ died for us." In this sacrament God takes the initiative and then we respond to what we have experienced. But you've got to have your eyes opened to experience it. So I think a lot of people come first and experience something of the community, and then the community itself becomes the body of Christ. In that context, that's why things like coffee hour are so important.

Now in the Mass setting, it really drives some of our folks crazy for any horizontal theology to be going on, So we keep it to a minimum. We have a little of it with the exchange of the Peace but that's really very subdued here.

But interestingly enough, that has grown over the last six years here. The first time we did it it was, Whoa, wait a minute!

That's so important when you put it in the context of a stylized liturgy. What we're doing, within the context of the Mass, is to say that if we have anything against our neighbor, we can, at least in that setting, leave our gift at the altar, make amends with our brothers and sisters, and then go to the altar and receive the gift.

That's an important thing in the whole dynamic. But it has to be understood that way, otherwise it looks like coffee hour in the middle of Mass. And that's why our folks responded against it, they think it's a little too tactile. But I remind them that Jesus put on skin, you remember, and touched skin, hence, that kind of dynamic of appealing to all the senses—our worship appeals to all the senses.

It's not just a head trip. Although you're not asked to leave your head at the front door, you have to be engaged with your mind as well. And there's that tension between the ministry of the Word and ministry of the Sacraments. I think that pulls people back into the Church. I know that's what pulled me back.

I grew up Southern Baptist, very active all the way through high school, and then I went away to college. During the two years of college before I went in the Navy—when I first went, I went to a large Baptist church in Dallas, and there was such a personality cult around the minister that it really turned me off. I think I was at that stage where I was struggling, and this became an excuse. When a person is really debating whether or not he wants to invest the time and energy in the Church, it doesn't take much to turn him off.

Anything, really, will do. So I walked out for two years. And I got in the Navy and there was this—the same thing you identified earlier—this sense within me that I needed to be in touch with God, and that was about as close as I came. I didn't know what that meant, even. But I knew I wanted to be in touch with God. The only language I had to express that wish was Baptist. That's all I knew.

So while I was on the ship, 150 miles out at sea, there was a fellow who was an Episcopalian. He and I started talking. He was from Washington, D.C., and we just started talking. He said, when I was explaining to him my views about God, "You don't really believe that stuff, do you?" And that was the light coming on for me. I said, "You mean there's another way?"

That was really a road-to-Damascus experience for me. It opened up a new horizon to me. After I got out of the Navy and came back to the States, I came back to Tennessee and went through confirmation classes, went to Vanderbilt, spent three years there, got involved with a parish, then went to Seabury.

But I'll tell you what really hooked me. We came back in after that conversation, back into port, and my new friend took me to the cathedral, in Jacksonville, Florida. It was Christmas Eve, and I had never done that before. The interesting thing was, before the Mass ever happened, I walked in there and I knew I was home.

They could have come jumping up and down and had Siva up there, because I didn't know what was coming next. But I knew it was the right place, whatever it was.

For example, the symbolism with the bread, of offering yourself; that's something that we've done here, that offering of ourselves, and it grows out of really reflecting on some of the changes in the Roman liturgy. Some of those are not bad.

But there is a guideline for deacons in the Roman Church that when the offering is brought forward, those symbols of our lives, it is handed *across* the altar—and I got to reflecting on that. And I thought, "How can I make that point here, that what we are doing is offering our lives?"

So what I have done is kind of a radical thing for Christ Church. I have opened the sanctuary doors, at that point, and instead of having an acolyte run out and block them from the sanctuary, I have the ushers come up to the altar and hand it directly to me. And then they turn and go back—they don't stay up, but they come into the Presence in that sacramental sense—and offer *themselves* at the foot of the altar. And we've had both very negative and very positive responses to that.

It scares them. A lot of them say, you don't go up *into* the sanctuary? You don't go into the holy of holies? But the point I'm trying to make is that you have to offer yourself there.

The ebb and flow of these renewal isues reminds me of the last four lines of T. S. Eliot's "Little Gidding": "We shall not cease from exploration,/And the end of all our exploring/Will be to arrive where we started."

To me that's the crux of the matter. We are rooted in God and we grow out, but we circle back. It's sort of like the structure of St. John's Gospel, the same thing; it comes back apparently to the same place, but it's at a different level. It's spiral rather than circular. So you keep coming back and you see it from a different point of view.

Hopefully, you're moving in a more and more rarefied atmosphere, in that you're moving closer and closer to God. Not that you become so heavenly minded that you're no earthly good, but in fact, you are moving in that way. It has to have a direction to it. That's the problem for a lot of folks, they don't feel that they're moving to God, and they're frightened, so they stay busy. And you can stay very busy in the church.

I don't think God has ever stopped revealing himself to us, I think we just didn't listen. Ten years ago, fifteen years ago, nobody would look to the church for answers, for the church was a laughing-stock in some ways. In the desire to become relevant, everything became relativized. I felt a lot of that myself.

But recently, the questions that come to me are, Why am I doing this? And what does it mean for me to be the spiritual leader—one of the spiritual leaders—of this parish? It seems to me that one of the tasks is to call people to some kind of awareness that God is active in this world. As Father Norris has said, either this is real or it's not. And I would add, if it's real, don't mess around with it. Don't play games with it. Remember the old saying: "God will not be mocked."

But I love the Episcopal Church's approach that grows out of affirming God's intent that we be united with Him. And while there is truth in the old 1928 *Book of Common Prayer* that there is no health within us, there is *help*, if we claim it. We can't do it on our own. But we don't have to. So there *is* help, and also *health*, in that sacramental sense.

Well, to continue: your comment about church growth interests me. One of the most obvious ways to measure growth is in terms of numbers. Interestingly enough, one of the things that called me back to an awareness of why I was doing all these things—all these activities, bazaars and bake sales and all —was a series of seminars I attended on church growth about a year and a half ago.

They did talk a lot about numbers, but the thing they talked more about was the difference between making decisions *for* Christ, which is salvation theology, and being disciples of Christ.

The extent that the Church can continue in the apostles' teaching and fellowship and continue in the breaking of bread and the prayers—to that extent, the church is no longer a "spectator sport."

To the extent that we can do that, we are going to make disciples. To the extent that we forget about that, we become country clubs.

None of our motives are pure, but God's motives are pure, in drawing us to Him. It is that sorting out of motives, always asking ourselves why we do the things we do along the way, sorting them out on the basis of what we believe, and then taking a step—that's important.

Something that has meant a lot to me—you talk about wanting to go to Bardstown [to Gethsemani, the Trappist monastary where Thomas Merton lived and wrote, near Bardstown, Kentucky: *Eds.*]. I copied this off the wall at the abbey; it's a prayer of Thomas Merton's.

It's a marvelous statement to me of how to move from our uncertainty, which sometimes can paralyze us, to the place where we can say with Merton:

My Lord God, I have no idea where I am going, I do not see the road ahead of me, I cannot know for certain where it will end. Nor do I know myself, and the fact that I think I am following your will does not mean that I am actually doing so. But I believe that the desire to please you does in fact please you. And I hope that I have that desire in all that I am doing. I hope that I will never do anything apart from that desire. And I know that if I do this you will lead me by the right road, though I may know nothing about it. Therefore, I will trust you always, though I may seem to be lost and in the shadow of death. I will not fear, for you are ever with me, and you will never leave me to face my perils alone.

—Thomas Merton, *Thoughts in Solitude*

Our belief really has to become incarnate in some kind of act. We have to have some kind of resolution, a way to make contact.

Your reference to Merton's *The Sign of Jonas:* this incredible falling back and returning, falling back, slipping back and recovering. The whole idea of "Am I sure I'm doing the right thing—but I'm not sure. . . . Lord, help my unbelief." This incredible dialogue is going on.

Maybe that's the whole thing about renewal. Maybe when you spend three days in the belly of a whale and get thrown up you have before you two roads: to go to Nineveh, or to go some other way. But you *know* that you have been in the belly of a whale. And that's a new piece of information for you. You've got to decide in light of that. That affects your next choice. You know when you're living under the sign of Jonas.

V · *The Once and Future Church*

The Spiritual Future of the Church in America

> You are not here to verify,
> Instruct yourself, or inform curiosity
> Or carry report. You are here to kneel
> Where prayer has been valid. And prayer is more
> Than an order of words, the conscious occupation
> Of the praying mind, of the sound of the voice praying.

> —T. S. Eliot, "Little Gidding"
> from *Four Quartets*

GEORGE

George is an Episcopal canon, and has served both as a parish priest and as the executive director of a large charitable organization within the church. He is bright, quick, fearless, and iconoclastic. He has a keen sense of irony and an unerring eye for the absurd. Also, to put it in his own words, "he's got religion."

You don't know this story at all, do you? Well, I went to a Baptist university in Texas; I attended Baylor. I started there as a ministerial student. After the first year, I knew I was not a ministerial student and certainly knew I was not a Baptist. But I didn't know what I was. I honestly did not know what I was. So I visited a number of churches.

236

One Sunday I visited St. Alban's Church [in Dallas]. And never in my life had I ever entered a church where the people who were there were focused on the *act* of worship, bowing down before God to worship. In all these years of going to the Baptist Church Sunday night, Wednesday night, revivals, and being preached at, sort of worshipped *at*, I had never, never in my life experienced bowing down and worshipping God— the Christian community as a worshipping community.

So I fell madly in love with the Episcopal Church but could not join it. I could not comprehend sacramental theology. I went to an adult Inquirers' class and couldn't quite grasp this notion of grace operating through things. I took an adult class in my hometown of Texarkana and my parish priest said, "George, you know sacramental theology is actually very simple. Have you ever had to kiss someone you didn't like, like an old aunt or uncle?" Well, that rang a bell. I had one uncle that I just couldn't stand and the thought of kissing him was enough to make me want to throw up.

Then he said, "Have you ever wanted to kiss someone that you really loved? A kiss is a kiss, but there is something radically different between a kiss of someone you love and someone you don't. And that's sacramental theology." That rang a bell. That finally made sense. I take a bath, that's one thing. I get baptized, that's quite another. That's God kissing me. I can eat, that's one thing. But to eat *this* bread and *this* wine, to eat the Body and Blood, that's literally to be kissed by God. It's the difference between those two.

So then I just went, hook, line, and sinker. I was so hungry for a Christian community in which, one, the community worshipped, and two, grace was encountered. It wasn't something I had to manufacture, it was something that could be given. I was sustained by it, and it was given to me on a regular basis.

This is how I entered seminary: I was teaching school in my

hometown. And my priest said to me one day, "George, don't you think you need to talk to me?" And I said, "Well, yes, as a matter of fact, I've thought about talking to you." But I had hesitated because I was very new. You see, I had been going to the Episcopal church since college, at age nineteen, and college was over, and I was now twenty-three. But that just re-activated all of that interest I had had as a teenager, as a ministerial student going off to college. Now it was re-activated on an entirely different level.

I had dropped out of the ministerial program in the Baptist church after one year. I was so terrible in college that I would corner the ministerial students and question them on the Virgin Birth and the corporeal Resurrection. And interestingly enough, two of my friends who were churchgoers at the time are now both professed agnostics.

Roman Catholicism—you know, I'm convinced upon closer examination, it's just the flip side of fundamentalism. In neither case do they set one free. The other day I was talking to you about Scott Peck's book. One of the things Peck stresses is that one of the things we know for sure is that God gives life, and anything that does not give life is not of God. And the same thing is true in the Church.

If the Church does not give life, then it is not doing the work of God. That's what fundamentalism was doing. It was never giving me life, it was always trying to absolutize a particular understanding of God and the world. I had to plug into that, otherwise I wasn't saved or was out of touch to such a degree that I was lost. Fundamentalism and Roman Catholicism are the same way, they focus on the negatives. Anglicanism walks that narrow ridge between the two.

I think one of the reasons I was comfortable in Anglicanism was the Reformation heritage, which was itself trying to find the reemergence of a more ancient heritage, not the creation of a new heritage. I don't know that I was aware of that when

I entered into it, but I knew that here was an environment in which, coming from fundamentalism, I could take some shape spiritually.

No one in my family was Episcopalian when I started. Now the majority of my family, aunts, uncles, cousins, are Episcopalian. Not because of me. In many cases, the pilgrimage was their own. My cousin Jeff came to church because of the Yellow Pages. And now he's senior warden and his mother and father are active, as are his wife and his kids. You ask Jeff where he found out about the church and he says, "From the Yellow Pages." I love it!

Jeff's experience isn't unique. There are probably a number of generic causes for coming back to the church. For example, that post–World War II rampant consumerism which most of us in my age bracket were just beginning to taste in the Fifties and Sixties. We were beginning to have things we never had before. When I was in college, I had three brothers and all four of us had cars in college. And three of us went to college at the same time.

Another example is the glitter of the world. It has so much appeal. The unfortunate thing is, you buy a car every two years, or you gain your trophies, you gain your college degree, you gain your professional degree. You can gain all these things but what have you got? The incredible divorce rate in this country, families falling apart—I think people are ready for something that's going to give them a sense of the eternal.

I think one of the reasons that there has been a renewal in the sacramental churches is that we've attracted so many converts from other religions. We at least provide a milieu in which the religious experience can be talked about and can even happen in myriads of ways. We don't absolutize any experience. It's all right for someone to talk about a conversion experience. But at the same time we don't see that as a contradiction to someone talking about the nature of the Sacraments being salvific and operative in their lives, on par with a conversion experience.

You know the story about the bishop of London once being accosted by a street preacher who asked him if he were saved. The old bishop turned and said, "My dear man, I *was* saved on Calvary, I am *being saved* now, and by the grace of God *will be* saved." In a way, the story does say that we Anglicans understand our faith in a historical context, and that salvation is both "now" and "on-going." I think another influence on people like me has been writers such as C. S. Lewis. Lewis was a layperson who articulated the faith for the twentieth century and probably did it more effectively than any preacher. A lot of people have come back to the church and re-embraced Christianity as a result of reading Lewis.

This return is partly the result of the broken promise of secularism. We thought we'd never have to reap the harvest. Now it's the Four Horsemen of the Apocalypse, they're all here: AIDS, insecticides, even plagues of locusts, the bomb, famine.

I think that many people are embracing fundamentalism but possibly they are doing it out of fear rather than out of any sense that this is the only thing that will set us free.

I would be inclined to say that where all renewal is taking place, both in Roman Catholic circles and in the fundamentalist circles and in the *via media* (Anglicanism), those people who are engaging themselves on the ends of the continuum really aren't changing much. They're simply replacing one set of gods with another set of gods. You know, instead of say, technology and consumerism, they've replaced it with spiritual masturbation. I don't see the difference. Hedonism is hedonism, it doesn't make any difference whether you're luxuriating with a fifth of alcohol and a beautiful woman on your knee in a luxurious salon, or whether you're just getting yourself off emotionally in a fundamentalist service. I do think that when you look at some versions of renewal and turn them over, and see the people who are embracing them, in many cases they're just substituting religion for some other form of self-gratification.

It's easy to buy into a system—and let's face it, Christianity is a system—if there's so little requirement, so little investment. There's a paradox there. Sometimes fundamentalist groups, in order to keep one addicted to this notion of salvation, are able to get their constituency to tithe, and to observe certain social restrictions: no smoking, no drinking, no dancing. Some of those things are good on their own. But it seems to me it's the right deed for all the wrong reasons. And it's the wrong emphasis, again.

I think there's a place for absolutism, but as an Anglican, I want to choose that out of free will. I want to choose that as an option for myself, as an option that brings life and not a kind of death, out of the restrictions it imposes.

Or if you observe restrictions, at least there's a recognition that there's a grace that's operative. It's the grace within that enables us to reason. It's a decision we make of our own free will. I guess renewal has always gone on and we're now at a point where it's raised into consciousness and we're seeing it and naming it. Buber's book, *I and Thou*, has always put me on caution about naming anything. If you name anything, you objectify it and therefore kill it.

There's always been some sense of renewal. At the demise of the Roman empire, people thought that the Church was going to disappear. Yet lo and behold, there were islands of spirituality that were just as vibrant, perhaps more vibrant, than at any time prior to that.

But I see hope. Even with all the flux and change, specifically in our church—I firmly believe that this kernel of good will always survive. That's probably the true tradition that will survive, the *real tradition*, regardless of what people wear or how it's said or the shape of the building.

* * *

I remember seeing a sociological study done after Billy Graham's first campaign—the big one in the Fifties, in New York —which found that church attendance, even synagogue attendance, shot up during the campaign. And then there was a marked decrease, even below the level prior to the campaign. So that suggests there's a positive short-term effect, but the long-range effects are negative. It's purely an emotional effect. That says something about the nature of renewal.

You see, I'm not sure what renewal really is. I do know that in the Episcopal Church in the last few years, where a kind of Christian humanitarianism has been stressed and where the emphasis has been on the humanitarian rather than on the Christian—when that took place, there was a marked decline in the quality of the church. Renewal really does have to be a combination of Christ and humanitarianism. And the accent has got to be on Christ in order for renewal to take place. You've got to "have religion."

One thing that sticks in my mind is a quote from Mother Teresa of Calcutta. She tells this when she is being interviewed. The Minister of Social Welfare was visiting the place in Calcutta where she does her work, and had seen what she and her sisters were doing. He said to her, "You and I are doing the same thing but there is a great difference between you and us. We are doing it for something and you are doing it for some*body*. And that is all. I think that explains the reason why the government's social programs have failed. They are just doing something."

The work that Mother Teresa and the sisters were doing was *sacramental*. It *incarnated* the work. And I think where renewal incarnates the religious experience, it's true renewal.

Remember, Paul says, "Always be ready to give an account of that which is within you, which is your faith." And nowhere else in the twentieth century have I seen it articulated so well. We do it *for* Somebody. It suddenly gives meaning to why you own a car or a house or go to work, a meaning which you can't find anywhere else. It's not the same as just reveling in the aesthetics, in the beauty of the liturgy or the music or the vestments; thinking not of the ascetic, only of the *aesthetic.*

Numbers, a head count, don't mean renewal. When I was on the West Coast last week, I went over to the Crystal Cathedral [the Reverend Robert Schuller's church]. (I love to call it the Crystal Palace.) One thing it *does* say is that a Christian community can build a great church in the twentieth century. It's still possible to build cathedrals. We live with this illusion that we're not capable any longer, we're past the great age of the cathedrals, past the age of faith. That we're not capable of making statements to the world about our love of God. I think it's tragic that we've lost that.

But on the other hand, I know that Schuller and that school of thought are still preaching that old Protestant ethic: if you work hard and do all the right things, then God pours out all these abundant blessings as your reward for being good. You never hear them say, however, what is also implicit: all the horrible things that are happening in the world. Famine in Ethiopia—the Christians in Ethiopia are really starving to death; you've got to account for the bad things, too. It's the salvation-through-works idea, and the American idea of progress. Work hard, be good, make money.

I am puzzled by the personality cult in many of the fundamentalist churches that are experiencing renewal. I don't know if this story is true, but it's told about Phillip Brooks, the preacher on the Eastern Seaboard who wrote "O Little Town of Bethlehem." He apparently was asked this question because he preached to packed congregations, and didn't preach in an exciting way. He wrote out his sermons word for word, he wore glasses, and he just kind of went back and forth across the text. But there was something going on. And he was asked what made a great preacher. He said, "It's the Gospel through personality." And it's true: the Gospel does work through personalities. We're incarnationalists and we're talking about God working in the world through the things of the world. Personality is one of them. But what happens so often is that the personality of the person becomes so central that there's no preparation made for the fact that that person might not be there tomorrow.

It seems to me that one of the primary responsibilities of the charismatic personality is that even the personality must die, as all things must die, in order for Christ to be born. Even though God uses the strong charismatic personality, that personality may be the very thing that puts stumbling blocks in people's way.

But numbers are a powerful thing—I love to see a full church. I would love to see my own denomination grow more rapidly. I often am depressed at the thought of how small and struggling we are. About the time we get on our feet, some crisis comes along and we lose half a million people. But I console myself by saying maybe it's this environment in which we're given freedom, we're given grace. And people can't handle freedom, they're afraid.

If you do not want to think, and you still want to be a religious person, there are two very good places for you to go: one is the Roman Church and one is fundamentalism. But Anglicanism is a terrible place to be. There's that old business about making auricular confession in our church. It's available. No one *has* to do it. But if God calls you to do it and you don't get there, you're really in trouble.

I think, in a way, that modern renewal is modern man coming to grips with the idea that he is set free and he's got to find some parameters for his vitality to flourish. I think that the popularity of Scott Peck's books is significant. One reason that he's able to communicate with so many people is because he's *not* using religious jargon. I think that's the kind of style that Christian writers are going to have to develop in order to communicate with the world. C. S. Lewis did it, Charles Williams did it. And even before Williams and Lewis, you saw it emerging in the late-nineteenth-century fantasy literature, with Morris and MacDonald right on up into the twentieth century.

I am convinced that one reason why science fiction gets bigger and bigger in bookstores, and science fiction movies are so popular, is because it is the only place that great tenets of the faith are being marketed today. Both children and adults are eating it up. Look at the morality of *E.T.* It was a morality play. Or *Star Wars.* And then, of course, you begin to see that the great Christian myth—which is true science fiction; as Lewis would say, is a myth that is *true*—the faith of the Gospel, is *real* science fiction.

"Science" meaning what? Knowledge. And fiction, coming from *facio, facere,* to make, making true, making truth. Ironically, it seems to me that the great eternal moral truths of the world are being proclaimed today more in fantasy and romantic literature than in mainstream fiction. And people buy it.

Traditional theology is fairy tale. It's the difference between myth and fairy tale. Maybe Grimm was correct in saying that fairy tale is simply broken and shattered myth. Lewis was always exempt from the criticism that his work was space opera or "mere fantasy" because so much of it was passed off as children's stories. Or the late-nineteenth-century stuff, for that matter—of course, it was romantic fantasy.

To get back to Mother Teresa, she says, "How do we prove that we love God? How do we prove that we love Christ with wholehearted, undivided love and chastity? By giving wholehearted free service to the poor, we believe it is to Jesus. . . . This thing, if it were not for Jesus, would not be worth doing."

I'm trying very hard in my own work to get people to come

back to a grasp of that. It's a major problem because agencies
are so institutionalized. They see themselves as just humanitarian service operations. But they're not. If they do it *for* somebody, that's back to incarnational theology again. And that
brings us full circle, back to where we started two hours ago.

JAMES

*James is an engaging, erudite man with a warm manner and
obvious affection for the people of the church, both laity and clergy.
He now is nearing retirement as diocesan bishop of a large urban-
based Episcopal diocese. We met with him in his office shortly after
he announced his approaching retirement to talk about some of his
experiences and reflections over his two decades in the episcopacy.*

Yes, I have seen it [the return to the Church] too . . . in my
week-by-week experience with the parishes, I have seen people
coming into the Church, coming back to it. One of the features
of the new prayer book, as you know, is the reaffirmation of
vows, and nearly every week there are people who had a
reconversion and would like to affirm this. They were
confirmed as children or in early adolescence, and then have
fallen away. Like you, they wanted something to reconfirm or
signify a new interest in the Church and the faith. And sometimes a spouse is coming into the Church at the same time, and
they do this together.

To talk to them as to some of the reasons why they've come
back is very interesting. Some of them have had a long period
of wandering in the wilderness, trying everything else, and
have come back to the Church. One of our greatest assets is that
we do provide a solid foundation of faith without being so
intellectually closed that people feel there's no room for intellectual honesty about their faith. Historically, we have stressed
that you don't have to make the false dichotomy between

science and religion, between the extremes of creationism and evolution. You don't have to check your brains at the front door every time you enter the church. I think sometimes, for all our confusion, that our lack of rigidity, for some people anyway, is a plus.

Then too, I feel a renewed sense of worship. That's certainly drawing people back, even drawing people from other, less liturgical traditions. The sacramental element is becoming very important to people. In the late fall of 1984 I attended World Communion Sunday in a Lutheran church in Oregon, and there ministers, priests, laity of every denomination, even the most Protestant of the denominations, were talking about a daily Eucharist. And while the Protestants move toward the liturgy, there's a renewed sense of interest among both Roman Catholics and Anglo-Catholics in Scripture and preaching.

There's certainly a movement, at least in the large cities, away from fundamentalism to the sacramental Church. A number of people have told me that when they began to investigate the history of their [fundamentalist] denomination, they began to go back fifty or one hundred years and then boom! Suddenly they were back at the New Testament. And they wondered, "What happened between 100 AD and 1850?" There must have been something; people were not totally unChristian in those years! And then they probed into it and began to discover the riches of historic Christianity. For many of them, those riches had been just an absolute closed chapter. No one ever mentioned the historic Church—as if the Church had been completely heretical and derelict and apostate from the third century until the Reformation! So that sense of a broader perspective on what it means to be a Christian is becoming very important today.

I keep hammering away at this point in sermons: if somebody asks if you're saved, if you're a Christian, for heaven's sake tell them yes. Don't say, "Well, I'm not sure, I'm an

Episcopalian." People are always trying to get you to say it in a particular way, that you've had precisely this or that experience. If they say "When?" you should say "Good Friday, at three o'clock!"

Another thing that marks the current renewal is the new emphasis on spirituality, prayer, the contemplative life. It's too bad the Church had to be reminded of these treasures which it has always had in its armory, by having people go to eastern gurus and find these values there. There's certainly a whole new interest in this area. One of the good things about the current renewal—it's not totally emotional, but also picks up on a return to the Scriptures as the Word of God.

Part of the original turning away from the Church represented a kind of turning away from the middle-class values and the false dichotomy that kids in the Sixties and Seventies saw between what their parents professed on Sunday and the way they may have been living during the week. Many of those students were the ones who dropped away from the churches of the Sixties because they themselves felt uncomfortable with middle-class morality.

The thing that skewed our perceptions a little is that the 1950s represented a kind of "bubble" in church membership. The period was almost an aberration. If you trace the history of overall church membership from colonial days, it grew at a steady pace until the post-war/Eisenhower years created the bubble. And therefore anything less than that is seen as a decline. In reality, statistically, it was an aberration. A lot of the Fifties churchgoers came in under social pressure. I remember that when I was a rector in the suburbs in the late 1950s, the minute you moved into that town, there was someone on your doorstep and you had to say where you were going to church. You had to go to one of two churches. It didn't mean you had to go every Sunday, but you had to *belong.* That was a strange phenomenon. And it made church membership in the Fifties seem much stronger than it actually was.

You mentioned that the decline in church membership parallels the enrollment drop in liberal arts colleges. There's a lesson to be learned there in terms of institutional skepticism. All structures were seen as bad, or at least questionable. In the Sixties and Seventies, all institutions and traditions were challenged. There was a general distrust of tradition. Now people have exhausted all those other avenues and we are looking back on what Christianity has to offer. What attracts people today are those versions of Christianity that don't require your checking your brains at the church door.

In this diocese, we sort of bottomed out in the early 1970s. I find a much stronger sense of commitment now in adult confirmands. Even though the birth rate is lower than in the Sixties, there aren't as many children being confirmed. And there's another change: confirmation is being seen as an *adult* commitment now. I see a great many adults coming for confirmation, even baptism.

In places where renewal is most successful, the real task is re-conversion; keeping people there and active—the ones who were there all the time. Getting them to read a new book, to go to classes . . . they'll say, "Oh, I know all this already!" Some of them stopped thinking and examining their faith the day they were confirmed. They hung in the Church even when the mass exodus started—but to get *these* people renewed and re-charged is a little more difficult. They kind of resent all this wave of new people—but the places that have been able to meet that challenge have succeeded.

We still have a big job ahead of us in trying to reintegrate Christianity into the life of the home. We also have to guard against the liturgy becoming an end in itself—and we have to recapture the sense of community of the early Church. That's much easier in a small parish than a large one, where you may not be missed for several Sundays. There's no geographical parish anymore, so we have to create our own definition of community.

I always tell people in my Inquirers' class and before confirmation that the Creeds and the Articles of Faith are not a sort of religious steeplechase. You can accept the Creed in its totality, but it may take years to accept every single individual tenet of the faith. We grow through participation. If you can believe that God was in Christ, reconciling the world to Himself, that's the real basis of faith. The great doctrine is the Incarnation and that's our basic belief. Without that, the Church is nothing.

But faith is not an obstacle course. The faith that is commending itself to people now celebrates life, but is also realistic about human sin and failure. And that's where renewal in the 1980s is leading us.

BENNETT

Bennett is the former bishop of Atlanta, and is presently the executive director of the Institute for Servant Leadership at Emory University in Atlanta. He tells a remarkable story of religious and ethical renewal in the business community.

I came out of a teaching ministry at Virginia Seminary, was elected bishop of Atlanta in 1971, and I enjoyed being bishop very much; I relished the chance to do something I felt the whole institution needed, in terms of some new directions and underpinnings with regards to the quality of leadership.

I spent most of my administrative energies on the business of creating a system that would evoke the most suitable people —get them into the training track and then support them until they went off to retirement and even beyond retirement. It's beyond retirement that I find is the most important time to be supportive.

We developed a womb-to-tomb, minister-to-the-minister program—and when that work was well in place and I could begin to see the fruits of it, I thought, Well, I don't know that I want to stay until I'm sixty-five. I'd like to get back into teaching, particularly into the area of continuing education for the experienced, especially those who, like myself, had no training for what they did so I thought I'd do something about that.

We bishops are just dumped into this office suddenly, you know, and there's lots to be understood that you're just not told about. Matter of fact, the joke is, you never really *do* learn it.

And I discovered, reading and talking—particularly with Robert G., who became my mentor—that there is this same kind of nonpreparation for all tasks in big institutions. I learned that the tour of duty for CEOs is decreasing steadily, the duration of their work. Disenchantment sets in rather quickly. And spiritual, inner depletion occurs. So the more I thought about that, the more I thought, Well, maybe we could expand the concept of leadership education to embrace all institutions, particularly since it was not the church that was the principal shaping agent.

At one time in the Middle Ages the really significant cultural-shaping decisions were made where the power was. Where the money was. Now, they are made in politics, big business, big government, big unions, big education, so that's where the church needs to make its influence felt. And that's the proposal I took to the president of the university about three years ago: let's start a "servant leadership" program for the people who make the decisions.

I said, "Really, I'd like to try this, what do you think?" And he said, "Let's do it."

And so, last November, I left the diocese at age sixty-three, figuring that I had one more trick up my sleeve before I ran out of gas. The diocese was wonderful in its understanding and there was a man right there whom they loved, ready to take my place, and carry right on. So I think that system is very healthy and in good hands and is happy with itself.

How to do *this*, I don't know. We are groping for a way in which to build those bridges between Christian commitment or moral sensitivity and the management of systems that are "in business to stay in business," one of which is the Church.

Because our theology is not survival, it's expansionist, and expansionist obedience means that you've got to pay attention to all the factors that go into the expansion of any kind of product: the right people, the right place at the right time, supported, motivated, embraced, and then—money. There's plenty of money in this culture, and those who know how, I think, prevail as institutionally successful and important.

There are some basic assumptions. The other underlying assumption is that institutions all come into being to enlarge and liberate human life. It's the meaning of America, it's the meaning of the Church. Any legitimately established institution has that purpose. To enhance human life.

And then those things that afflict the human spirit, that make us fearful, oppressive, and tyrannical, oppress all institutions: those are the forces, it seems to me, that the leader is constantly dealing with in himself and in his system.

The common worldly ethic tends to be "Sure, do it unto them before they do it unto you!" Which is, of course, self-destructive. Both ethically and practically. If you can really historicize the self-destructive character, that's what its basic policy is. But what, for example, is to turn the American automobile industry around, except paying attention to some of the things that motivate a more successful industry?

To give you an idea of what we're trying to do here at the Institute for Servant Leadership, we give seminars that are of five days' duration, at least so far. We only began it last November; we've had two so far. I'm here now designing another retreat in November. See the schedule: we try to multiply these here. It's a beautiful location, close enough so that they can keep in touch with Atlanta by telephone—but even that's discouraged.

At any event, we just try to combine some fundamental things, three actually: ethics, business, and theology. Theology being the undergirding approach, and that's my job. And I really mean this: I don't know how to do this yet. Except I am beginning to get some illumination, beginning to get a little clearer as time goes on.

At the November seminar about two-fifths of those five days, maybe three-fifths, are spent interacting, and the evaluation so far of the two experiences we have had shows that the most valuable experience they've had is the interacting. There is loneliness in all of us, a rootlessness and an aimlessness, or at least a wonder: "Are my values going to work? Or will they stand in the way? How do I measure success? What is success anyway?"

And more than anything else, we discovered that people in responsible roles help each other. The chief criticism is that we are not clear enough yet about servant leadership in conceptual terms, and we know that. But in that two-fifths didactic approach, we try to pull into the concept of servant leadership the disciplined insights of theology—that's one thing—and ethics, which is the bridge between theology and business, or institutional management.

So we need to find a way in which to enlarge on the practical aspect of this so that they can get handles on how to function as servant leaders. We are unashamed that there is a retreat component here that draws on the intuitive spirituality in people. It's not a business course—Harvard can do that—but we've discovered through our own research that businesses, the big corporations, value two attributes in the people whom they ask to assume major responsibilities: those are integrity, and sensitivity to other people.

But most companies have no plan to encourage or reinforce,

enlarge upon, or interpret the meaning of these two attributes that they most depend upon. They expect the people whom they most need to have those attributes when they get there and to find ways to nourish them on their own.

In the business world, it's "*Be* it, but don't talk it." We want to talk it. We note that the "being it" is much more appropriate and truly fulfilling, and that's about as far as I can say we've gone.

As far as our participants are concerned, let me just give you some statistics. In the first seminar we had fifteen people. Fourteen of them were there because I knocked on their doors. The second seminar, we had fifteen people and twelve of them were there because they had their doors knocked on. In the seminar scheduled in November there are twenty-three signed up. That means we'll have eighteen, and only half of them are there because I knocked on their door.

In other words, people have begun to knock on *our* door. Or others recruit them for us, I don't know. That's an encouraging shift. My own assumption is that if this is not self-recruiting ultimately—for example, as in having contracts with companies that want their executives to have this kind of exposure—that's what I am hoping for eventually. That's what I am aiming for: that the program becomes self-supporting. Right now, it's largely grants. And that's okay too. We like a capital investment, we're trying not to make any money the first couple of years. Five years out—well, we'll see.

Now the consequences, if you're interested: these are both owners of businesses who were present at the first seminar last December. One man told me that that five-day period turned his life in another direction. He was content with the status quo, he was making money, and he has since formed a corporate board. It was a very closely held private company, all decisions made by the CEO and executives, and it has expanded and taken on a whole new product line at immense capital risk. And I am a member of his new board. So I'm now a corporate director!

It's been a wonderful, eye-opening experience for me, to see how a big company functions. The policy statement of that reorganized company is really a remarkable piece of work.

The other effect has been to change the extent to which another company in Atlanta, a development company, has taken some of its profits and poured them into development of housing for the poor in Atlanta's Grant Park. That has been done through some kind of federal linkages.

I want to be responsive to your purposes. You've asked for names of people. I understood you to be writing a book on people who are recently returned to the Church. Fascinating! I just wish we had more time because I would like to know what you have found out about that. A sea-change, you call it.

And a publisher in New York really *did* buy a prospectus for such a book? They're waking up. And you've had adventures on your trip already, with all the people whose lives you've touched! That's evangelism, it really is. Your lives have been enriched.

Our seminars, I would hope, may eventually bring some people into the church, but I don't think so yet. Most of these people are in earnest about their church affiliation, but don't see in their church affiliations much help in making the connections between what they do in church on Sunday and how to run something practically as a money-making operation on a Monday. But they're ready to try to learn. They see how urgently this servant model is needed in business and feel sometimes a little helpless to get it installed.

I hope we can stay in touch. We'll put you on our mailing list. And I do want to read your book.

ELFVIN

Elfvin is a marvelously jovial and earnest young priest in a small church near a university in Des Moines, Iowa. He has a gift for putting people at ease and sharing his own insights with them. We talked to Elfvin for only an hour, but we felt that we had known him all our lives. His opening remarks were in response to questions about people returning to the church after a long absence.

I would like to think that almost everybody eventually finds his or her way back to the Church. Maybe in a new way, because the faith you left isn't the faith you want to keep. Often you find something that's much more viable, something that was always there, but you just hadn't seen it before.

So I appreciate your sharing your story. I hope we see more and more of that, people staying away for a long time and for a variety of reasons, and saying, "If there were someplace else I could go and get the same thing I get from the Church, I would. But there isn't, so I'm in church."

A person with a similar story who comes to mind is Janice B., who had been in St. Timothy's parish years ago and left the Church for a period of time. She had been . . . well, I guess it was around the time of her divorce that she left the Church. Just didn't want the hassle. And in quite a matter-of-fact way she would tell you: "I stopped praying, I stopped the whole thing." I don't remember the exact year, because we often talked together during that time. But she's finally back at St. Timothy's. She came here after her time of absence and gradually became more comfortable with the church. Her daughters, oddly enough, continued at St. Timothy's all that time, and the whole family is finally back together at this parish in West Des Moines.

Janice leapt to my mind, but there are others, like our Altar Guild president, for example. She was baptized just a few years ago, had certainly known about the Church a long time before that. But it was only two years ago or so that she finally got around to doing that and attaching herself to a congregation. And there must have been a reason.

I don't know if the fellow I'm about to tell you about is what you're looking for, but let's see if it fits. He grew up as a Baptist and then for a time even attended the First Federated Church here in town, which is a very outgoing, nondenominational church that really is its own denomination. He went there for a time with great enthusiasm for the church. But he eventually had no part of it at all, he just rejected the whole experience. He married a lady who had been a Roman Catholic. I don't know if she continued to go to church, or if he made fun of her religion, or what—I have no idea.

I'm not sure exactly what transpired. I won't say he ever completely lost his faith, but I will say he got more and more disappointed in what he found in the Church. He rejected the Federated experience, and he didn't want to be a Catholic or a Baptist.

So years later, his brother got married in this church. The girl he married had some ties here. He came to this church just for a wedding service and in the course of it said, "This is really *right*. This isn't nearly as crazy as I had thought." And he's been here ever since. That's got to be four years ago.

We have some college students here. We certainly take ministry to them as a very serious mission of this church. Recently, we were going through a renewal drive to knock out walls and put in an elevator for handicapped people. One of the things we talked about was instead of trying to find parking where we are—was just close it up and move the whole parish somewhere else.

One of the major objections to that, although economically I don't think it would have been too difficult, was that we had a unique ministry to the university campus with our presence here, near fraternity row. And the students who had studied here and made a commitment to religion during their college years—you can't just abandon that kind of mission because, in fact, one of the appeals of the Church is to take somebody who actually has a brain and can think about theology and make it sound like respectable sense to him. And if that isn't represented on a college campus, I don't know where else it will be.

I think very often we get people who come from various traditions, and in college they will experiment a bit and go around to various churches and look for some answers. This church doesn't have all the answers. If it did, it certainly hasn't grown that way. But I think we have enough of the right answers so that it is a mission given by God to be here for people who need it, especially for people in academic circles who need it.

There's been a kind of sea change in universities also. The students are more receptive to the liberal arts now than they used to be. A few years ago, it was just, "My opinion is as good as yours, it's all opinion anyway, so why bother?" Just misinterpretations of John Dewey's educational philosophy. You get that same sort of thing in religion. I can remember in the late Fifties and early Sixties, a lot of us felt that religion was a sort of antiquated, outmoded, anthropological oddity, and no one really had to take it seriously anymore. Now people go back and reread the books that took them away from the Church and find they had thrown the baby out with the suds all the way through.

That's very easy to do, you know. And I think there's a natural tendency on the part of all students to do it. Even in seminary. Last summer, I attended an advanced seminary program and my disappointment was twofold. The first part was that while I was there, I thought I was trying to find out what kind of a minister I might make and no one seemed interested in that question. What they *were* interested in was whether or not I had read the text, and did I know what it said. I felt as though we were missing the most important part.

The second thing is that I thought that the community—the seminary community itself—was entirely too cautious when it came to advancing the tenets of the Christian religion. When you come right down to it, the Resurrection, like it or not, is very much what we're about. The Resurrection! If there were no Resurrection, we could probably just gather in a philosophical club somewhere and talk about the nature of the world.

It seems to me that in the academic environment—liberal arts or whatever—we must concede that much has been done to proclaim strongly that the only right answers are scientific answers after all. In philosophy, it's like Charles Sanders Peirce's fixation of belief: a classic example of that. But we live in an age which lives with that continual verification of the present time being the be-all and end-all.

When you're on the campus and you're talking about Resurrection, people say, I don't know what you're talking about. Let's go at this a different way. How could we socially improve the world and the demographics? Then they all say, "Oh, well, *this* we understand." So we all sit down and talk about demographics and social programs. And the Church quietly goes away, even when you're in seminary, because they want the academic credentials so badly.

I went to Princeton this summer because I wanted to see if anything had changed in all these years. One thing had, and I was scared to death. This program that I was in at Princeton, they really did want to find out what I *thought*. And I found out I don't think nearly as much as I should. That's more threatening than the other would be. They didn't want just my final opinion: they wanted all the steps. You try to sort that out, and it's a scary business.

But most people's essential attitude, about the things that are genuinely religious, is still to put them at arm's length. I talked to a guy at Princeton about the Holy Spirit—didn't get to the Resurrection, that's too big a question—I was just talking about the Holy Spirit, and he said, "Well, we've got a student here who's really into the Holy Spirit. He took a test, and did a terrible job, and I flunked him. He came to me afterwards and said, 'Look, the Holy Spirit came to me and told me what to do on this test.' And the professor said, 'Well, you'd better consult Him again because the Holy Spirit told me to give you an F.'"

So the student was there, sort of scratching his head, trying to figure things out. What the professor was really trying to say was, I don't know what the Holy Spirit is or where he is, I just don't want to talk about it. I came back to the professor saying, "If you don't want to talk about it, then the only people who are going to be talking about the Spirit are all the kooks who don't understand it anyway. You know, you've run away from it, not because you don't believe in it but because you think it's too hard. But if it's hard for you, think how hard it is for the other people."

I don't know if he was going to take my advice; he isn't necessarily going to listen to me. But the point is that the Church in the academic environment has often backed away from *being* the Church, because it wasn't comfortable in proclaiming the Gospel. No wonder people lost their way, or lost interest. You talk about people losing interest in the Church. Years ago the Church stopped talking about its essential message.

And finally, what exactly constitutes a human being? My son works for a little country club and polishes golf balls. There's a race to find out who can have the best golf clubs and the biggest car. Yet, we must all concede that this is a very empty thing. You can't measure a human being by what he owns. Surely it's something on the inside.

Even the basic things in life are less important than this.

They aren't unimportant; we have to be able to eat in order to ask the questions. But that is less important than what you're eating *for*.

Recently I was in Philadelphia and a friend of mine got lost. We had been told very carefully about what route to take—you go through the park on that lovely drive and so forth—but we missed a turn. And we wound up in the most incredible ghetto expanse that I had ever seen.

I don't know, it's just something about the way Philadelphia is built, it's just a closer city, the homes and the apartments, it's just very tight in the way doors line up vertically. There was just a great sea of hopelessness. And you try to find an answer to that. If only someone could begin to address that in a way that could be heard, in a way that would really make a difference!

It's a problem that just doesn't go away. *All* the people around need to hear and understand and feel that community. They need to experience what it means to be truly God's people.

As you say, I suspect that people sort of intuit that and that's why they are coming back to church. I don't think they understand it rationally, I don't think they have made all the connections, but I think that is one of the reasons why people come back to the Church.

I grew up in a scientific community. Both my parents were engineers and we had a scientific explanation for everything. But we were also a part of the Church. I always felt, at least from the sense in our family, that science would eventually solve every problem. We all really believed that science had all the answers and sooner or later we'd advance to the point where we'd have all the answers, and wouldn't need this crutch called religion. But that myth, that science is omnipotent, has been exploded much more rapidly than I would ever have thought.

There was also a movement, . . . a kind of a Bohemian thing, a sort of romance about being lost twenty or thirty years ago. There was a whole generation of people, of college students and intellectuals, who thought being lost was so marvelous . . . a whole generation of people just wallowed in being lost and knew there was no God, and no hope, and all was despair, and all was nothingness, and it was just marvelous. Because then you had no ethical obligations to anybody.

Remember that great scene in Woody Allen's *Play It Again, Sam* where Woody cannot get a date and he goes to the art museum? There is something being subtly said about people who hang around art museums, there is a certain type, and it's very much what we were just describing: the cynic who's decided the whole world is garbage in the first place and that what we need to do is to find a way to express the Infinite Void.

Then Woody sneaks up to a woman and says, "What do you see?" and she says, "I see the utter depravity of mankind, the hopelessness of the world, the total galactic void, the emptiness of everything," and Woody says, "Okay, what are you doing Saturday night?" And she says, "Committing suicide." And he says, "How about Friday?" There's so much in that! You're right. It was so in vogue to be empty.

Maybe Gail Sheehy was right in the article you mentioned: we've passed that point now, the despair and the romance of being lost. The renewal movement—of which religion is only one symptom—also includes a renewal of patriotism, and the recognition that it's okay to be patriotic, interested in the values of the country and home and church and so on. It's no longer so vogue-ish to be in despair all the time.

People who are returning to the Church are finding that they now have a whole new vocabulary. How marvelous it is to be able to say, "Well, the Lord arranged this for us or made this happen," whereas a few years ago, we wouldn't have said this. We'd have said "good luck" or "random factors," as Commander Spock would say, made it happen.

It's really a miracle, isn't it? Who would ever have thought in the 1960s that we would be sitting here in Des Moines, Iowa, in the 1980s, talking about religion?

GREGORY

Gregory is a strikingly handsome, articulate man with a gentle manner, piercing gray eyes, and a ready sense of humor. A former Benedictine monk, he was ordained priest in the mid-Sixties and has spent fifteen years as rector of a pastoral-size parish in Chicago. He is widely sought-after as a spiritual director and retreat leader. An aura of genuine spirituality surrounds the man; you can sense it in everything he says and does. This conversation with him took place on a rainy spring afternoon in Easter Week when we asked him to reminisce about parishioners who had returned to the Church.

Well, I'm not one who remembers very well, as you know . . . not individual stories, anyway. But I do find a repeated pattern in people, a search for something deeper and more fundamental than even the good things of secular life. Many of the people now returning to the Church have everything, have always had everything, materially speaking. Yet they had a sense that there must be more to life than this. A spiritual hunger, the ultimate desire for a direction—that's what motivates many of them.

Many people went to college in the Sixties and Seventies and decided that there was nothing to religion. They did EST and yoga and encounter-group therapy and finally came into the Church a decade or two later almost by accident—to discover that this was what they had been looking for all this time. They just didn't know it.

It's strange. In talking about the spiritual hunger that some people experience . . . the other side of that coin is, we get people who are attracted by the externals only. And then it's interesting to see the difference between those who find those externals a means to an end, and those who rest in the externals. And if they get caught in the trappings, those externals become passé, almost distasteful to them, and they move on to something else. They'll fall away almost always. They touch the community, the Church, and then they move on. They haven't reached through the "vesture, gesture, and posture" to the real sacramental Church . . . and so they get satiated with liturgy and vestments and music and don't move on to anything deeper.

One source of disillusionment, too, is the extent to which a church can become secularized. This was the disillusionment of many with the post-Vatican II Church: the feeling that God was absent and the sociologists had taken over.

I think the Sixties saw a real change. Many people, when the social upheavals of the Sixties came along—and the Church did get involved in and respond to social issues—still, many dedicated people did not really accept or understand these social forces and their impact on the Church. There were a lot of real activists in the Church. And more left than came in, so that accounts for the overall lowering of membership, I suppose . . . that's when I was in the monastery, so I didn't have a lot of direct experience with this period when people were leaving.

Now there's a general movement back toward conservatism. Perhaps people realize it's all right to think about institutions again. Of course, after any revolution comes a retrenchment, and the Sixties were certainly a revolution. There's that dimension too. Some of the people who are now in the church are the revolutionaries of the Sixties come home again.

It's always interesting to me to see how one movement after another sweeps the country. And clearly the Church, because it lives in society, has to be affected by all this and has to respond to it. The Church by itself doesn't make the culture, but it lives in it and has to respond to it. I don't know how one balances all this; how we avoid losing our souls in succumbing to one fad after another, how we hold on to the fundamentals of faith. The secret is to remain contemporary, involved, in touch with all these things, but also in touch with the deeper fundamentals and with one's personal and cultural roots. One of the reasons churches as institutions tend to be conservative is to maintain that continuity—that sense of a tradition and a unique identity within the tradition.

We're in a transition decade and we really don't know what will come next. We don't know what role the Church will play. But traditionally, in transitional times the Church plays an important role. The Dark Ages, for example, are really a misnomer, as Ralph just said. The Church perpetuated whatever culture we had. It was the *only* place where culture was preserved and valued.

Historically, at the end of these transitional periods, things fall into place again and people begin to have definite beliefs —whereas ten years ago, they might only have believed in whatever was popular that day. So in the 1980s the Church is becoming an important social force again.

Maybe the common element in all this is a spiritual hunger. But burn-out is the biggest problem. And it's a paradox, isn't it? People come because of this intense spiritual hunger, they find a place in the Church, they want the satisfaction that comes with contributing something. But they get so caught up in the externals that they lose the ability to accept the original gift of grace. It's Wednesday of Easter Week: already that glory [of the Easter Vigil] is fading into the past. If only we could avoid that, even we as clergy. To paraphrase St. Paul, after preaching to others, we don't want to find ourselves castaways!

In an ordination sermon for a young seminarian, I once said,

"If you don't let Christ come into your life every day, ever more fully, and guide you in all you do, you'll fall flat on your face as a priest." Those are hard words. It's very hard to do that.

Some will say the Church is just like any secular institution. Of course it is "just any secular institution" in one sense. If you look at it superficially, you see people involved in all sorts of business, even if it is "religious" business. If you look at it only on a superficial level, you can certainly say that. But there's another dimension—not just "the Church as institution" but the Church as the sacramental Body of Christ.

In the same way, "renewal" can mean anything from a charismatic TV preacher to certain modern, gaudy styles of vestments and free-standing altars. But renewal as we are talking about it here can also be a wonderful thing. Literally, it means to *make new* our life in grace, in prayer, in sacrament.

Almost more fascinating for me than why people return is why they left in the first place. I'm not sure . . . people have zeal and commitment for a time, and somewhere along the way, the initial glory goes; it does for everybody. And the day-by-day, year-by-year drudgery takes over. It's like a relationship—it's all glory and sparks flying at first. But then something quieter, deeper—hopefully—takes over in its place. But that doesn't always happen in the Church. And I don't know why that is.

There are the precipitous things: people who leave "because they changed the liturgy" or because they changed choir directors. Or those who didn't like the sermon, or the hymn, or because the priest didn't wear a biretta one day. It's obviously not trivial; it's very important to the person at the time. But their priorities aren't straight. If it's more important to have one person as choirmaster, hear one hymn sung, one sermon preached, then obviously that person's spirituality hangs on the wrong thing in the first place.

To come to church for what you can "get out of it" is a mistake. It's another case of having the wrong priorities. You don't come, first of all, to get something but to give yourself back to God in worship and praise. And yet we hear that—I hear that—all the time: "I don't get anything out of it anymore, Father, so I don't come." But if the Church really is the body of Christ on earth, our presence enlivens and enriches that body and makes it an ongoing thing.

That's the area in which something really *has* happened. People now come back to the Church to give . . . to give *themselves* to God. They've gradually fallen away from giving, have learned to ask only what they can *get*. Now there's a whole new dimension they must learn to deal with. Now they're in a situation in which they get so much out of it that they want badly to put something back *into* it. That spiritual hunger I spoke of—in a way, we can interpret that hunger as a desire to receive, a desire to be fed. We get from Our Lord an overwhelming abundance, more than we need, can ever need.

But the hunger can also be interpreted as a need to give ourselves *to* something, to make a total surrender to God. To me, that's what that basic offering, that gift of ourselves every Sunday, is all about. The liturgy doesn't start with the procession into the church with crucifer and acolytes and torchbearers and clergy, but with ourselves, when we roll out of bed and shower and drive to the church: *that's* the beginning of the liturgy. We symbolize this when we enter the church and take that wafer from the bread box and put it into the ciborium— we're giving *ourselves* to be carried up to the altar as an offering to God in His risen Son.

But God doesn't give us anything as a reward for good behavior. We can't receive what is given unless we open our hearts and accept the workings of grace. I think the people who leave balk, somehow, at self-surrender, at giving *themselves* in this way . . . if only they could come to understand that unless we are open to Him, we can't receive His grace. That dimension is always there: God's giving is totally free, but we can't receive the gift until we can open our hearts to Him.

FRANK

Frank is a quick, engaging, articulate man in his mid-forties who has recently become Bishop Coadjutor of a large urban diocese. He was rector of a large East Coast parish for over a decade and has supported the ministries of women, minorities, and the handicapped and a wide variety of lay ministries. He is well-known as a spiritual director and has participated in a thirty-day retreat on Ignatian meditation. Our conversation with him begins as we speculate together on the phenomenon of the generation of the Sixties returning to the Church.

The people I have dealt with most are people who were very much social activists in the Sixties. They genuinely believed that if we just tried hard enough and were clear enough about our thinking, we really could bring in the Kingdom. I think that the naïveté of that time—and I certainly was part of it too —involved a real overlooking of *sinfulness;* of the way in which grand schemes could become aggressive and manipulative, and, conversely, how various patterns of resistance could emerge in the process of trying to get something done. Often they came out of oneself, if one wanted to be the initiator of the project and there was someone coming along who had actually a better vision of the whole—the initiator might find ways to sabotage him or her.

In any event, lots of people became profoundly disillusioned. Also, we can't overlook the fact that the Church is organic and processive—and sometimes these dramatic assaults on a previous consciousness, within the Body of Christ, simply produce greater resistance instead of bringing about a conversion. And so many people showed an incapacity to be compassionate toward limitations. Some people were actually converted and brought along toward a new consciousness—yet that didn't seem to happen very much. Instead, there was an attitude of "I'm right and you're wrong," and the anger that this produced—and the disaffections . . . "Well, the institution's hopeless," "They're all hypocrites," "They don't move fast enough."

I think particularly of a friend of mine. I consider him a friend; actually, I didn't even know him until he came back. A gay activist, central in starting Integrity and all the rest of it. Actually, he was into every cause imaginable, had hair out to here—everything about him suggested challenge and confrontation. Anyhow, just to use him as an example: he renounced his orders when the General Convention in Denver said that no one who is "an active homosexual" is appropriate for the ordination process. So he turned in his orders at that point.

Then he went off and started a restaurant in Philadelphia. It was immensely successful. And he kept saying to himself, "I don't need the Church, this is much more real. People are more honest and human, there's less hypocrisy."

Then—I'm not quite sure what moved him, but he went to a liturgy in a church in Philadelphia. And something sort of . . . *pierced* him. And he was in confusion for a while, because he realized that as much as he hated the Church and rejected it, there was some bond there that couldn't be turned yet into fully formed words.

In any event, he went—he kept going to that church. And then he went to see the assistant bishop, who was very much a liberal activist. And the bishop told him that he needed spiritual direction, and sent him to me. And that's when I first met this person, after having observed him at a distance in the

Sixties as the most radical of the gay activists. By now he had his hair cut and looked quite different. And I remember listening to him and saying to him "Repent."

At which point he burst into tears.

And so began a very marvelous season for me and also for him, in which he basically caught up with some of the things he had so definitively rejected, and in very personal terms.

And now I'll generalize again. The thing that's been so interesting to me is that people who acted out of their own *unredeemed* energies, motivated by consummate good will and a desire to save humankind, went through a disillusionment, saw the Church as a part of the pattern of falseness. They really went through a death.

Since you call your book *The Road to Damascus,* I think Paul is very helpful here. Paul, as I see him, had built a whole structure of piety to offset a low self-worth. But this piety was self-generated. According to his own confession in Galatians, it exceeded even the boundaries that were established by tradition—that kind of obsessive-compulsive drive. Which I think many of these people [the Sixties radicals] had: they were going to go beyond the limits to bring in the Kingdom.

And then the whole thing fell apart. They weren't quite hit over the head by Jesus on the road, but the whole structure of their piety fell apart. And they realized that salvation was not to be found in unrelenting self-generated efforts to change the structures of society and the Church. They had to have the real experience of poverty, disillusionment, alienation from the Christian community—and I think probably, too, of a season in which they had to come to terms with their own profound self-alienation. They projected this alienation onto the institution, but much of their disaffection had to do with throwing oneself too unreservedly into massive movements of revolution and change. And when the movement didn't succeed, you couldn't feel good about yourself; the movement hadn't justified your efforts. So you were back once again with your fragility and incompleteness.

And that kind of experience of one's own interior poverty has really brought a number of people to a deeper place, a more honest place, both in respect to themselves and in respect to the Lord. And so there's really been a conversion, a dying to self, a dying to the projections that one had created out of his or her own imagination. Those projections were fired by goodwill, even grace, up to a point—but ultimately were evil since they involved exceeding the limits of the grace actually being offered. It was a distorted generosity, a trying to do too much, that then becomes bitterness, anger, and finally ends in the collapse of the project.

I think people went through that kind of disillusionment which involved coming home to the truth of themselves and the limits of what an institution can do, and back to a recognition of the *absolute* primacy of grace.

The people that have come to me for spiritual direction over the last few years are ready to hear, "You can't do it by yourself." It's a relief for them to hear it. It's a new beginning. This is in no sense that kind of vacuous passivity that we associate with much of fundamentalism—"Just sit back and God's going to take care of everything." There's a sense of personal responsibility, but grounded in the notion that one has to cooperate with grace. One can't overrule it, one can't exceed it. And therefore there's a capacity to listen that wasn't there before. There's a capacity for compassion that comes from being able to accept one's limitations. In saying yes to oneself, one can say yes to the frailties, foibles, incompleteness of everyone else. And you don't get quite as angry. The zeal is tempered now. Even grand schemes are less likely to be imposed on someone but to be, instead, lived out in the limits of your and their humanity.

People who come to this point in their spiritual journeys

sense that they are changing, that they are in process. They sense that they are becoming something different. They can't put a finger on the exact change or the trigger point, but they sense it. Some of them even speak of being *formed* or *shaped*.

Week before last, I was reading William Law and ran across the phrase "the process of Christ," which I found quite marvelous. I think that Christ *is* a process—Christ *happens* to us, and Christ happens through the very circumstances of our lives. The shaping and the forming go on, and a word—a word is formed, sometimes even below the level of consciousness. And then something triggers it. The gay activist going back to the liturgy couldn't tell me what it was, but *something* was released and began to move toward consciousness that he knew intuitively had been there the whole time. Although he didn't have access to it and anger had helped bury it . . . The same with Valerie's experiencing the crucifix that triggered the Donne poem "Goodfriday 1613."

It strikes me, too, that the Resurrection happened when everyone was asleep. The people had to cope with a sudden shift that had occurred, that was imposing a change of consciousness on them. But no one was there to see it. It just sort of happened, there between nightfall and daybreak, and people had to try to catch up with it. We've been trying to catch up to it ever since.

Along that line: as I read Paul—and Paul's been a very important person to me—the real conversion begins with the stoning of Stephen. Paul is there and he's not aware, consciously, of being pierced by the living Word in the radiance of Stephen. But the very fact that we're told that he began with a new earnestness to harry the church would suggest that something had shifted. Something told him, "Stamp this out or it may get you." Then the road to Damascus becomes simply the curious moment when for reasons unknown, the word comes to consciousness and the shift occurs. We may not hear that word for weeks, months, even years, but it's there. It's there.

For my friend that I've used as my primary example, but for plenty of others as well, there is a sort of zero point. I see this traveling into death with people—people who did not have an articulated faith, sort of cultural, nominal Christians who suddenly discover they have leukemia—that sort of thing. It's amazing to me that as everything is stripped away, and the person is brought into closer proximity with the simple fact that he or she *is*, with no way of distracting the self from that primary reality, with distractions or fantasies—when he or she has simply to deal with being at the heart of existence, the person finds something. And not out of the wish to be rescued from a desperate situation. But when you get to the thin place where fundamental reality is being experienced, that's where God is. It has to be an experience of God if God is truth and reality. And so people find faith, almost by accident, when they're brought to the zero point. Not out of a spirit of "Get me out of this and I promise to worship You." It's just there, at the deepest level.

Then on the other side of it, in spiritual direction, you're dealing with an incredible gift to share. People are not looking for a piety of escape any longer. Everything is profoundly existential: Where does Christ touch me? Where does my own unfolding connect with the whole notion of "what we shall be, as yet to be revealed . . . growing from glory to glory as we reflect His image," as Paul says? All that notion—that assimilation of a pattern and deep personal integration—is central to the new spirituality, as opposed to an older, exterior rule.

I must say that in spiritual direction, too, you'll often get someone who's gone through a conversion. Then you must spend months disconnecting him or her from a fundamentalist background, a self-castigating evangelical heritage. These people are prisoners of that interior sensor, the inauthentic conscience.

This new emphasis on spirituality is changing the Church as well as the people coming back. At the heart of it is a clear understanding that my life experience is a dimension of Scripture; that I need to appropriate and create and affirm my own life experiences as a part of discipleship. This, as opposed to a notion that the discipline, the life of the Church, is over here, mysticism is over here—and I have to climb this incredible mountain and use *these* skills and acquire *this* vocabulary before I can really think of myself as a fully articulated Christian. The whole notion that God is already in the heart of your own lived moment and you need to listen to those moments, and the Gospel will give you a vocabulary for talking about them—or discerning certain movements and invitations within the givens of your human reality: that is the way the new spirituality in the Church is moving now. It is a much more existential approach to Christianity.

I'd say, too, that people are able to use a faith language without embarrassment, which is lovely—and without having to say in apology, "I'm not a fundamentalist, but . . ." Now we can talk about where Jesus is in our lives this week without feeling ridiculous.

I think Jung has been very helpful here. Under the banner of "scientific inquiry," he's given people access to the numinous dimension and the mystery of life. Persons who were reluctant once just to be persons of prayer now can look at some of the Jungian structures and metaphors and say, "Well, I'm not totally rational . . . there's a whole other dimension to me, and that's okay."

I was thinking, as we were talking, of Simone Weil's conversion. She had gone off to the Abbey of Solesmes for Easter—she was not yet a person of faith, [she was] a Jewish intellectual with no particular religious ties. Someone gave her a book of George Herbert's poetry—she was interested in "English literature of the seventeenth century" and all that. She read "Love bade me welcome" and she thought that she was just reading a beautiful poem. Later she noted in her diary that as she read it over for the third or fourth time, "Jesus Christ came down and possessed me totally." Yet she thought she was just dabbling in literature, as you two were dabbling in music that Easter Sunday!

I recently did a retreat for some seminarians who are graduating this May. In their reflections there was a common thread: a constant of being chased by the hound of heaven and not being able to get away—of offering all sorts of rationalizations, and then by some quirk, the realization zapping them—all the while going to church and saying, "I'm only here for aesthetic reasons, it has nothing to do with belief."

To dream about the Church in the next decade for a moment: I think a lot is happening and will happen in terms of what I call support groups. People who have had some kind of common experience, who see their spirituality as something profound to be lived and not simply an external decoration . . . in a very healthy way, they see they can't do it alone. They see that you need other travelers—in fact, many of the renewal efforts in the Church at the present moment have this sense of continuing support groups. I find, for instance, that the increase of one-on-one spiritual direction has a lot to do with people recognizing the fact that they may have had these shattering, highly personal experiences, but the *content* is common to the Christian community. They need to figure out what faithfulness is going to mean in terms of their own lives— which involves sharing the journey with other Christians, very much like an AA group.

Right now, I see this element like leaven. It's all so innocent —these marvelous, wonderful personal experiences—but in consequence, the Church will ultimately become much less hierarchical—at least, it will *live* less hierarchically.

We're coming to see that if we really take the liturgy seri-

ously, liturgy can identify the Church to itself. If we use lay
ministries intelligently and well in celebration, the liturgy
becomes human-scaled. If we do it right, we are again enacting
the central mystery of the Church. We're *playing,* in a way—
playing out the reality of the Church. And things should follow from it—for example, the community exchanging the
Peace in this formal liturgical context must mean that we are
to support one another and be Christ to one another, beyond
the confines of a formal liturgy.

So we really *need* the other members of the body of Christ
in more than a formal liturgical context. If liturgy identifies the
Church to itself and if we take renewal seriously, we will find
those two assumptions make drastic differences in the body of
Christ. "We are members of one another," and therefore ought
to share—*need* to share—in one another's journeys, pay close
attention to them. Sharing these pilgrimages as we're doing
here—that's what the next decade of the Church will be about.

Epilogue

There are two ways of getting home; and one of them is to stay there. The other is to walk round the whole world till we come back to the same place.

—G. K. Chesterton, *The Everlasting Man*

KANSAS CITY, MISSOURI

We got a room in the Travel Lodge on the west side of Kansas City, Missouri. The temperature was just above 100 degrees, and we had to carry the three trunks and all our equipment inside to keep them from being stolen.

Across the street stood a shabby four-story apartment building, with graffiti-strewn doors and torn curtains hanging out through broken window panes. A police car and a paddy wagon were parked in front, and people hung over the balcony railings to watch three men being led out at gunpoint and shoved into the paddy wagon. Several men talked to the policemen. One woman kept waving her hands in an upward motion, as if she were throwing leaves from a basket into the air. Eventually the cops drove away and everybody but the young men went back into the apartment building.

For some reason, the clerk behind the desk seemed suspicious of us. She examined my American Express card closely, and scratched at the signature with her fingernail. She held my driver's license up to the light. I asked if she had a room for two nights. She replied that I would have to pay for the first night the next morning and then ask for another night.

While I was signing the register, she called a maintenance man to unlock a room that had been sealed for nonpayment. A grateful but sullen guest followed the maintenance man to his room.

As we got on the elevator, a ragged, unshaven man in his fifties got on. His left arm was in a cast and his face was covered with bruises and cuts. He was drinking what appeared to be bourbon from a bottle in a paper sack. He said hello, got off with us on the third floor, and ambled down the hallway.

It took three trips to transfer all of our luggage from the van to the room. The injured man rode up and down with us each time. The last trip, he invited us to his room for a drink. We declined, but thanked him anyway.

After the seedy room in Des Moines, the Kansas City Travel Lodge was palatial! I showered and then spent about an hour on my notes. A cold Coke took the edge off the fatigue of the trip.

I pulled the drapes away from the huge picture window and set up Valerie's typewriter, then settled down on the bed and opened the second of the Saberhagen novels. Across the room she typed her notes from yesterday's interviews. In the background three blocks away, the crumbling spire of Old St. Mary's Church stood, surrounded by vacant lots and boarded-up stores, its red bricks stained with city-soot.

In the streets, hard-eyed young men yelled to the girls in the apartment-building windows. Outside, in the hallway, the injured man was waiting for the elevator.

The next day, we rode down on the elevator again with the injured man. This time, he was almost sober and told us that he had been in the county hospital for a week. He had been in an accident (hit and run), had broken his arm, and was heading home. He didn't tell us where home was. I told him what we were doing. He looked at us, smiled, and shrugged his shoulders. When the elevator door opened, he got off, looked back at us and smiled again, then headed for the liquor store down the street.

We saw him for the last time on the morning of the third day, as we were checking out. I was telling the new cashier about our trip, that we were interviewing people who had been away from the Church for a long time and had returned. He was singularly uninterested: he looked up at me, shoved the American Express voucher at me, and said, "Sign here." I signed the voucher and turned to leave.

The injured man, who had been listening, asked, "How long was you away from the Church?" I replied that I had been away for twenty-five years.

"But you're back now, huh?"

"Yes, I am."

"Was it what you expected?"

"No, it wasn't."

"But you're glad you're back?"

"Yes, I am."

"Well, I might go back, too, you know? What do you think?"

"It might not be what you expect."

"Well then, maybe I *should* go back!"

We laughed and I shook hands with him and wished him well. The cashier shook his head at us and filed the voucher. The suspicious woman who had been on duty two days earlier stood in the doorway to the inner office. She turned and walked away, shaking her head.

As we went out the door, our new friend smiled. "You two be careful and have a good trip."

We got in the van and pulled out of the driveway. The injured man's scarred face was framed by the aluminum door. We waved goodbye and he raised his good arm and waved back. We headed for Oklahoma City. It was already in the nineties.

ARKANSAS BORDER, AUGUST 1984

I thought we would never find a service station. We had been on the road for four hours before we finally rolled up to a dusty Exxon station just east of the Arkansas border. I got out to get a drink of water and Valerie headed for the ladies' room. A sun-bronzed young boy in jeans and a brown tattered tank top came out as I started the pump. He didn't speak.

I gave him my credit card, tripped the meter, and started to fill the front tank. He looked at the Illinois plates and asked how far we were going. I told him who we were and what our trip was about.

Suddenly, the boy's face brightened and he said, "You know, I'd like to go to church."

"Why don't you?"

"I ain't got enough money."

"What do you mean?"

"Well, it takes money to go to church. I got a wife and she just had a baby. I'm working on three jobs—I pump gas here on Saturday and Sunday, and I work out at the chemical plant from four A.M. to noon on weekdays, and I work for a record company setting up equipment in the afternoon—just to make ends meet. But I used to go to church. And I just don't feel right to go without putting something in the plate, you know?"

"Do you really want to go to church?"

"Yeah, I guess I do."

"Let me make a suggestion. Pick out the church you want to go to and go to it. After church, ask the minister or pastor or priest or whatever he calls himself if you can talk to him. Tell him what you just told me. He'll probably get up and give you a hug and tell you to forget about the money and come to church. If he doesn't, then get out of there. You're in the wrong church. Keep trying until you find a place that welcomes you just the way you are. You'll find your church."

"I don't know if I could do that."

"How badly do you want to go to church?"

"Well, maybe I will try it."

I signed the voucher, bought a can of iced tea, and got in the van. "Take care, and don't forget what I told you."

When we reached the highway, I looked back and waved. He was still standing at the pump, shielding his eyes from the sun. He waved as we headed down the road. Our next stop was Little Rock, Arkansas.

CONYERS, GEORGIA, THE MONASTERY OF THE HOLY SPIRIT, AUGUST 1984

We left Mack's house at noon today and started back to Atlanta to pack. But on the way home we decided, on impulse, to make a side trip to Conyers to the Trappist monastery.

The road winds and winds; we miss our turn. It is hot and a thunderstorm is brewing. At last we get to the monastery, a group of low, graceful buildings looming ghostly white in the overcast summer twilight.

We find the chapel and go in. The Evening Office is already in progress. We sit in the back, in the visitors' stalls, and listen. The voices rise in the heat to the very rafters, and fill the great half-empty chapel.

At the end of the Office, the monks file out in order. At the end of the procession is one lame brother. He walks slowly, a little behind the rest, genuflects to the altar, then hesitates, looks back toward the visitors' stalls, smiles, and bows to us. We bow back to him, the three of us alone in that holy place, observing the ancient Office, keeping the vigil together.

GETHSEMANI, KENTUCKY, AUGUST 1984

We are on our way to Louisville, but this is our one indulgence of the trip: we plan to spend the night in Bardstown and drive into the city tomorrow after we see Thomas Merton's grave. But conventions ruin our plans; the small town is over-run with tourists and there is no place to stay.

We make our way to Gethsemani slowly, over winding country roads, until we reach a small sign that says simply TRAPPIST and points toward another narrower, even more winding road. At last we reach the famous Trappist house which Thomas Merton immortalized in the phrase "the four walls of my newfound freedom."

Once inside, we inquire where Brother Louis is buried. After much blushing and hesitation, a young brother tells me that he is very sorry, the lady cannot visit Brother Louis's grave, which lies inside the enclosure where women are not allowed. I do not beg for special favors; I understand the rules. But secretly, I am heartsick that we have driven so far and now I can't go within a hundred feet of the grave.

So Ralph goes instead, with camera, inside the enclosure to visit the plain black marker, while I talk with the stammering young brother who has had to play reluctant gatekeeper. He takes pity on me and gives me many pictures of Merton and shows me the photos on the wall, and a big map of the Trappist houses across the United States.

Finally, Ralph comes back with half a roll of film and a pine cone and two acorns from Brother Louis's grave. And with that I will have to be content.

OCEAN SPRINGS, MISSISSIPPI, ST. MARY THE VIRGIN, AUGUST 1984

This has been a trip of contrasts: heat and welcome coolness, affluence and decay, cathedrals and dives, priests and street-walkers, and everywhere, kids bopping up and down the half-melted sidewalks in time to soundless Walkmans. In the car we listen to our Wagner tapes and Palestrina masses; it is a way we make our own kind of statement, I suppose.

Other contrasts: the beautiful cathedral in Kansas City with its Tiffany windows and breathtaking rood screen, and up the hill, the shell of what was once the city's equivalent of Ascension, now with broken and boarded windows, and vines winding in and out of the boards. Or the open, inviting courtyard of the small cathedral in Oklahoma City where Canon Haugh sits at lunchtime, contrasted with the huge mausoleum of a church where "Evangelist J." preaches on special Sundays and other state occasions.

Sunday we left after the Eucharist and headed due south, on our way to Little Rock. Had it not been for the dictum, rigidly enforced in me since childhood, that one never receives twice in one day, we might have stopped and gone to Communion again.

For Sunday morning found us at a huge church on the outskirts of a middle-sized city. It is the most prosperous church in the area, with a congregation of over three thousand and a budget that runs into the millions each year. We entered the church through a side entrance and took in the scene: well-dressed people, an altar banked with late-summer blooms ("a floral statement," the church bulletin was pleased to call it), a twelve-foot-high statue of Christ, arms outstretched like a butterfly pinned to a board, chromed halo gleaming by spotlight.

The sanctuary party numbered over fifteen; they showed the flag and trooped the colors and sang "The Star-Spangled Banner." The assistant pastor preached so fast that it sounded like a foreign language. And while the organ played "Just as I Am" in mellow tones, seven hundred people raced to Communion, tripping over one another in their eagerness to get to the altar rail. It was pandemonium. We left without feeling we had been to church at all.

At coffee hour, everyone complimented the clergy on having finished the service in just under an hour. There were pastries and petit fours from the best bakery in town, served on silver trays. There were silver samovar urns full of steaming coffee and tea, linen napkins and heavy, ornate coffee spoons laid out on a polished mahogany table that gave me back my reflection when I bent over the sugar bowl ("One lump or two, dear?" inquired the exquisitely coiffed gray-haired lady who poured). Everyone was friendly and flawlessly polite, interested in the two slightly bedraggled strangers who came with tape recorders and cameras, wanting to talk about renewal (renewal!) on this bright, steamy August morning.

It was oppressively affluent and correct and somehow dead. They were all such *good* people, all of them. But somehow the Spirit, like many of their fellow members, was absent that day. Perhaps He too preferred the solitude of the outdoors to that country-club surrogate with its imposing façade and manicured lawns.

Now in the truck, I slept fitfully, listening to my tapes, scanning my notes, looking for the common thread in all this. Tonight we would spend the night in another anonymous, slightly seedy motel, with children splashing in the pool and strange cars cranking up in the middle of the night: another strange bed, strange city, strange shower, strange mirror that gives back a reflection itself a little strange. Tomorrow night, thank goodness, we will be among friends. George's Texarkana cousins have offered us a place to spend the night.

In Texarkana there is Southern hospitality to spare; a huge catfish dinner, good conversation, a chance to meet Father George's two engaging cousins, Jeff and Marilyn. Jeff tells a wonderful story of locating the church where he is now a vestryman by calling every listing in the Yellow Pages until he found one that "sounded good to him."

In the evening, bliss: a water bed for two weary travelers. And the next morning, hot, freshly brewed coffee in a real kitchen to speed us on our way. It was a welcome respite from

Travel Lodges and Day's Inns, and we left refreshed and ready for the next leg of the journey.

Then we are off to Ocean Springs. In the past year, I've picked up yet another skein of my past life: I have traced down and begun again to write to dear Father Robert Manning, the priest who presented me for confirmation years ago. He is now in ill health and is on dialysis three times a week. But he is alive, and happy, and as full of spirit—indeed, of the Spirit—as ever. Now in less than twenty-four hours I'll see him again. He is staying with the rector of St. John's tonight; he has been supplying for the church during vacation.

Ocean Springs is an enchantingly pretty, small Gulf Coast city just a stone's throw from Biloxi. Father gets us a motel room at the edge of the water. In the morning we go for long walks along the gulf and photograph the gulls swooping down for their morning crumbs, smell the sharp fishy odor of the water, and pick up shells to take back to the motel. Several still hold their crabs, and I shriek when my lovely shells start walking about the bathtub. We photograph an old church with only the tower left; all but the bell tower and a bit of the stained-glass windows and the altar was destroyed in a hurricane. The women of the town saved the fragments and lovingly pieced them back together, so Father tells us.

Father picks us up at the motel and we drive across the bridge to Ocean Springs. I can't believe our good fortune to have found him, after all these years. We go to dinner at a lovely little country inn on the water's edge, where we eat delicious crab claws and raw oysters, and talk for hours. He remembers all his "kids," as he affectionately calls us pagans whom he patiently prepared for confirmation year after year.

After dinner Father drives us back to the motel. "I have a surprise for you," he says. "Tomorrow morning, if you like, come over to Saint John's and I'll say a Mass. And then go 'round the town a bit. I thought that since it's the Feast of Saint Mary the Virgin . . ." His voice trails off. But there's no need to say more. Of course we'll come.

After our morning walk, we drive through still-shady winding roads lined with antebellum houses in various stages of decay and regentrification; Spanish moss hanging from trees, air heavy with honeysuckle, wisteria dripping from porches. At last we get to St. John's, a tiny 150-year-old clapboard church ringed with gnarled live oaks. Father greets us outside and takes us in to admire the exquisite woodwork of the altar and choir stalls, the lovely miniature Della Robbia–style Stations along the walls.

And then the Mass: Father and his one acolyte, a young man in sweatpants and jogging shoes, and a woman from the local bookstore, and Ralph and me. We sit in the choir stalls just a few feet from the altar. For the first time in over a decade, I hear the lovely cultivated Gulf Coast voice saying the familiar words of the Mass with that utter conviction, that utter simplicity, that only the Real Ones know.

And the Presence is suddenly there, so real, so intense that it is almost palpable. When Father Manning offers the Mass with a special intention "for Ralph and Valerie and their pilgrimage, and for the Feast of Saint Mary the Virgin," we know: this is the high point of our journey. It is for this that we have come four thousand miles: to kneel in this room, at this altar, and take the Bread and Wine from these hands, to bring the journey full circle from its inception a decade and more ago, from its new beginning on Easter of 1983. Yes, we understand why we are there, why we are all there, and why He is there as well.

We don't want to say good-bye, but we must. But we take away with us a special gift: that rare moment when the sun streamed in benediction through the plain colored-glass windows of the little clapboard church and Our Lord suddenly stood among us, as surely present as He was absent this past Sunday in the suburbs.

I will sit up late tonight, writing Father Manning a letter, a letter to thank him and Our Lord for the miracle on the road to Damascus.

Afterword

In the old days, on Easter night, the Russian peasants used to carry the blest fire home from church. The light would scatter and travel in all directions through the darkness, and the desolation of the night would be pierced and dispelled as lamps came on in the windows of the farmhouses one by one. Even so, the glory of God sleeps everywhere, ready to blaze out unexpectedly in created things. . . .

—Thomas Merton, *The New Man*

We shall not cease from exploration
And the end of all our exploring
Will be to arrive where we started
And know the place for the first time . . .

—T. S. Eliot, "Little Gidding,"
in *Four Quartets*

MARCH 30, 1986, THE FEAST OF THE RESURRECTION

Easter Sunday: a gloriously bright day, unseasonably warm for Chicago—70 degrees and rising: a day as unlike that damp, chilly Easter three years ago as one could imagine.

In our living room, a vase of tulips looms white in the early-morning light. The manuscript of *The Road to Damascus* is on my desk, buried in a sea of papers and Ralph's theology texts, awaiting the copy editor's blue pencil and the ending which I must somehow write this week.

Last night we sat in darkness, my friends and I, for what seemed like hours, waiting for the Great Vigil of Easter to begin at the Church of the Ascension. Then suddenly the little procession materialized at the rear of the darkened church and the blessed fire was kindled, the grains of incense imprinted on the Paschal candle.

This morning, still half-asleep, I remember bits and pieces of the liturgy: Father Brian chanting the *Exultet;* the church suddenly ablaze with candles as we proclaim three times "Jesus Christ, the light of the world"; the Gloria ringing out with a sudden joy for the first time in six weeks as the purple covers were stripped from the shrines and candles replaced on the altar; Ralph, as crucifer for the Vigil; acolytes carrying, very solemnly, big pots of white lilies to place at the foot of the Paschal candle; Father Norris's voice rising suddenly in a beautiful mozarabic tone, clear as a bell in the spring night, a great pure sound rising from the smoke and dust to the very rafters in a poignant reminder of why we are here.

Then afterwards the bells, the glorious Easter hymns, the jubilant organ postlude, and on to an Easter feast. David and Jim had made Russian Easter bread. The table in the church hall was filled to overflowing: we all brought whatever we had given up for Lent, and in abundance. Surfeited with hugs and kisses and handshakes, chocolate bunnies and candied strawberries, we dragged ourselves home at three A.M.

This morning I am tired, but with the exultant, clean fatigue that comes at the end of Holy Week. Ralph and I, through some quirk of scheduling, end up as torchbearers together in the eleven A.M. processional. We move at a stately pace, following the thurifer's stride. Absurd that we should have to walk so slowly; despite my aching feet, I want to leap for joy.

Twelve-fifteen and the service is nearly over. I don't think I can stand for another minute. I am feeling the effects of three hours' sleep last night. But just now, Father Norris's voice soars once more like pure joy into the rafters of this strange holy place that we have come to call home. And I remember again why I was there sitting in that pew exactly three years ago; why I am standing here now in cassock and surplice, with my aching feet and end-of-Holy-Week exhaustion.

A shaft of light hits the crucifix on the high altar, striking sparks of light from the outstretched arms.

"Let us go forth into the world in peace, alleluia, alleluia," Father intones.

"Thanks be to God, alleluia, alleluia," we answer.

And I know, just now, how the story of *The Road to Damascus* ends.

Books and Other Resources

The following list is not meant to be exhaustive, but covers only those books and resources mentioned in this book. Popular books in the field of religion may be found in almost any bookstore or library. For reference works such as ecclesiastical dictionaries and biblical commentaries, and for a deeper look into contemporary religious thinking, a visit to the bookstore or library of your local theological seminary is well worth the time and effort.

Alban Institute, The, c/o Loren B. Mead, 4125 Nebraska Ave. NW., Washington, DC 20016.

Altizer, Thomas J. J. *The Gospel of Christian Aetheism.* Philadelphia: Westminster Press, 1966.

———— (with William Hamilton). *The Death of God.* New York: Bobbs-Merrill Co., 1966.

Bloom, Archbishop Anthony. *Beginning to Pray.* New York: Paulist Press, 1970.

————. *Courage to Pray.* New York: Paulist Press, 1973.

The Book of Common Prayer (Episcopalian). New York: The Church Hymnal Corporation, 1979.

The Book of Discipline (Methodist). Nashville, Tenn.: United Methodist Publications, 1984.

Buber, Martin. *I and Thou.* Translation by Walter Kaufman and G. S. Smith. New York: Scribners, 1970.

Carnes, Ralph L. and Valerie B. *The New Humanities.* New York: Holt, Rinehart and Winston, 1972.

Chesterton, G. K. *The Everlasting Man.* New York: Doubleday and Co., 1974.

Church Teacher, The (bi-monthly publication for church-school teachers), c/o 2504 N. Roxboro St., Durham, NC 27704.

Copleston, Frederick, S. J. *A History of Philosophy* (6 vols). Westminster, Md.: Newman Press, 1946–60.

    Copleston is also referred to in "The Existence of God—A Debate," by Bertrand Russell and F. C. Copleston in *A Modern Introduction to Philosophy,* Paul Edwards and Arthur Pap, Eds. New York: The Free Press, 1957. This is a reprint of a debate that was originally broadcast in 1948 by the British Broadcasting Corporation and was published in *Humanitas.*

Cox, Harvey. *Religion in the Secular City.* New York: Simon and Schuster, 1984.

Crowley, John. *Little, Big.* New York: Bantam Books, 1983.

de Chardin, Teilhard. *The Phenomenon of Man.* New York: Harper and Row, 1959.

Dix, Dom Gregory. *Jew and Greek.* New York: Harper and Row, 1953.

————. *The Shape of the Liturgy.* New York: Seabury Press, 1982.

Eliot, T. S. *The Complete Poems and Plays, 1909–1950.* New York: Harcourt, Brace and Co., 1958.

The Episcopalian (monthly publication). 1201 Chestnut St., Philadelphia, PA 19107.

Faith Alive (or Faith Alive Weekends), President and Executive Director Fred C. Gore, RD 3, Box 250, Unit B2D, Hockessin, DE 19707.

The Charles E. Fuller Institute of Evangelism and Church Growth, P.O. Box 989, Pasadena, CA, 91102

Grierson, Sir Herbert, Ed. *The Poems of John Donne*. London: Oxford University Press, 1960.

Greely, Andrew M. *The Jesus Myth*. New York: Doubleday, 1973.

Hartshorne, Charles. *The Divine Relativity: A Social Concept of God*. New Haven, Conn.: Yale University Press, 1948.

———. *The Logic of Perfection and Other Essays in Neoclassical Metaphysics*. LaSalle, Ill.: Open Court Publishing Company, 1962.

Holloway, The Rev. Richard. *The Anglican Tradition*. Morehouse-Barlow Company: Wilton, CN: 1984.

———. *The Killing*. Wilton, Conn.: Morehouse Barlow, 1984.

———. *Signs of Glory*. New York: The Seabury Press, 1983.

Hume, David. *Dialogues Concerning Natural Religion*. Critical edition edited by Norman Kemp Smith. Oxford: Oxford University Press, 1935.

The Institute for Servant Leadership. The Rt. Rev. Bennett J. Simms, Executive Director, 6 Bishops Hall, Emory University, Atlanta, GA 30322.

James, William. *Varieties of Religious Experience*. London: Longmans, Green, 1902.

Kant, Immanuel. *The Critique of Pure Reason*. Translation by Norman Kemp Smith. London: The Macmillan Company, Ltd., 1958.

Kushner, Harold S. *When Bad Things Happen to Good People.* New York: Schocken Books, 1981.

Lead Consultants, c/o John Savage, P.O. Box 664, Reynoldsburg, OH 43068. (800) 828-6556; (716) 586-8366.

Leech, The Rev. Kenneth. *Soul Friend.* San Francisco: Harper and Row, 1977.

Lewis, C. S. *The Four Loves.* New York: Harvest Books, 1960.

———. *Mere Christianity.* New York: The Macmillan Company, 1952.

———. *The Pilgrim's Regress.* New York: Bantam Books, 1981.

———. *The Screwtape Letters.* New York: The Macmillan Company, 1982.

———. *Surprised by Joy.* New York: Harvest Books, 1955.

———. *Till We Have Faces.* New York: Harvest Books, 1956.

Mandino, Og. *The Christ Commission.* New York: Bantam Books, 1981.

Marshall, The Rt. Rev. Michael. *Renewal in Worship.* Wilton, Conn.: Morehouse-Barlow, 1982.

Merton, Thomas. *Bread in the Wilderness.* New York: New Directions, 1960.

———. *The Sign of Jonas.* New York: Harvest Books, 1953.

———. *The Seven Storey Mountain.* New York: Harvest Books, 1976.

Mother Teresa. *Words to Love by.* Notre Dame, Ind.: Ave Maria Press, 1983.

Peck, M. Scott., M. D. *People of the Lie.* New York: Simon and Schuster, 1983.

————. *The Road Less Travelled.* New York: Touchstone Books (Simon and Schuster), 1978.

Peirce, Charles Sanders. *The Collected Papers of Charles Sanders Peirce.* Edited by Charles Hartshorne and Paul Weiss. Cambridge, Mass.: Harvard University Press, 1931–35.

Rothange, Arlin J. *Sizing up Your Congregation.* Education for Mission and Ministry Office by Seabury Professional Services, n. d.

Russell, Bertrand. *A History of Western Philosophy.* New York: Simon and Schuster, 1945.

Sayers, Dorothy. *The Mind of the Maker.* New York: Harcourt Brace, 1941.

Schmemann, Alexander. *For the Life of the World.* Crestwood, N.Y.: St. Vladimir's Seminary Press, 1973.

Schumer, Fran. "A Return to Religion," *The New York Times Magazine,* April 15, 1984.

Sheehy, Gail. "Retreat Is Out, Renewal Is In," *The Chicago Tribune,* August 6, 1984, section 5, pp. 1, 3.

Through the Year With Thomas Merton: Daily Meditations From His Writing. Edited by Thomas P. McDonnell. Garden City, N.Y.: Image Books, 1985.

Ware, Archimandrite Kallistos. *The Orthodox Way.* Crestwood, N.Y.: St. Vladimir's Seminary Press, 1980.

Whitehead, Alfred North. *Process and Reality.* New York: The Macmillan Company, 1929.

Williams, Charles. *All Hallows' Eve.* Grand Rapids, Mich.: William B. Eerdmans, 1982.

————. *Descent of the Dove.* Grand Rapids, Mich.: William B. Eerdmans, 1939.

————. *War in Heaven.* Grand Rapids, Mich.: William B. Eerdmans, 1982.

OTHER SOURCES

Donne's "Goodfriday 1613. Riding Westward" is from Sir Herbert Grierson's edition of Donne's poems, *The Poems of John Donne.* London: Oxford University Press, 1960.

The passage from Acts is from the Revised Standard Version of the Bible, New York: Thomas Nelson and Sons, 1952.

All Prayer Book citations, except for the one designated "The 1928 Prayer Book," are from *The Book of Common Prayer,* 1979 (The Church Hymnal Corporation, N.Y.).

A Glossary of Common Religious Terms

As a book of interviews and personal stories, *The Road to Damascus* covers the experiences of people in many religious denominations. Consequently, some of the religious terms used in the book may be unfamiliar to the reader, depending on his or her religious preference. The following glossary is not meant to be exhaustive, but only to clarify certain terms that are used in this book. For more elaborate but easily understood explanations of religious terms, especially those of the sacramental church, we recommend the excellent (and inexpensive) *A New Dictionary for Episcopalians* (Minneapolis: Winston Press, 1985) by the Reverend John N. Wall Jr. A more extensive reference is *The Oxford Dictionary of the Christian Church* (Oxford: Oxford University Press, 1958).

ABSOLUTION   The pronouncement by a priest or bishop that sins confessed have been forgiven. In Episcopal liturgies, absolution usually comes between the general confession and the Peace.

AGNUS DEI   Literally, the "Lamb of God" in Latin. The Agnus Dei is also an anthem sung or said after the Eucharistic prayer ("Lamb of God, you take away the sins of the world").

ALTAR GUILD   An organization, found especially in sacramental churches, that is made up of lay people who assume responsibility for washing altar linen, cleaning Eucharistic vessels, repairing vestments, and performing other duties related to preparing the altar for public worship.

CHALICE   The cup in which wine is consecrated during the Holy Eucharist, and from which each communicant drinks.

COMMUNION, HOLY COMMUNION   A common expression for the Eucharist; also used to denote that portion of the liturgy of the Mass that is associated with the Eucharistic prayer. Communicants participate in Holy Communion by eating and drinking consecrated bread and wine which is believed to be the body and blood of Jesus Christ, either symbolically (in most Protestant churches), spiritually (according to Calvin), or actually (according to the doctrine of transubstantiation). Holy Communion is thought to have been instituted by Christ during the Last Supper.

CONFIRMATION   Confirmation is a sacrament in which, after appropriate study and reflection, commitments made at the time of baptism are reaffirmed. Since baptismal commitments are often made on behalf of infants, confirmation is sometimes erroneously thought of as a "re-baptism" ceremony. Only previously baptised persons are eligible for confirmation; however, Confirmation is a rite separate from baptism both in substance and intent.

CROSS   The cross or Crucifix is the universal symbol of Christianity. Its original referent is the wooden structure on which Jesus was crucified. The *Sign of the Cross* is a gesture made in remembrance of Jesus' crucifixion, and involves touching (in sequence) the forehead, the center of the chest, the left side, and then the right side of the chest with the fingertips of the right hand. In the Eastern Orthodox Church, the sign is made from right to left instead of from left to right. Miniature crosses or crucifixes are worn as jewelry by most Christians. During the middle 1980s, rock-music stars have affected the wearing of crucifixes as ironic decoration.

EPISTLES   Sections of the New Testament that are thought to be letters from the Apostle Paul to various readers. In Episcopal services, Epistles are read between the Old Testament and Gospel texts as part of the "Liturgy of the Word."

EUCHARIST   See *Communion,* above.

EVENING PRAYER   One of the two "Daily Offices." The form for Evening Prayer may be found in the Book of Common Prayer (or "Prayer Book"). Also referred to as the Evening Office.

EVENSONG   A more formal, more elaborate sung version of Evening Prayer, usually preceded by a Mass and often followed by the Benediction of the Blessed Sacrament.

FOUR GOSPELISTS   The authors of the four New Testament Gospels, usually identified as Matthew, Mark, Luke, and John. Although his Gospel follows Matthew's in the Bible, contemporary New Testament scholarship usually recognizes Mark as the first Gospelist. The three other Gospel authors were undoubtedly aware of Mark's Gospel when they wrote their own, since although written at a later time, much phraseology is common among Mark and the other three. Each Gospel, however, also has material not in common with the others, denoting different sources and different objectives on the part of the individual authors. Consequently, modern scholars have speculated about a hypothetical document which they call the "Q" source. "Gospelist" and "Gospeller" are sometimes used to denote the person who reads the Gospel during a liturgy.

GENERAL CONFESSION   A confession of sins made during a liturgy by the entire congregation, as opposed to "private confession," which is made to a priest, individually and in private.

GLORIA IN EXCELSIS   A traditional spoken or sung as part of the liturgy of the Holy Eucharist ("Glory to God in the highest . . .").

GLORIA PATRI   A sentence spoken during the Daily Offices—for example, at the end of the Psalms and Canticles: "Glory to the Father, and to the Son, and to the Holy Spirit, as it was in the beginning, is now, and will be forever, Amen."

GOSPEL   Literally, "Good News," and usually a reference to one of the four New Testament Gospels (see *Four Gospelists,* above); but often erroneously used as a synonym for "truth."

GRACE   A gift from God—unsought, and often undeserved, but always to be treasured.

GREAT VIGIL OF EASTER   The chief vigil of the Christian year: an evening liturgy in celebration of the resurrection of Jesus Christ and in anticipation of the Feast of the Resurrection of our Lord (commonly known as Easter).

HIGH CHURCH   A term, often used derisively, to denote an Episcopal Church that is closer to Catholicism than to Protestantism in its liturgy. "Low Church" denotes the opposite orientation.

HOLY MYSTERIES   Far from the trivial sense in which it is often mistakenly interpreted, the *Holy Mysteries* as mentioned in the Episcopal Eucharistic liturgy's post-communion prayer ("we thank you for assuring us in these Holy Mysteries that we are living members of the body of your son and heirs to your eternal kingdom") refer not to a vague supernaturalism, but to the concrete and current actuality of Christ's sacrifice for us as embodied in the liturgy of the Eucharist. In short, communion is neither merely symbolic nor merely a remembrance of a past event, but is a present recapitulation of Christ's sacrifice and our own saving participation in that sacrifice through our participation in the liturgy of the Eucharist.

HOLY SPIRIT   The comforter and sanctifier sent by God after the resurrection of Christ; the third person of the Trinity.

HOST   The unleavened bread used in the Eucharist, which represents the body of Christ. It is consecrated, then broken and distributed by the priest. The term is often restricted in its usage to denote only the wafers that are used instead of unleavened bread loaves. Some use the term to refer only to the large wafer, or "priest's host."

HIGH MASS/SOLEMN HIGH MASS   A Eucharistic liturgy with full ceremonial, done at a church's high altar, as opposed to a "Low Mass," which is a simplified version of the Eucharistic liturgy, and which is usually done at an altar table or "low altar."

INQUIRERS' CLASS   Classes held in the Episcopal, Roman Catholic, and other Churches for persons interested in learning more about the Church; usually attended prior to confirmation, sometimes as a requirement for confirmation.

KYRIE ELEISON   Literally, "Lord have mercy." Usually said or sung at the beginning of a Mass.

LOW MASS   Simplified form of the High Mass (see above).

MASS   The liturgy of the Holy Eucharist (see *Holy Eucharist*, above). The term is derived from the Latin word *Missa* (dismissal), which was traditionally used at the end of the liturgy when the Eucharist was over and the congregation was dismissed.

MASS OF THE CATECHUMENS   Traditionally, catechumens (persons who had not yet been baptised or confirmed) participated in the Mass only up to the beginning of the Eucharistic prayer, then left since they were not yet allowed to communicate.

MORNING PRAYER OR MORNING OFFICE   One of the daily offices of the Episcopal Church, the form for which is found in the Episcopal Book of Common Prayer (see *Evening Prayer*, above).

OBLATE   A person who is affiliated with a monastary, but whose association does not involve taking full vows. The term is derived from the Latin *oblatus*, which is also the source of "oblation," or gift.

OFFERTORY   That portion of the liturgy of the Eucharist that denotes Christ's sacrifice for all people and the participation of the congregation in that sacrifice. The term is often erroneously limited to the act of bringing the elements (bread and wine) and collection plates to the altar.

PEACE, THE   The liturgical exchange of greetings and the wish for God's peace for each other by participants in an Episcopal Mass.

PRAYER BOOK   A universally accepted shortened reference to the Episcopal Book of Common Prayer.

PRAYERS OF THE PEOPLE   A portion of the Liturgy of the Mass, in which formal intercessions are made either by or on the behalf of the participants.

PRELUDE   A musical piece played before a religious service begins.

RESURRECTION   The return from death to life of Jesus Christ.

SACRAMENTS, BLESSED SACRAMENT   The visible signs of Christ's instituted grace to the worthy. Different denominations recognize different numbers of sacraments. In the Episcopal Church, for example, there are seven sacraments: Holy Eucharist, Baptism, Reconciliation of a Penitent, Confirmation, Matrimony, Unction of the Sick, and Ordination to Holy Orders. *The Blessed Sacrament* usually refers to the Host (see *Host,* above).

SANCTUS   A responsive anthem used in the liturgy of the Holy Eucharist.

SANCTUS BELL   A bell that is rung during the Eucharistic prayer at the consecration of the elements and at the call for Communion.

SCRIPTURE   The Bible: the Old Testament, New Testament, and (for some demoninations) The Apocrypha.

SECOND COMING   The looked-for return of Christ to the world.

SISTER   A member of a religious order, as in ". . . a Sister of the Order of St. Anne."

STATIONS OF THE CROSS   A Lenten liturgy, commemorating Jesus' passage through the streets of Jerusalem, and the stages of His crucifixion at Golgotha.

TRINITY   The three-in-one unified nature of God: Father, Son, and Holy Spirit.

VIRGIN BIRTH   The birth of Jesus from the Virgin Mary.

WOMEN'S GUILD   A popular auxilliary church service organization for women.

About the Authors

Valerie Carnes, a former Associate Professor of English at Roosevelt University, is Vice President of Words Unlimited (a Chicago-based technical writing firm), has a Ph.D. in Renaissance Literature, is a licensed lay reader in the Episcopal Church, and is a member of the Commission on Education for the Episcopal Diocese of Chicago.

Ralph Carnes, the former Dean of the College of Arts and Sciences at Roosevelt University, is President of Words Unlimited, and has a Ph.D. in Philosophy and the Humanities. He is a recent graduate of Seabury-Western Theological Seminary, and is a Postulant for Holy Orders in the Episcopal Diocese of Chicago.